A Guide Through the Theory of Knowledge

Second edition

A Guide Through the Theory of Knowledge

Second edition

Adam Morton

University of Bristol

First published 1977

Second edition 1997

2 4 6 8 10 9 7 5 3 1

Blackwell Publishers Ltd
108 Cowley Road
Oxford OX4 1JF
UK

Blackwell Publishers Inc.
350 Main Street
Malden, Massachusetts 02148
USA

British Library Cataloguing-in-Publication Data

A CIP catalogue record for this book is available from the British Library.

Library of Congress Cataloging in Publication Data
Morton, Adam.
    A guide through the theory of knowledge / Adam Morton. – 2nd ed.
      p. cm.
    Includes bibliographical references and index.
    ISBN 0-631-20004-5 (hardcover: alk. paper). – ISBN 0-631-20005-3 (pbk.: alk. paper)
      1. Knowledge, Theory of. I. Title.
    BD161.M84   1997
    121 – dc21
                                       97-3879
                                          CIP

Typeset in 11 on 13.5 pt Bembo
by Best-set Typesetter Ltd., Hong Kong
Printed in Great Britain by Hartnolls Ltd, Bodmin, Cornwall

This book is printed on acid-free paper

Contents

Foreword for Students

This book is meant as a simple introduction to the main issues and theories in the theory of knowledge, also known as epistemology. This is a subject that has many paradoxes and intellectual traps, and touches on some deep and mind-boggling questions. An introduction to the theory of knowledge should not ignore the traps or trivialize the deep questions. But it should try not to wallow in the difficulties or allow controversies about some of the questions to obscure the clear answers to others. So I have tried to find a route through the subject that concentrates on what is clear and definite, while keeping the big questions in view. On some topics I have views which are not shared by all philosophers. (There is no philosopher who has not.) I have tried to make it obvious what is my opinion and what is the consensus of most contemporary philosophers.

At the end of each chapter there are two kinds of questions. *Reading questions* are meant to check your understanding of the chapter. If you find any of them hard to answer, you should read the relevant section over again, and if you are still puzzled, ask for an explanation in a lecture or discussion group. *Thinking questions* are meant to make links to further topics, to raise doubts about the line taken in the main text, and to provide general intellectual stimulation. They are possible topics for essays. Not being able to answer the thinking questions is definitely not a sign of not having understood the chapter, but trying to think out answers to them will often give you a better sense about the questions behind the questions. At the end of each chapter there is also a list of titles for further reading, with an explanation of the relevance of each item. These lists are a good place to start in looking for suitable reading matter when you are planning an essay. (You can use the index, too, to find more discussion of many topics.)

At the end of the book is a Glossary with definitions of technical terms in philosophy used in this book. Many of these words are printed in **boldface** when they are first used in the text.

Teachers should notice that there is an appendix for teachers at the end of the book.

Many of the issues discussed here have been fascinating philosophers for centuries, and recent work on them has brought out more of their capacity to intrigue and stimulate. I hope that this book makes the standard problems and theories clear to you; but I will have failed if it does not also make it clear to you why these are still fascinating questions, which every person can gain from considering. The more you think about them, the more their fascination grows.

Acknowledgements

In the first edition of this book I thanked Hartry Field, Gil Harman, Glenn Kessler, Cliff McIntosh, Milly Morton, George Pitcher and Eric Rosen. Thanks again. I am grateful to Steve Smith at Blackwell Publishers for suggesting a second edition, and to Nathalie Manners for unobtrusive editorial support. Five anonymous readers for Blackwell gave extremely valuable advice on revising the book, and Andrew Pyle and Stephen Wilkinson read all of the almost-final draft and caught a remarkable number of mistakes and bad ideas. Martin Poulter gave me sharp comments on chapter 9. Susanna encouraged the mooses.

1. Beliefs and their Qualities

1. Defending and Attacking Beliefs

Any person has many beliefs. You believe that the world is round, that you have a nose and a heart, that $2 + 2 = 4$, that there are many people in the world, and some like you and some do not. These are beliefs about which almost everyone agrees. But people disagree too. Some people believe that there is a God, and some do not. Some people believe that conventional medicine provides the best way of dealing with all diseases, and some do not. Some people believe that there is intelligent life elsewhere in the universe, and some do not. When people disagree, they throw arguments, evidence and persuasion at one another. Very often they apply abusive or flattering labels to the beliefs in question. 'That's false', 'That's irrational', 'You haven't got any evidence', or 'That's true', 'I have good reason to believe it', 'I know it'.

We use these labels because there are properties we want our beliefs to have: we want them to be true rather than false; we want to have good rather than bad reasons for believing them. The theory of knowledge is concerned with these properties, with the difference between good and bad beliefs. Its importance in philosophy comes from two sources, one constructive and one destructive. The constructive source is that philosophers have often tried to find better ways in which to obtain beliefs. For example, they have studied scientific method and tried to see whether we can describe scientific rules which we could follow to give us the greatest chance of avoiding false beliefs. Rationalism and empiricism and Bayesianism, described later in this book, are constructive philosophies of this sort. The destructive source is that philosophy has often been caught up in the conflict between one set or system of beliefs and another. For example, people with religious faith sometimes try to find philosophical reasons for believing in God, and anti-religious people sometimes try to find philosophical reasons for why it is irrational to believe in God. So the **theory of knowledge** – or **epistemology** as it is also called, from the Greek word *epistēmē* meaning **knowledge** – can get involved both in trying to find better ways of acquiring beliefs and in criticizing the beliefs we already have.

This chapter introduces the basic ideas and terminology of the theory of knowledge. It connects the search to improve our beliefs and to referee the conflicts between different systems of beliefs with the fundamental ideas of the subject. The central idea here is the importance of questions about the kinds of beliefs we want to have. The chapter ends with two extreme views, deep scepticism and radical externalism, to show the importance of these questions.

2. Epistemic Ideals

Until recently, most philosophers working in the theory of knowledge have not paid much attention to the different ways in which beliefs and the ways we acquire them can be satisfactory or deficient. They have not asked: What qualities do we want our beliefs to have? And what qualities do we want them not to have? One reason for this is that philosophers have often thought that the answer was obvious: we want our beliefs to be true and not false. As we will see later (especially in chapter 5), this answer is *not* obvious. But, focusing on the desire for truth, most philosophers until recently have described various ideals for beliefs: ways in which our beliefs and the ways we get them could be perfectly organized. Rationalists described an ideal in which arguments as forceful as those in a mathematical proof could demonstrate the truth of all the beliefs we need. Empiricists described an ideal in which evidence from what is seen, heard or otherwise perceived could give adequate evidence for all our beliefs. A contemporary epistemic ideal, defended by the Bayesian movement in probability theory and the theory of knowledge, aims to describe ways in which we can discover exactly how probable each of our beliefs is, given the evidence we possess.

In the course of this book we will discuss each of these ideals. One important question to ask about each of them is: Are human beings capable of satisfying this ideal? Can we have beliefs that are like this? But another equally important question is: What would be the price for satisfying this ideal? In order to have beliefs like this, would we have to lose something else of value?

A very simple epistemic ideal is that of **coherence**. Coherence is having beliefs that not only make sense individually, but which hang together in a pattern which makes sense. If I believe that all cats are intelligent, believe that my neighbour's pet is a cat, and also believe that my neighbour's pet is stupid, then my beliefs are incoherent. They cannot all be true, and I can start with some of them and give good reasons for disagreeing with others. My beliefs could be incoherent for other reasons too. I might believe many things which amount to strong evidence for something, and yet believe the opposite. This often happens when people deceive themselves. Suppose, for example, that someone knows that her child gets into fights at school, knows that the teachers are afraid of the child, knows that many other children are not permitted to play with the child, but still deceives herself into thinking that her child is a well-behaved little angel: such a person's beliefs will not be coherent.

Why should we want our beliefs to be coherent? One reason is that incoherent beliefs tend to include many false beliefs. Another is that incoherent beliefs are hard to defend against people who challenge or attack them. So coherence is an ideal that we could set ourselves. We could try to make our beliefs as coherent as possible. This does not mean that any person's beliefs could ever be totally coherent. Every human being will probably always be subject to bad reasoning and self-deception. That's the way we are. But it is an ideal we can try to achieve. It is also an ideal that someone might decide not to aim for, probably because it was thought to conflict with some other ideal, such as the ideal of having interesting new ideas. So even for this very simple epistemic ideal, there are questions to answer about the price of aiming for it, and how near to achieving it human beings can actually come.

3. The Basic Concepts

In discussing beliefs, philosophers use a number of central concepts. It is hard to define any of them in terms that all philosophers would accept, for the definitions are usually tied up with theories about knowledge, just the theories that we need to compare in this book. But if you consider the examples below, you will almost certainly conclude that they are concepts you are already familiar with. Everyone uses them in everyday life, in a general and imprecise way, even if they do not use the words for them that philosophers do. (In what follows I will often write a word in *italics* to indicate that it is a word worth noticing, or in boldface if it is among the epistemological terms listed in the Glossary at the end of the book.)

Rational/irrational

George has a date with Shoshana, who is blonde. She decides at the last minute not to go out with George that evening, but to stay home and study instead. George is furious, and decides that all blonde women are evil. He will never trust a blonde again. This is especially strange since his mother and sister, who have always treated him with the greatest kindness, are blonde. But from that day on, however friendly, considerate or helpful a blonde woman is, George always interprets her behaviour as evil.

George's belief that all blonde women are evil is an **irrational belief**. It comes not from careful thinking, but from a sudden angry impulse that continues to grip him. (Speaking more carefully, we might say that the way George came to have that belief was irrational: it was irrational of George to acquire that belief at that time in that way.) We might say that it was a crazy or a stupid belief, though George may be neither crazy nor stupid. Many philosophers think that a lot of people's beliefs, including beliefs handed down through the generations, are irrational. In some important way they are like George's belief about blondes. Superstitious beliefs, like, for example, the belief that it is bad luck to have a black cat cross your path, are good candidates for being irrational. Some philosophers argue that all religious beliefs are irrational, and some philosophers think that it is irrational to believe in an objective difference between right and wrong. Many other philosophers, needless to say, disagree.

Contrast George with Sonya. Sonya has a cruel father, and her brother is a drug dealer. Neither shows any affection or consideration for her. Indeed, with the exception of two of her teachers at school, all the men who have played any role in her life have been baddies. Yet, when asked her attitude to men, she says: 'There are a lot of bad ones. But I've met a few decent ones, so I have some slight hope for them.' This does not seem irrational. It is a **rational belief** to the extent that it does not claim more than the evidence available to her suggests, and leaves open possibilities that are not closed off by that evidence. One conclusion to draw is that very often a rational belief will have to be more subtly expressed than an irrational one in response to the same evidence. The rational belief will less often say 'all' or 'never'.

True/false

Suppose that there is some mechanism in the universe which ensures that whenever a black cat crosses a person's path, something bad happens to that person in the near future. No human being knows of the existence of this mechanism, which works by physical principles which humans will never understand. Then the belief that it is bad luck to have a black cat cross your path is *true*. (So the belief that the probability of bad events is unchanged by a black cat's crossing your path is *false*.) But still there may not be any good evidence for it: the combinations of cat-crossings and bad occurrences are too subtle for us ever to notice them. Then the belief that black cats are bad luck is true even though there is no good evidence for it; true even if the belief that it is true is irrational. So irrational beliefs can be true. That may be a surprising conclusion, but it is clearly right. A less surprising conclusion is that rational beliefs can be false. There can be very strong reasons for believing something although it is false.

Evidence

Scientists do experiments to find **evidence** for and against scientific theories. Detectives hunt for evidence showing who committed crimes. Evidence can take many different forms. The behaviour of animals in a learning task, the pattern of light in the view-piece of a telescope or microscope, a letter confessing to an action; all these and many others could count as evidence in suitable circumstances. Very often when evidence is produced, it is in order to convince someone to change their mind, from belief to disbelief, from disbelief to belief, or from neutrality to either. The evidence then has to be believable by the people who are to be convinced, and in addition has to be such that when they think about it, they will, if they are rational, find some tendency to change their beliefs. So evidence produced by the defence in a court case might be testimony that even a juror who was inclined to convict would take seriously. Similarly, evidence for a scientific theory might be the results of an experiment that even someone who believed a rival theory would have to admit was definitely carried out and definitely gave the result it did.

Reasoning and argument

When evidence supports a belief, it makes people think that the belief might be true. Because of the evidence, they perform some reasoning that tends towards the belief. There are many kinds of reasoning. Sometimes to persuade someone, you do not produce any evidence at all, but say, 'Suppose for the sake of argument that . . .' and then go on to draw conclusions. A defence lawyer says: 'Suppose that someone besides my client was hiding in the house that night', and then shows how that mystery person could have committed the crime and planted her client's stolen wallet near the scene. The jury thinks about this, and is led through steps of *reasoning* by the lawyer's *argument*. Then they may conclude: 'Someone else just might have done it' or 'If someone else could have got into the house, then someone else could have done it'. Sometimes reasoning can show that a belief is true without using any evidence at all. For example, suppose a student says to a librarian: 'This book was due on February 1st and it is now March 1st, and the fine is $1 per day, so I owe $29', and the librarian replies: 'But this is a leap year, so you owe $30'. The librarian's reasoning shows that the student's belief is wrong, without producing any new evidence.

Justified/unjustified

Consider Toshiro, who lives in Tokyo and knows nothing about North American animals. He has never seen a moose or a chipmunk, and does not know what sorts of animals they are. His family is taking a trip to Seattle, and on the plane they give him a book, in English, with the title *Animals of North America*. In fact the book is a joke, and most of the information in it is wrong. In particular, the photo and description of a moose are of a chipmunk, and the photo and description of a chipmunk are of a moose. In Seattle he goes to a zoo and sees a moose. He believes that he is seeing the animal called 'chipmunk'. That is clearly not a silly thing for him to believe, given what he has read and what he sees. On the basis of that information his belief that he is seeing what is called a chipmunk is a **justified belief**. His sister Sumiko, who has much more information about North American animals, looks at the big ruminant with the wide horns and at once thinks 'That's a moose', and her belief is also justified. Many theories of knowledge are theories of when a person's beliefs are justified. A belief is justified on the basis of information which makes believing it a better strategy for getting to the truth than not believing it. Often people draw conclusions that are not justified by the information they have. For example, if Sumiko thinks that since moose have horns and since 'mouse' sounds like 'moose' then mice have horns, then her belief is unjustified on the basis of her information, unless she also has some reason to believe that animals whose names in English sound alike are similar.

Knowledge/ignorance

Toshiro was *ignorant* of the names of North American animals. We are all ignorant of many things: there are many questions we do not know the answers to. Probably no human knows whether there is life on other planets. Probably no human knows how to achieve universal peace. Probably no human knows whether there are infinitely many twin prime numbers (like 3 and 5, 11 and 13, 1,001 and 1,003). There are many people who have beliefs about all these things, and some of their opinions are rational, and some are justified. But it does not follow that any of these opinions count as *knowledge*. To know that there is life on other planets, a person would have to have a powerful theory of how life develops or have direct evidence produced by such life. To know how to achieve universal peace, someone would have to have a recipe for producing peace and a very convincing reason that showed how and why it would work. To know that there are infinitely many twin primes, a person would have to have a correct mathematical proof of this fact. In short, and very roughly, to know something, your mind has to be linked to the fact, and that link has to be a top-quality reliable one. This makes knowledge seem very special and very rare. Yet we talk as if we know many things. Just about every person knows the names of his or her friends, and knows that they have a nose in their head. Most people know that the earth revolves around the sun, and that twelve multiplied by thirteen is a hundred and fifty six. One sign of this is that most people can be relied on to give reliable information about these things. Seen this way, it is not surprising that there are many controversies about knowledge: about what knowledge is and how much knowledge we have. For it is at the same time something that seems very hard to achieve and something that we think we have quite a lot of.

None of these explanations was a real definition. There were too many vague, unexplained terms in them: for example, the idea of a 'top-quality reliable' link between a mind and a fact. Later in this book more precise definitions of some of these terms will be considered. (See chapter 6 for more about knowledge, and see question 15 at the end of this chapter for more about the difference between justified and rational beliefs.) But the explanations will probably have reminded you of enough about these concepts that you can understand them. The important point to grasp now is that all these words can be used to describe desirable and undesirable, good and bad, features of our beliefs. It is not at all obvious that there is only one kind of desirable feature of beliefs, so these good and bad aspects can cut across one another in complicated patterns. In particular, note the following three complications.

A good result can be obtained by a bad method. For example, a true belief can be arrived at by irrational reasoning. You see a spider, and because you are scared by its hairy legs, you think it must be poisonous. That is bad reasoning, but it may be that the spider is poisonous all the same. There are many examples of this in the history of science. For example, William Harvey in the seventeenth century came up with the theory that the blood in the body circulates, leaving the heart by the arteries and returning by the veins. He reached this conclusion by thinking: the heart is like the sun and the blood is like the earth, so, since the earth revolves around the sun, the blood must revolve around the heart. This is not very convincing reasoning, to put it mildly, but it led him to a true conclusion. (He later did experiments and found better evidence for his idea.)

A bad result can be obtained by a good method. For example, Toshiro in the example above was not reasoning badly when he thought that the large animal in front of him was called a 'chipmunk'. Or consider a scientist who tests a million samples of a drug on a dozen species of animals and finds no harmful side-effects. In the absence of contrary evidence, she is justified in concluding that the drug is harmless. But it may turn out that in some species under some conditions the drug is fatal. Her justified belief was false. (This example is related to questions about induction, discussed in chapter 4.)

Opposing beliefs can both be justified. Toshiro and Sumiko both had justified beliefs, in terms of the different evidence available to each of them. People thousands of years ago were not stupid when they thought that the earth was flat and the sun revolved around it, just as we are not stupid in believing that it is spherical and revolves around the sun. Relative to the evidence available to ancient people, their belief was a sensible one. Note, though, that opposing beliefs cannot both count as knowledge. If the earth is really flat, then we are wrong in thinking that we know that it is spherical.

These three complications are similar to complications that arise whenever we are applying several different kinds of good and bad qualities. In particular, they are similar to complications that arise in ethics, when we are trying to understand the good and bad qualities of human actions. There too we find that a good result can be obtained by a bad method, as when someone attacks a rival out of petty jealousy, and thereby accidentally prevents the rival from committing a murder. And we find that a bad result can be obtained by a good method, as when a person saves the life of a drowning swimmer, who then commits several murders. Opposite actions can also be justified, too, as when two people are in a burning building and one rushes out so that she can survive to take care of her children and the other rushes in to save some children who are trapped inside.

The analogy with ethics is far-reaching. We apply many of the same labels when evaluating actions and reasoning: careful, sloppy, reliable, clumsy, (in)accurate, (ir)responsible, effective, pointless and so on. We have in everyday life standards and criteria for both the ways we act and the ways we form our beliefs, which philosophy can try to understand and perhaps even improve.

4. The Basic Questions of the Theory of Knowledge

Philosophers contributing to the theory of knowledge have tried to judge how good our beliefs are and how good they could be. They want to evaluate the beliefs we actually have and to suggest ways in which we could get better beliefs. These two aims are obviously connected: if a philosopher thinks that our beliefs are generally rational and true, then he or she is less likely to suggest radical changes in the ways we get new beliefs, whereas if a philosopher thinks that our beliefs are a mass of confusion and falsity, then he or she is likely either to suggest very different ways of getting new beliefs or to despair. So there are three central questions that the theory of knowledge tries to answer:

What qualities should our beliefs have?
What qualities do our actual present beliefs have?
What qualities could our beliefs have?

The answers to the first question might seem obvious. We want our beliefs to be true, rational and based on evidence. But suppose that a philosopher persuaded you that we are not capable of getting very many true beliefs. Then you might settle for aiming at rationality rather than truth. Or suppose a philosopher persuaded you that using reasoning to base beliefs on evidence will result in far fewer true beliefs than some other method: for example, relying on the authority of some tradition. Then you might settle for aiming at true beliefs rather than beliefs based on evidence.

Nearly all philosophers want us to aim at both truth and rationality. They differ, though, on the relative importance of these and other good qualities of beliefs. (For more on this see chapter 5.) Philosophers divide into what might be called conservative and radical camps on the question of how much better our beliefs could be than they are. In the early days of the scientific revolution philosophers were very optimistic about the possibilities for human knowledge. They proposed ways of basing beliefs on reason and evidence which they hoped would lead to beliefs which were both more rational and more often true. (Some of these ways are discussed in chapters 2, 3, and 4.) Many of these philosophers were looking for ways of using reason and evidence which would make it unnecessary to rely on faith or on tradition and authority. Earlier philosophers had tended to be much less optimistic about how much better our knowledge could be. And more recent philosophers, in the nineteenth and twentieth centuries, are also less prone to suggesting radically new ways of obtaining beliefs. So in this respect philosophers writing after the early years of modern science are more like philosophers who wrote before those years. One important difference, though, is that modern philosophers usually consider scientific method to be among our normal ways of acquiring knowledge. Still, philosophers in the twentieth century in particular have tended to analyse the way we actually get knowledge rather than propose radical new ways of acquiring it. (The most radical suggestions have tended to come from Bayesian epistemology, discussed in chapter 9.)

5. Two Extreme Views

To see how different answers to the three questions above can be combined, consider two very extreme views, deep **scepticism** and radical **externalism**. ('Scepticism' and 'externalism' are standard terms in the theory of knowledge. I add the labels 'deep' and 'radical' to show that I am describing particular forms of these positions.)

Deep scepticism

This answers the question 'What qualities should our beliefs have?' with 'We should be able to give good reasons to show that they are true'. It answers the question 'What qualities do our actual present beliefs have?' with 'We cannot give good reasons why they are true'. And it answers the question 'What qualities could our beliefs have?' with 'Human beings are not capable of having beliefs which they can know to be true'. Deep scepticism thus gives a very strongly pessimistic description of the possibilities for human knowledge. (Some milder form of scepticism might be less pessimistic.)

What reasons might there be for deep scepticism? Here are three arguments for it.

Mistakes in reasoning. Most of what we believe is based on evidence. For example, we believe that some medicines cure some diseases, by reasoning from evidence about particular people with those diseases. But it is easy to make mistakes in reasoning. One small mistake can make a whole chain of reasoning go wrong. One safeguard is to check our reasoning; But this is not really a safeguard, as the checking is itself reasoning and can just as easily go wrong. Suppose that there were some profound flaw in the way human beings think. This would spoil all our reasoning; but since it would also spoil the reasoning we use to check our reasoning, we would never know that our thinking had gone wrong.

Perceptual illusions. Very often things are not the way they seem. Often when we rely on seeing or hearing, we form false beliefs. One reason for this is that there are many illusions: mirages, tricks of perspective and of light, ways in which the human visual system does not work perfectly. (These are discussed at greater length in chapter 2.) And then there are dreams and hallucinations, in which people often think they are perceiving things which do not even exist. We are aware of illusions and hallucinations because they contradict the rest of our experience. But that only means that small errors can be caught. Big errors, in which a large range of our perception is illusory, are much less likely to be caught. (In a dream you usually do not know you are dreaming.) So there could be illusions that permeate right through our perception, which we will never recognize as illusions.

Our poor track record. Humans have often been wrong in the past. We once thought that the earth was flat, and now we think it is spherical. The ancient Greeks thought that matter was composed of atoms, and then science thought that it was continuously divisible like a fluid, until in the late nineteenth century scientists began to believe in atoms again. Newton, in the eighteenth century, thought that light was composed of particles, but later, scientists decided that it was composed of waves instead – until Einstein showed that there must be light particles, called photons. Any scientific theory will eventually be shown to be false. And the theory that succeeds it will also eventually be shown to be false. Yet scientific beliefs are the ones we have most reason to think true; if these beliefs are false, then there is little hope for all our other beliefs. So we have reason to conclude that almost all our beliefs are false. I shall not evaluate these three arguments. You should, though, consider seriously how convinced by them you are. (See questions 8 and 11 at the end of this chapter.) Instead, I shall describe a very different position, radical externalism.

Radical externalism

This answers the question 'What qualities should our beliefs have?' with 'Truth is the most important quality of beliefs; other features such as rationality are simply ways of making it more likely that a belief is true'. It answers the question 'What qualities do our actual present beliefs have?' with 'Many of them, especially beliefs about the world around us, are true'. And it answers the question 'What qualities could our beliefs have?' with 'There are many ways in which human beings, individually and in co-operation with one another, can be reliable sources of true information about their environment'.

Here are three arguments for radical externalism.

Evolution. Human beings evolved in an environment not too different from the one we now inhabit. Our ancestors lived on the surface of this planet, dealing with objects of roughly the sizes and shapes that we now encounter. Our human and non-human ancestors were sensitive to the same frequencies of light and sound as us. If our senses and our ability to use the information we get from them were not generally accurate, we would have died out thousands of years ago. But we are still here, a testimony to our ability to form true beliefs about our environment.

Intuition. When people defend their beliefs with conscious chains of reasoning which they express with words, they make many mistakes. But in the course of everyday life we learn many routines of thinking which work well, especially if we do not stop to think about them. For example, people are pretty good at simple arithmetic, as long as it stays simple. But if you ask a person to state the reasons why he or she believes that 340 − 89 = 251, you are likely to get a confused and erroneous answer. Moreover, we have skills, such as the ability to find our way from one place to another or the ability to understand one another's moods and facial expressions, which we do not understand very well, but which get us satisfactory results. We usually do not get lost on the way home, and we usually understand when another person is angry with us. These everyday routines and skills are sources of beliefs, such as the belief that 340 − 89 = 251, that to get home you must turn left at Elm Street, or that the person you are speaking to is on the verge of violent anger. Since our everyday lives depend on these beliefs, and since our everyday lives work reasonably well, we can conclude that the routines and skills we use are fairly reliable sources of true beliefs.

Co-operation. People acting in groups can easily do many things that would be impossible for individual people. This applies not only to hunting and building houses, but also to knowing. A member of a society can know information learned generations before and passed down from one person to another. Language is essential to this, and so is the disposition to trust what other people say unless there is some reason to disbelieve them. In modern times a lot of our beliefs depend on very complex networks of co-operation. For example, you believe that television sets pick up radio waves coming through the air, but you probably cannot give a good description of how they do this, or even what radio waves really are. And you believe that antibiotics such as penicillin are effective against many bacterial diseases; but if you are like most people, you do not have any good idea of how antibiotics are made or how they work against bacteria. But this information is available to you via your links with other people: you can read books, ask for advice, and consult experts. So the whole community in a way has a more complete knowledge of many things that individual people do not. Functioning as part of a community, trusting others so that you can put your different bits of information together, an individual person can have reliable access to many true beliefs. Individual people can rarely have this knowledge using just their individual resources, and they usually cannot give a fully convincing explanation or justification of it. But that does not deny the fact that the beliefs are trustworthy and true.

Deep scepticism and radical externalism are very different views. But notice that they are not simple opposites. For they start from different answers to the first question, 'What qualities should our beliefs have?' Deep scepticism assumes that the most important quality of our beliefs is that we can be sure that they are true. It then tries to show that we cannot be sure that many of our beliefs are true. On the other hand, radical externalism assumes that the most important quality of our beliefs is just that they are true, whether or not we can be sure of it. It then tries to show that many of our beliefs are true, even if we cannot be sure exactly which ones. Both deep scepticism and radical externalism may be wrong. But until we have decided which are the most important qualities for our beliefs to have, we should not feel that if one were to be right, the other would have to be wrong. Given the assumptions each one makes about the aims of belief, they could both be right.

Issues connected with deep scepticism and radical externalism will get more discussion in later chapters. (See especially chapters 3, 5, and 8.) For now the important point is how answers to the three questions shape theories about knowledge. Do we want our ways of acquiring beliefs to produce true beliefs, rational beliefs, beliefs that are true and rational, beliefs that we can be sure are true and justified, or what? How much more true, more based on evidence, or more rational could the beliefs of human beings be? The theory of knowledge tries to answer questions like these. It is important to see the interaction in these questions of considerations about what kinds of belief we could have and considerations about what kinds of belief we want.

Reading Questions (For the distinction between reading
questions and thinking questions see the Foreword for Students.)

1   Section 1 mentioned constructive and destructive functions of the
theory of knowledge. It also gave examples of searching for better
ways of acquiring beliefs and of criticizing beliefs: which of these
was the constructive function, and which was the destructive
function?

2   Section 2 gives examples of epistemic ideals. It then suggests that
we should consider whether they can be achieved by human
beings. How might the rationalist ideal not be achieved by human
beings?

3   Section 3 claims that rational beliefs will tend not to be wide
generalizations expressed with words like 'all' or 'never'. Could we
express any rational beliefs using these words?

4   Section 3 had examples of rational and irrational beliefs. Would it
be more accurate to speak of beliefs which it is rational or irrational
for a person to hold at a particular time? Give examples.

5   Section 3 said that there can be very strong reasons for believing
something although it is false. Give an example of this.

6   Consider the following four cases. (They are all Canadian cases, for
no special reason.)

(a)   Alberta is enjoying a rare warm break in a cold winter. It is
January, and she is in Calgary. She is about to travel to
Edmonton, 250 km to the north, for a week. She thinks: 'I'll
leave my winter coat behind; it's so nice today that it's sure to
stay warm.'

(b)   Victoria is waiting for the 12.05 ferry from Vancouver to
Nanaimo. She is wearing an expensive watch which has never
gone wrong and which is reset every noon by a time signal
from the British Columbia observatory. She looks at it and sees
that it says noon. She thinks: 'It is noon, so I had better hurry
to get the ferry.'

(c)   Arthur is waiting for the plane to take him from Thunder Bay
to Winnipeg. He has a watch which works one day in three.
He looks at it and thinks: 'It is noon, so I have plenty of time
before the plane leaves.'

(d)   William is waiting for the plane to take him from Winnipeg to
Thunder Bay. The airport clock says 11:42 a.m. and he thinks:

'The plane boards at 1 p.m. so I can spend fifteen minutes finishing my coffee and still have more than an hour before I have to be at the gate.'

In which of these is the person's belief rational? In which is it justified? In which is it knowledge? Classify them into Yes, No and Perhaps.

7   Section 4 said that if you thought that we were not capable of getting very many true beliefs, then you might want to have rationality rather than truth as your aim. It also said that you might want to have truth rather than evidence as your aim if you thought that basing beliefs on evidence would result in few true beliefs. Why?

8   In section 5 the second argument for deep scepticism said: 'We are aware of illusions and hallucinations because they contradict the rest of our experience. But that only means that small errors can be caught. Big errors, in which a large range of our perception is illusory, are much less likely to be caught.' Why might someone think this?

9   The conclusion of the first argument for radical externalism is that the routines and skills we use in everyday life are fairly reliable sources of true beliefs. Why only fairly reliable?

Thinking Questions

10   Consider canny Cassie. She is a great guesser. She has hunches about which teams are going to win basketball or football games; she has intuitions sometimes that a news bulletin or a newspaper headline is false; she often has a conviction about unannounced schedule changes of television programmes; and just occasionally she has a terrible foreboding of an impending disaster. We all experience these things; but Cassie is different in that her hunches, intuitions, convictions and forebodings are nearly always right. When she has a belief about the future, it is nearly always true. When she is asked about this, she says: 'I don't know where my beliefs come from and I know no reason why they should be true. In fact, I don't expect that my beliefs about the future are any more reliable than other people's.' But she is wrong: her guess-based beliefs *are* more reliable than other people's.

Suppose you are about to travel to New York by plane. Cassie says to you: 'Don't take that flight. I don't know why I feel this, but I really don't want you to take that flight.' Is Cassie's belief rational? Suppose you take her seriously and believe that you shouldn't take the flight. Is your belief rational? Suppose that while taking Cassie seriously, you continue to believe that no person can know the future. Is that belief then irrational?

11   Here is part of the first argument for deep scepticism: 'Suppose there were some profound flaw in the way human beings think. This would spoil all our reasoning, but since it would also spoil the reasoning we use to check our reasoning, we would never know that our thinking had gone wrong.' Is it so clear that we could never tell if there was a flaw that affected all our reasoning? Suppose, for example, that people always estimate probabilities wrongly. Would we never notice this fact about ourselves? Might there be other kinds of problems about our reasoning which would be forever hidden from us?

12   Here is part of the second argument for radical externalism: 'If our senses and our ability to use the information we get from them were not generally accurate, we would have died out thousands of years ago.' Is this true? Can you think of kinds of inaccurate perception which would not interfere with a species' survival? Might there be kinds of inaccurate perception which would actually increase the survival chances of a species?

13   Consider the ultimate virtual reality machine. It plugs into both your sensory and your motor nerves and connects them to a hyper-powerful computer which stimulates all your senses with exactly the input they would get from a real environment and changes these stimulations exactly the way they would change if you were really moving your body so that you interacted with this real environment. Of course the environment that the computer simulates is completely different from your actual environment. Suppose you had been in such a machine from birth. Would you have any reason to believe you were not living a real life in the environment you seem to find around you? Would your beliefs (for example, that you are reading a philosophy book at this moment) be rational? How does this relate to deep scepticism?

14   How does the ultimate virtual reality scenario relate to radical externalism?

15   In section 3 rational beliefs were described in terms of the way a
     person acquires the belief at a particular time. Justified beliefs, on
     the other hand, were described in terms of the relation between
     the belief and the information on which it is based. Very often
     rational beliefs will be justified, and rationality and justification will
     coincide. But not always. Consider two examples. Neither of them
     makes an open-and-shut case, but discuss their implications for the
     distinction between rationality and justification.

   (a) Genevieve wants to know whether the coin in her hand is fair
        (that is, whether there are equal chances of heads and of tails if
        it is tossed). She tosses it four times, and it comes down heads
        three times. A friend who has a Ph.D. in mathematics tells her
        that if the head is fair, there is a 2/16 chance that it will come
        down heads at least three times in four throws. She thinks that
        since this probability is pretty small, the coin is probably biased.
        In fact, her friend is wrong, and there is a 5/15 chance that a
        fair coin will come down heads at least three times in four
        throws. Is Genevieve's belief that the coin is biased rational? Is
        it justified?

   (b) Gunther is taking part in a psychological experiment. The
        experimenters tell Gunther that they are giving him a powerful
        drug which will make all people look like his mother. Gunther
        believes them, although the 'drug' they give him is actually
        pineapple juice. The point of the experiment is to test whether
        he will think that women look like his mother just because he
        expects them to. Gunther's mother is a telephone repair per-
        son, and has been called to fix a telephone in the psychology
        department. By mistake she walks into the laboratory where
        Gunther is. 'Hello mom', says Gunther, for a moment thinking
        it is his mother, before doubt sets in. Is Gunther's momentary
        belief that the woman in front of him is his mother rational? Is
        it justified?

16   Assume that an epistemological theory we may call 'traditionalism'
     is true. According to traditionalism, it is rational to hold a belief
     which many others in your culture believe and have believed, even
     if there is no strong evidence that it is true, as long as there is no
     strong evidence that it is false. (Take 'strong evidence' to be
     evidence that would make it rational to hold the belief indepen-
     dently of the traditions of your culture.) Then, as in question 15,

we have a way in which it might be rational to hold a belief even though you had no justification for believing it. It all depends on what you mean by 'justified'. Suppose that a person lives in a culture in which some religious beliefs are widely held. Suppose, moreover, that there is no direct evidence for the existence of God – no evidence that should convince a determined atheist – and there are no logical arguments proving the existence of God. Contrast the following two definitions of 'justified':

(a) A person is justified in holding a belief B if either she knows of evidence that would be accepted by someone who doubted B which makes it rational to hold B, or she understands a logical argument which leads from her present belief to B.

(b) A person is justified in holding a belief B if, given her other beliefs, it is reasonable to add B to them.

Assume that traditionalism is right. Describe in detail a person's beliefs and the person's situation (evidence, beliefs of other people, etc.) which would make that person's belief in God rational but not justified, according to (a) but not according to (b).

Further Reading

Accessible discussions of belief, reason and the aims of the theory of knowledge are found in chapters 1 and 2 of Martin Hollis, *Invitation to Philosophy* (Blackwell, 1985), and in chapter 1 of W. V. Quine and Joseph Ullian, *The Web of Belief* (Random House, 1978). Chapters 1 and 2 of Adam Morton, *Philosophy in Practice* (Blackwell, 1996), are also relevant. Chapter 1 of Jonathan Dancy, *An Introduction to Contemporary Epistemology* (Blackwell, 1985), begins with scepticism as a basis for covering some of the same ground as this chapter. Dancy is not an introductory book, though. Issues about how the aims of epistemology have changed during its history are discussed in Mary Tiles and Jim Tiles, *An Introduction to Historical Epistemology* (Blackwell, 1993). Fundamental distinctions between rational and justified beliefs are made and challenged in chapter 1 of Alvin Plantinga, *Warrant: The Current Debate* (Oxford University Press, 1993), which also discusses the resemblances between standards in morals and those in epistemology. Selections from classic philosophical works relevant to this chapter can be found in John Cottingham, *Western Philosophy: An Anthology* (Blackwell, 1996). See part I section 7, David Hume, 'Scepticism Versus Human Nature', and part I section 10, G. E. Moore 'Against Scepticism'. (These are Cottingham's titles, not Hume's and Moore's.)

2 Perception

1. The Issues

We have knowledge of many things because we can see, hear, smell or touch them. So any account of the ways we can and could acquire our beliefs must discuss perception, the use of our senses to learn things about the world around us. There are two central questions in the philosophy of perception. The first is: How do we obtain information about our environment by using our senses, and when is this information accurate? The second is: How does perception provide us with evidence for or against our theories and beliefs? These questions arise very naturally when one reflects on two observations. First, people's senses often deceive them, and things are often not as they seem to be. Second, one of the marks of science and of responsible thinking is a careful use of facts gathered from unprejudiced observation.

Philosophers trying to answer these questions run into a very basic problem. To understand how reliable perception is, we might begin by learning some facts about perception, learning how the eyes and ears work and what kinds of illusions affect them. And to understand how far evidence from perception can support theories about the world, we might begin by seeing how perception is related to the world around us, to learn what range of facts connect with the visible spectrum of light reflecting into our eyes, sounds that we can hear entering our ears, and so on. But this seems to run round in a circle. To learn how the eyes and ears work, we have to study them scientifically: but why should we trust these scientific theories before we know whether the perceptions they are based on are reliable? And to learn how perception connects with the world, we have to study the world scientifically: but why should we trust this scientific picture of the world?

Contemporary philosophers take this problem less seriously than philosophers in the past have. Since the middle of the twentieth century many philosophers have thought that they can use theories based on perception to study how beliefs can be based on perception, without going round in circles. One of the main purposes of this chapter is to explain why this is so. In doing this I shall describe a number of different philosophical attitudes to perception. Some of these theories allow themselves to use facts and theories from the psychology and physics of perception. Other theories want to base what they say just on common sense, logic and the meaning of words.

2. The Concepts

Perception is what happens when one becomes aware of objects and situations around one through the use of the senses, such as sight, hearing and touch. We sometimes describe what someone perceives in **relational** terms. That is, we just say what object or event the person perceives; for example, we might say that someone sees a cat, and hears her, and touches her. Sometimes we also want to say what information about an object or the person's surroundings has been gathered in perception. We might say that someone hears the cat come in through a window, and sees that she has hurt her foot, and feels that there is a thorn in it. These descriptions are **propositional**; they involve propositions, assertions about what is perceived. It is important to note that we can also say things like 'He sees that all his cats are asleep' in a situation in which someone does not get all the information at one glance, but gathers it bit by bit and then puts it all together mentally. One cat may be asleep on the rug, another on the bed, and the third on top of the refrigerator.

As a result, it is quite natural to use the vocabulary of perception, to talk of seeing and hearing and feeling, in cases that involve thinking and remembering as much as they involve the use of the senses. In extreme cases, as when one says that someone sees that torture is wrong or hears that Microsoft has dropped fifteen cents, it seems clear that the use of perceptual terms is purely 'cognitive' – that is, that it is the brain rather than the eye or ear or skin that is doing the perceiving. But in many other cases, such as that of the person who sees that his three cats are sleeping, it is not clear that we can make a distinction between the cognitive and the perceptual, between pure thinking and pure perceiving. Most perception seems to involve thought as well as the use of the senses.

If we describe a person's perception in propositional terms, we ascribe true beliefs to that person. The person who hears the cat come in through the window, and then sees that she has hurt her foot, first believes that the cat is coming through the window, and then that she has hurt her foot. When we describe someone's perceptions in relational terms, we also assume that the person acquires beliefs about whatever is perceived. However, some of the beliefs may be false. For example, if a person sees a cat but thinks that it is a bowling ball, it is still true that that person saw that cat. And even when we describe a perception propositionally, we are not ruling out the possibility that false beliefs are acquired along with the true ones. To someone who sees that a cat is limping, it may seem that it is the right front rather than the left front paw that is being favoured, and this may be false. The person acquires the true belief that the cat is limping and the false belief that the right front paw is being favoured.

The beliefs that are acquired as part of perceiving are called **perceptual beliefs**. There is not an exact line between perceptual beliefs and other beliefs, just as there is not an exact line between perceiving and thinking. But obviously some perceptual beliefs are nearer to pure perception. The belief that there is a grey shape in front of you is *more perceptual* than the belief that there is a cat nearby, which is itself more perceptual than the belief that your cat has come home. This does not mean that there must be completely perceptual beliefs.

Perceptual beliefs can be true or false. (In the examples above, one person gets the true perceptual belief that there is a cat coming in through the window, and another the false perceptual belief that there is a bowling ball right in front of him.) The belief that the cat has hurt her foot is a borderline case of a perceptual belief, and the person's belief that cats are not bowling balls is not any sort of perceptual belief. False perceptual beliefs don't feel any different from true ones. If I look at my cat and think that she is asleep, she may actually be waiting for me to pass by so that she can sneak outside or she may be asleep. It *seems* the same to me in either case. We may also say that I receive the same *visual appearance* whether or not the cat is sleeping. The visual appearance is of the cat lying on the rug with her eyes closed and her legs folded under her and her nose tucked under the tip of her tail. In this case the visual appearance is true to the cat. (Or at any rate, the part of it I have described is; we might go on to say that the appearance is, to me, one of a sleeping cat, and this part may be false.) However, visual appearances (also appearances from hearing, touch and other senses) may be quite unlike the facts. It may appear to me that off in the corner of my field of vision a curtain is moving, when actually my cat is tipclawing outside.

Appearances are a fundamental aspect of perception, for humans at any rate. When we see or hear, things look or sound one way or another; they have visual or auditory appearances. Almost every person experiences most of their waking life a rich variety of perceptual appearances from all the senses. Only some of the richness of perceptual appearance is captured in our perceptual beliefs. (To make this vivid: look at any scene you have seen a hundred times. Search and you will find some feature of it which you had not known was there – you had no belief about it – but which was part of the way the scene looked to you.) So appearance and belief are both basic aspects of perception. Yet the relation between them is not simple, as we shall see.

3. Empiricism

One of the most influential movements in the theory of knowledge, and perhaps one of the most influential movements in philosophy, is **empiricism**. Empiricism was developed by philosophers such as Locke, Berkeley and Hume in the seventeenth and eighteenth centuries, and has contributed ideas that are still central to philosophy. The most important of these ideas is a picture of the way in which beliefs are justified. According to empiricism, a belief is justified when it is connected by good reasoning to evidence obtained by perception. Moreover, perception can give us beliefs that are certain enough that they can be the evidence for all beliefs that can be justified at all. (A possible exception is beliefs about mathematics and logic, which are not supported by any evidence at all.)

Empiricism can be seen as giving answers to central questions of the theory of knowledge, described in the last chapter. To the question 'What qualities should our beliefs have?', it answers: 'They should be based on sure evidence obtained by perception.' To the question 'What qualities do our actual present beliefs have?', it answers: 'Many of them are not supported by adequate evidence. In many cases the evidence can be found, but in some there is no evidence and the beliefs should be abandoned.' To the question 'What qualities could our beliefs have?', it answers: 'We could, potentially, have only beliefs that are based on perceptual evidence.' Empiricism is thus both a very down to earth and a very idealistic philosophy. It is down to earth because it aims to base all our beliefs on what we can see, hear and touch. And it is idealistic because it thinks that human beings are capable of reforming their beliefs so that they are all based on perception.

A theory that gives such a central role to perception must be as clear as it can be about the nature of perception. The empiricist account of perception can be described in terms of the two central questions of the philosophy of perception, introduced in section 1 of this chapter. The first was: How do we obtain information about our environment by using our senses, and when is this information accurate? According to empiricism, when we use our senses, we receive distinct units of information, which Locke and his followers called 'ideas', but which more recent empiricists call 'sense-data'. These **sense-data** describe the shapes and colours that a person is seeing, the pitches and timbres that she is hearing, and so on. They correspond both to visual appearances (or appearances from other senses) and to beliefs that are as close to pure perception as beliefs can get.

The second basic question of the philosophy of perception was: How does perception provide us with evidence for or against our theories and beliefs? According to empiricism, the ultimate evidence for all our beliefs comes from sense-data. There are two features of sense-data that make them the ultimate evidence. First, there is nothing that can give evidence for them; they're at the end of the line in terms of evidence. And second, they are certain; they are evidence that cannot be doubted by the person who has it.

Both of these features are controversial, and later philosophers have attacked them energetically. But empiricists did have reasons for assuming them, which arise out of the ways it is natural to defend a belief if it is challenged. Suppose you think that your cat is on the kitchen counter making 'I want to be fed' noises. If someone doubts this belief, you will give evidence for it. You might begin by saying, 'She was here on my lap a moment ago, and then I heard her footsteps going towards the kitchen.' If you are challenged to say how you know she was on your lap, you would say 'But I saw her'. Notice how when we give evidence for a belief, we move towards describing what we have perceived. But suppose that your questioner still does not give up. 'How do you know that you saw her?' 'Well', you might say, 'it looked like her: I certainly saw a black and white cat-shaped figure.' Notice how when your perceptual belief is challenged, you defend it in terms of a more perceptual belief, and ultimately in terms of appearance – that is, in terms of the way things look or sound or feel to you. Sense-data are the information you get from these beliefs, at the end of the line of justification, about your perceptual appearances.

There is a central insight here (which empiricists took over from Descartes). It is that your perceptual beliefs are more certain than your other beliefs, and that your beliefs about your perceptual appearances are more certain than your other perceptual beliefs. In short, you know for sure how things look, sound and feel to you, and no other person's challenge is going to make you doubt that you are having the perceptual appearances you do have. So sense-data are well suited to being the ultimate evidence, in terms of which all beliefs must be justified.

There are two other reasons why we might take perception to be a good source of evidence for beliefs. The first is that perception makes a fairly direct connection between a physical fact and a person. Light reflects off the cat into the person's eyes and causes cells in the retinas of the eyes to stimulate the optic nerve to transmit information to the brain. This process is complicated but reasonably reliable, and probably much less complicated than most of the other ways in which facts affect our thoughts. So it is natural to think of perception as a very basic way of discovering facts. (Note that although empiricists are no doubt influenced by this reason, it is one they have to be careful with, since for them the beliefs about the connection between facts and the brain are among the beliefs that they want to justify using evidence from sense-data.)

The other reason for taking perception as a source of evidence is that perceptual beliefs are relatively independent of other beliefs. If I come to think that my cat has been abducted by aliens, then when I hear her coming in through the window, I will think that it is some other cat, but I will still see that a cat is coming in, and she will still look the same way to me. The more perceptual a belief is, the less it will be affected by changes in other beliefs. As a result, there is less danger of circular reasoning when using perception for evidence. There is less danger that someone challenging the evidence will be able to say that if you hadn't already held the belief you are finding evidence for, you would not have held the belief you are using for evidence.

The appeal of empiricism as an epistemic ideal is clear. It offers us a picture of a wide range of beliefs, including those of common sense and science, all based on very firm evidence obtained by perception. (This is the appeal of a variety of epistemic ideals and theories, known as **foundationalism**. Foundationalism is discussed in chapter 5, especially section 2.) If we could meet the empiricist ideal, we would be able to give reasons for all our beliefs, and though we might not be completely assured that all our beliefs were true, we would have pretty good assurance that they were as true as we can make them.

The appeal of the ideal is clear. But what is its price? And how near to achieving it can human beings come? Unfortunately, after some three hundred years of considering, refining and arguing about empiricism, the consensus among philosophers is that the full empiricist ideal would have a very high price, and is not an ideal that humans can come very near to achieving. There are two main reasons for this.

First, *more certainty means weaker evidence*. The evidence on which scientific theories are based is rarely absolutely certain. For example, the chief source of evidence for theories in astronomy is observations made through telescopes. Astronomers try to make these as carefully as they can, and to make as few unnecessary assumptions as possible when describing their observations. But they are not totally certain. When an astronomer says that she has seen a new star appear at given co-ordinates in the sky, it is always just possible that she has instead seen some optical malfunction of the telescope, or has been hallucinating, or that some activity by extra-terrestrials has caused a bright light to appear at the appropriate spot in the sky but much nearer the earth than it appears to her. And even when the evidence takes the form of a photograph of the light collected by the telescope, a lot of interpretation has to be added before the photo can be used as evidence. Is this really the film that was at the telescope's focus at the time in question? In what direction was the telescope pointed when the light was collected? Which marks on the film represent light focused down the telescope, and which represent either light from other sources or effects of the film's development? Were atmospheric conditions above the telescope distorting the paths of light rays to it? All these questions can be answered if there seems to be serious doubt about them. But answering them usually involves other sophisticated equipment and other not completely certain observations.

The point is that in science the technique for finding evidence is to use unusual situations and complex experimental apparatus to find tell-tale effects of natural processes. Doubts about the evidence are resolved by other evidence and other experiments. This will not answer all possible doubts. It is not meant to. Usually in science some particular theory has to be defended against doubters who support some other particular theory, and the evidence has to be chosen so that both of these sides can take it seriously, but not so that non-scientists or sceptical philosophers will be impressed. So if astronomers are debating the origins of quasars, they need evidence that will be interpreted in the same way by astronomers who believe in steady state and Big Bang theories of the origin of the universe, who believe in different theories of the evolution of stars, the distribution of mass in the universe, and so on. But they do not have to worry what doubts or interpretations will occur to mystics who believe that the stars are angels dancing around the earth with messages for mankind, or to sceptics who suspect that telescopes produce images of things that do not exist.

This is very different from the technique suggested by empiricism, which aims to qualify the content of observations until they could not be doubted by anyone, no matter how little they know or what other beliefs they hold. The ultimate certain evidence, according to empiricism, is not 'There is a supernova at time t at co-ordinates r, θ' or 'There is a bright event at t, r, θ', but: 'It seems to astronomer P that at time t she saw a bright light at what she thought was location *r*, θ, and which she assumed to be produced by light from beyond the earth.' When you appreciate the difference between this kind of evidence and the evidence that is actually used in science, you cannot feel very optimistic for the empiricist aim of basing all our beliefs, particularly scientific ones, on absolutely certain sense-data.

The second reason for doubting that the empiricist ideal can be attained can be summed up as: *Very basic beliefs are very hard to find evidence for.* Suppose that you are an empiricist and that you take the best evidence to be your sense-data, information about how things look, sound or feel to you. You want to use this evidence to support beliefs about the world around you, such as the belief that you are on the surface of planet Earth, occupying a human body, and surrounded by other humans. On the way to these beliefs, or as a consequence of them, you will want to find evidence for the belief that there is a physical world around you which causes your sense-data by stimulating your senses. But very basic beliefs like these are not easy to justify in terms of sense-data. In effect, it is not easy for an empiricist to show why the deep scepticism discussed in section 5 of chapter 1 is not right. By asking that all beliefs be supported by absolutely certain evidence, empiricism may be guaranteeing that very few beliefs will be supported.

The problem of showing why it is reasonable to believe that our perceptions are really caused by a physical world around us, sometimes called the problem of the existence of the external world, is a very serious one for empiricism. So is the problem of showing why it is reasonable to believe that the human beings you are surrounded by have minds like yours and experiences similar to yours, which is called the 'other minds problem'. (The other minds problem is discussed in the first five sections of chapter 7.) Note that the other minds problem makes the external world problem harder. For one of the sources of your belief in the external world, and in fact of almost all your beliefs, is what other people tell you. But if the words of other people are not the result of thoughts, information and knowledge held by those other people, then you should treat everything that people say to you with great suspicion. The danger is not that other people may be lying to you as much as that their words may not mean anything at all: what you take to be meaningful speech giving you information about the world might just be random sounds. In order to provide evidence for many of your beliefs, empiricism would have to give evidence to show why you can rely on what other people tell you about past times, distant places and experiences you have not had. For it is your links to other people's beliefs and experiences that provide you with most of the evidence you have for most of what you think you know.

4. Some Experiments

In this section I summarize four experiments about appearance in visual perception. They suggest some reasons why the empiricist ideal is difficult for us to attain.

Experiment 1: seeing as

In figure 1 there is a drawing of a duck. Look at it. It is easy to see the duck in the drawing. Actually, the picture can also be seen as a rabbit (see the duck's beak as the rabbit's ears). If this paragraph had begun by saying 'Figure 1 contains a picture of a rabbit', you would have seen it as a rabbit when you first looked at it.

The picture does not look the same when it is seen as a duck and when it is seen as a rabbit. One thing this shows is that some visual impressions are not determined by the image on the retina of a person's eyes (since the image on the retinas, the sensitive regions at the back of the eyes, is the same when a person sees a duck in the drawing as when the person sees a rabbit in it). It also shows that some visual appearances cannot be completely described in a simple geometrical way, as the distribution of

Figure 1. Pictures that change their meaning. The duck-rabbit (b) is particularly striking, because it is perfectly placed between two kinds of examples (a and c). At one extreme is the reversing cube (a), which can be seen two ways, each of which represents a different geometrical configuration – is the starred corner at the front or the back? At the other extreme are figures that vary in terms of their expressive meaning; (c) looks like Charlie Chaplin or like Hitler. The duck-rabbit shares with examples like (c) the feature that its changes of meaning are not simply changes of the geometrical figure it represents, and shares with examples like (a) the feature that its meanings clearly differ in what it is seen as, and not in the way one reacts to it. It is thus ideally suited to illustrate the moral: appearances are not uninterpreted pictures.

light and dark points in space. For in these terms too there is no difference between the duck-appearance and the rabbit-appearance. A visual appearance is not a picture. (It is perhaps a picture plus some sort of explanation of the picture.)

This experiment also shows that our expectations influence how what we see appears to us.

Experiment 2: perspective

In this experiment subjects observe circles from various angles. They are asked to draw the visual impressions that they have of these circles seen at these angles. (They are asked to draw what they look like, not what they think they are.) Some subjects draw all the circles as circles except those which are seen at extremely great angles. Other subjects draw all the circles as ellipses except those which are seen at extremely small angles. But all subjects draw less eccentric (more circular) ellipses than those which the corresponding circles will throw on their retinas. Moreover, the less sophisticated subjects, especially those with less knowledge of psychology or of perspective drawing, draw the rounder ellipses, and the more sophisticated subjects draw the flatter ones. But even the most sophisticated subjects do not draw the ellipses as flat as they should be according to the rules of true perspective drawing, or as they should be if their visual appearances correspond to the images on their retinas.

The conclusion here is that people's beliefs about a situation – in this case, the belief that the figures are circular – influence their perception of it. We make the appearance resemble the way we think the reality is.

Experiment 3: the upside-down world

Subjects spend a period of days, or sometimes weeks, wearing glasses which turn the image upside-down. At first it looks as if everything is upside-down: the sky is beneath and the earth above. Then there is a fascinating transitional period in which some things at some times appear inverted, and some things do not. Finally the subject says that things look normal: the sky seems above and the earth beneath. Then the subject takes off the glasses and everything seems upside-down again!

This is an intriguing experiment, and hard to draw firm conclusions from. It certainly shows that a person's visual impression of the world is not just a matter of the input from their sense-organs. It suggests also that the input from the sense-organs determines the visual impression, in a way that depends in part on the beliefs and tendencies to behaviour that they produce. Thus, as long as subjects had not learned to use their senses to guide their actions when they were wearing the glasses, they had an upside-down impression; but when they had learned how to get around wearing the glasses and manipulate objects properly, then the world stood on its feet again. There is a lot more that can be said about this experiment, and others like it; more detailed descriptions and analyses of them are well worth reading. (For one thing, it is not perfectly clear how the world does appear to someone who has got used to the inverting glasses; I have glossed some things over.)

Experiment 4: wise babies

Modern technology allows us to make observations of young babies that would have been impossible not long ago. One recent technique is to monitor babies' eye movements to see what features of their environments they dwell on. It turns out that even very young babies do a surprising amount of structured looking. They tend to look much more at unexpected objects and situations than expected or familiar ones. In one experiment infants as young as two and a half months watch a ball roll behind a screen which is then lifted revealing the ball at rest at an end wall. Then, when they are familiar with this, they see two kinds of event. In one, the 'possible' event, a box is placed in the path of the ball, the screen is lowered, the ball rolls, and the screen is raised, revealing the ball at rest by the box. In the other, the 'impossible' event, a box is placed in the path of the ball, the screen is lowered, the ball rolls, and the screen is raised, revealing the ball at rest by the end wall, as if it had passed through the box. Infants looked longer at the impossible event, suggesting that it was surprising, and thus that at the age of two and a half months they are on the way to thinking of the world as containing solid objects which cannot pass through one another.

5. Evidence without Certainty

Empiricism, at least in the traditional form in which it was described in section 3, gave us no good account of how perceptual beliefs are justified. It led us into a swampy maze. The four experiments I have just described suggest why. They suggest that empiricism makes a false assumption about perceptual appearances. In assuming that all our perceptual beliefs can be based on sense-data, empiricism supposes that when we perceive something, we first start with information about appearances, and then use this as evidence for a belief about what we are perceiving and what it is like. These experiments, and others described in the psychology of perception, suggest that this is wrong.

The experiments do not suggest that there is nothing to the notion of an appearance, for they rely on subjects' being able to describe how things look to them, and express in other ways what visual impressions they have. If we take appearances to be specifications of how the world looks, sounds and so on to people – which they report when asked about their impressions – then there clearly are appearances. But what the experiments suggest about visual, and presumably other, appearances is that they are not purely collections of information gathered by the senses, and that perceptual beliefs are not obtained by reasoning from them. For the way a person's environment appears to the person at any moment depends on that person's previous state, their beliefs and desires and habits, just as the acquisition of perceptual beliefs does. For example, in the first experiment (seeing as) the figure looks like a duck or like a rabbit depending on what the person looking at it believes he or she is going to see. In the second experiment (perspective) people represent the appearances of the things they are seeing in ways that make them more like the shapes they know these things really have. And in the third experiment (upside-down world) the appearance that information from the senses leads to is shaped in part by the practical purposes which the information is going to be used for. The fourth experiment (wise babies) suggests that we arrive at the outlines of some beliefs about how things really are so early in life that they are in effect shaping our perceptions from the very beginning.

Perception thus begins with sensory inputs or patterns of stimulation, which are probably not beliefs of any kind, and by combining these with beliefs that the person already has, makes perceptual beliefs *and also appearances*. Appearances are not produced at the boundary of the mind; they are produced by a complex interaction of sensory input and pre-existing belief. They are thus not very well suited for the role of ultimate basic evidence, since they depend on beliefs themselves. To people with different beliefs, the same things will appear different, so the appearances cannot always provide impartial evidence to suggest which beliefs are true.

There are several possible reactions to this situation. The empiricist ideal of absolutely certain evidence, based on the sense-data of individual people, which will give good reasons for our beliefs, is impossible. So we could try for a less demanding ideal. We could want evidence that was less than certain. We could want evidence based on something other than perceptual appearances. We could want perceptual evidence that gave reasons for less than all our beliefs. Nearly all contemporary philosophical theories of knowledge retreat from the full empiricist ideal in all these ways, to a greater or lesser degree. Before asking exactly how much we should retreat in each way, we should remember the point made in chapter 1, that there may be many different qualities we want our beliefs to have, and it is far from clear that a single ideal can meet them all. Do we want beliefs that are completely beyond doubt, or beliefs that fit neatly with scientific knowledge, or beliefs that we can use in everyday life? Beliefs that a community of people can use for their combined scientific and practical projects, or beliefs that a single person can use to gain as much knowledge as she can all by herself? Different kinds of perceptual evidence may be right for these different purposes.

Behind the details of empiricism there was a vaguer ideal, of holding beliefs because they are supported by evidence that can be seen, heard or otherwise sensed. The nearer we can get to this ideal, the more confident we can be that we are not holding beliefs just because we have been taught them in childhood, or because they are written in textbooks, or because other people believe them. How much of this vaguer ideal could remain if we retreat from full-strength empiricism? How much can we expect our beliefs to be shaped by our perceptions, if we accept that how we interpret our perceptions – how things seem to us and what perceptual beliefs we form – is always going to be influenced by the beliefs we already hold. To see some of the possibilities and issues, consider an imaginary extreme case.

Imagine two tribes or societies that have very different mythologies and differ throughout their opinions about how the world works. They live on different islands, and have no contact with each other or with any other societies. Perhaps one society believes in many gods who take an interest in individual animals and individual things, while the other society believes in one magical spirit found in everything and believes that individual animals and things are aspects of this spirit and thus fundamentally the same. (So the one society sees the universe as a collection of many things, and the other society sees the universe as one thing showing itself in many ways.) Suppose that from a certain point on, the two societies are exposed to all the same data and observations, in the same order, for a number of generations: the same weather, the same events in the day and night sky, the same diseases and harvests, and so on. Moreover, suppose that these new observations refute all the original opinions of both tribes. Now it might seem plausible that if these societies were composed of sensible, intelligent people, then after all these years and with the original divergent opinions no longer on the scene, their opinions would be more or less the same. But this need not be so. Faced with each new observation, each society could evolve its doctrines in a very different way, because the doctrines they had before making the observation were different, and because the parts of the different doctrines that did not get changed, at the stage in question, could influence the changes that did get made. For example, one society might treat as an interesting hallucination what the other society treated as divine revelation. (On each island, water freezes to ice crystals one day, something they both previously thought impossible. On the first island they take reports of this as a dream sent by the spirit to show that everything can turn into everything else, since everything is the same. So afterwards they think that perhaps liquids can turn into solids. On the second island, they take the reports to be relating something so impossible – substances that the gods had kept apart becoming one another – that they can only be lies or illusions sent by evil forces. Anyone who claims to have seen water freezing is put to death.) In this way, at the end of the process, although each society's beliefs are based on the same body of observations, the responses they have made may be very different.

This story suggests how perception may support and lie behind our beliefs, theories and opinions, without determining exactly what they will be. To use an analogy, our beliefs are like the position and orientation of a leaf blown by the wind. The wind represents experience and observation. The only force leading to change in position and orientation is the wind, but the changes that it produces depend on the initial position and orientation. Two leaves initially near to each other and pointing in similar directions could, when blown by a strong, uniform wind, end up in quite different places pointing in quite different directions, because of the small original differences.

This way of looking at the effect of perception is meant to bring out both its capacity to move our beliefs towards the truth and the limits of that capacity. The limits are easiest to see: the beliefs of the two societies in the example are very different even after they have been influenced by a long period of similar perceptual evidence. If either one is true, the other one is false, and it is just as likely that both are false; so exposure to perceptual evidence does not seem automatically to produce true beliefs. But there is another side to the same story, which reveals more of the power of perceptual evidence.

Think again about the example of how observations of water freezing were understood by one society as a message from the spirit and by the other as an illusion. In each case the interpretation was determined by two main factors: the society's beliefs about what kinds of facts could possibly be true and its beliefs about how perception works. Both societies believed that what seems like real perception can be the effect of good or bad spirits; so the fact that one society believed that freezing was just possible made it interpret the experience as a true message, while the fact that the other society thought that freezing was out of the question made it interpret the experience as a delusion. The conclusion might have been different if the two societies had also had strong beliefs about how perception works. We in our culture believe that nearly everything that seems like perception and which happens when people are awake and behaving normally is real perception. And if several people seem to see something, and can also touch, hear and smell it, then we are very reluctant to think that they are not really seeing it. Moreover, we have beliefs about how perception occurs. We think that seeing is the effect of light reflecting from objects into people's eyes, and we have complex beliefs about exactly how this occurs. So if we are in doubt about whether something is really perception or not, we can try to test the situation further: we can try to discover how light and sound are being transmitted, and so on. We know some of the causes of hallucinations, and we know how mirages work and the principles behind many optical illusions.

What this suggests is that perception can enlarge our true beliefs under certain special circumstances. Suppose that we know enough about the causes of perception and illusion to be able to tell in most cases which is which. Suppose, moreover, that this really is knowledge – it does tell us when our perceptions are giving us true perceptual beliefs. And suppose lastly that even if there are many falsehoods and unanswered questions in our beliefs about the world, we are not totally mistaken about the kind of environment we live in. Then we can gather information by using our senses, either simply perceiving as much as we can or using sophisticated scientific strategies to observe special and unusual situations. And much of what we observe will be true. We can use our imperfect knowledge of perception to tell us which perceptions to trust and which to reject, and then use the ones we trust to increase our knowledge and thus improve our understanding of perception. And so on, round and round.

If our beliefs are not too mistaken to start with, and *if* our understanding of perception is not too inadequate, we can expect to be able to use our senses as part of a slow process of weeding out false beliefs and replacing them with others nearer the truth. It would not be completely misleading to call this position *naturalistic* empiricism, contrasting it with the simple empiricism discussed earlier in this chapter. For it assumes a conception of the role of the senses in connecting us with the natural world around us, and uses this to explain how the senses can provide us with evidence. (See sections 5 and 6 of chapter 9 for more on naturalism.) But it does make some large assumptions: if and if. Many philosophers would not grant these assumptions. For example, philosophers sceptical of our capacity to know much about the world would not grant them. And if our beliefs about the world are deeply mistaken, then, according to this position, evidence from perception is not going to improve them. That is surely correct: no theory of perception could show how to learn the truth if we are locked into virtual reality machines, or live our lives in drug-induced hallucinations, or are duped by superior beings who amuse themselves by feeding us misleading information. If any of these are true, then, when we try to base our beliefs on perceptual evidence, we are as likely to make them more false as more true.

Reading Questions

1   Suppose I write a book in which I say: 'Everyone should believe anything that Adam Morton says.' The book has other surprising claims in it too. Someone doubts whether the book is a trustworthy source of information, and another person says: 'The answer to that question is in the book too: in chapter 1 it says that you should believe what it says.' What is the problem here, and how does it relate to the issues in section 1?

2   Which of the following beliefs are more perceptual and which are less perceptual?
(a) A blind person's belief that grass is green.
(b) A person's sudden realization that another person is very angry.
(c) An experienced hunter's belief that there are moose droppings at his feet.
(d) A musician's belief that her instrument needs tuning.

3   Why might beliefs about mathematics and logic be exceptions to the empiricist claim that all beliefs are based on perception?

4   Which of the following is nearer to being a report of a person's sense-data?
(a) I see a moose.
(b) I am experiencing a shape in front of me with a central brown region and below it four vertical regions and above it a head-shaped region connected to yellow-grey spreading areas.
(c) It smells like moose.

5   Consider the example in section 3 of doubts about the interpretation of photographic evidence in astronomy. One doubt was whether the image on the film was caused by light coming down the telescope. How might this doubt be resolved, and how would this require other equipment and other observations?

6   Why is there a problem for empiricism from the fact that, as section 3 expresses it, your links to other people's beliefs and experiences provide you with most of the evidence you have for most of what you think you know? You hear what people say, and you see what they write: is this not empirical evidence?

7   Why is it important in experiment 1 that if the description had begun by saying 'Figure 1 is a picture of a rabbit', you would have seen it as a rabbit when you first looked at it?

8   How does experiment 3 show that a person's visual impression of the world is not just a matter of the input from their sense-organs?

9   Why might the conclusion of experiment 4 be difficult for an empiricist to accept?

10   The myth of the two islands suggests that sensible and intelligent people can react in different ways to the same evidence. But one society believes that ice is a hallucination. How could this be sensible or intelligent?

11   'We can use our imperfect knowledge of perception to tell us which perceptions to trust and which to reject, and then use the ones we trust to increase our knowledge and thus improve our understanding of perception. And so on, round and round'. How can this cyclic process result in anything but more and more evidence for the same beliefs?

Thinking Questions

12   In section 2 a person sees a cat and thinks it is a bowling ball. How wrong could you be about something and still be perceiving it? Suppose that someone thinks that the black spot at the edge of her visual field is a floater in her eye, when actually it is the image of her cat in the half-light. Is she seeing her cat? Suppose that there is a row of identical buttons along the top of a chair, and placed among them is the nose of a cat hiding on the far side of the chair, the only part of her that is visible. A person sees the row of buttons and takes the nose to be simply another button. Does he see the cat?

13   Some beliefs are more perceptual than others. But, according to section 2, there do not have to be completely perceptual beliefs. Supposing that there are not infinitely many beliefs, does not every person have to have some beliefs that are their most perceptual beliefs? And are these not then completely perceptual for that person?

14   Is it true that your beliefs about what things look like are more certain than your beliefs about how things really are? Consider this story. A bank employee catches a very brief glimpse of the face of a robber. He cannot give the police any usable description of what

the robber looked like. A week later he sees a woman for an instant through closing elevator doors. He knows that she was the robber he saw. But again he cannot give any definite description of what she looks like.

15 Is it true that you know for sure how things look, sound and feel to you? Consider these possible counter-examples:

(a) A person wonders why he finds a portrait in a gallery disturbing. It looks to him both attractive and angry. In fact, the portrait closely resembles his mother, to whom he has a very ambivalent attitude. He does not know what it looks like to him.

(b) A person goes into a restaurant and has the best meal of her life. She tries to reproduce the special taste of that meal at home. But she finds she cannot, because although she remembers the meal very vividly, she does not really know what it tasted like.

(c) A person is trying to describe a singer's voice. 'She has a very high soprano', she says. 'No', someone else says; 'it is not high; it's just squeaky. You don't know what it sounds like.'

16 The example of the astronomical observations depended on the fact that astronomy uses complicated equipment such as telescopes. Can similar points be made for sciences, such as field biology, which do not need sophisticated equipment?

17 Suppose that, as argued in section 3, evidence in science does not refer to the experience of particular people. Could an empiricist still argue that scientific evidence is valid only when it is based on the experience of particular experimenters? After all, each experiment is performed by a particular person at a particular time, and the report of the experiment depends on what that person experienced.

18 The conclusion drawn from experiment 2 is that we make the appearance resemble the way we think the reality is. Describe some alternative interpretations of the experiment that block this conclusion.

19 The conclusion drawn from experiment 4 is that two-and-a-half-month-old babies are on the way to thinking of the world as containing solid objects which cannot pass through one another. Describe an alternative interpretation of the experiment that blocks this conclusion.

20   Section 5 suggests three retreats from the empiricist ideal. We could look for (a) evidence that was less than certain, or (b) evidence based on something other than perceptual appearances, or (c) perceptual evidence that gave reasons for less than all our beliefs. And it also suggests that we might associate these retreats with the search for (i) beliefs that are completely beyond doubt, or (ii) beliefs that fit neatly with scientific knowledge, or (iii) beliefs that we can use in everyday life. Which of (a), (b), (c) would be a suitable means for getting beliefs of which of the kinds (i), (ii), (iii)?

21   Section 5 also suggests that we could look for (1) beliefs that a community of people can use for their combined scientific and practical projects, or (2) beliefs that a single person can use to gain as much knowledge as she can all by herself. Which of (a), (b), (c), described in the previous question, are suitable means for getting beliefs of kinds (1) and (2)?

22   In the example of the two cultures on the two islands, the starting beliefs of the two cultures are very different from ours – so different that they will disregard perceptual experiences that we would regard as important evidence. So what is the point of wondering what conclusions a long run of perceptual evidence would lead them to?

23   The conclusion of the chapter is that perception can only lead us to true theories about the world if our beliefs about it are not too mistaken to start with. Could more evidence and more theories give us any confidence that our starting beliefs were not radically mistaken?

Further Reading

A very readable introduction to issues about perception, covering both philosophical and psychological theories, is Robert Schwartz, *Vision* (Blackwell, 1994). There is a very simple discussion of the philosophy of perception in chapter 9 of Adam Morton, *Philosophy in Practice* (Blackwell, 1996), which focuses on empiricism. A good collection of philosophical papers on perception is Jonathan Dancy (ed.), *Perceptual Concepts* (Oxford University Press, 1988); the papers by Lewis, Dretske, Armstrong and Grice are most likely to be helpful to a non-advanced student. Chapters 10 and 11 of Jonathan Dancy, *An Introduction to Contemporary Epistemology* (Blackwell, 1985), discuss perception from a more advanced level than this book.

Accessible texts in the psychology of perception are Lloyd Kaufman, *Sight and Mind* (Oxford University Press, 1974), and Irvin Rock, *Introduction to Perception* (Macmillan, 1975). Iona Rock, *Introduction to Perception* (Open University Press, 1978), is an extremely clear and helpful exposition in two short volumes. Experiments on the perceptual skills of small children are described in chapter 3 of J. Gavin Bremner, *Infancy* (Blackwell, 2nd edn 1994).

Two stimulating books on the overlap between philosophy, psychology and art theory are Richard Gregory, *Eye and Brain* (McGraw-Hill, 1966), and E. H. Gombrich, *Art and Illusion* (Pantheon Books, 1960).

For the views on perception of the British empiricists see David Hume, *An Enquiry Concerning Human Understanding*, chapters 2, 3, 7 and 12, and John Locke, *An Essay Concerning Human Understanding*, books I and II. For discussions of the empiricists see Roger Woolhouse, *The Empiricists* (Oxford University Press, 1988); chapter 10, sections A and B, of John Cottingham, *Rationalism* (Oxford University Press, 1988); Barry Stroud, *Hume* (Routledge, 1988); and chapters 6 and 10 of Jonathan Dancy, *An Introduction to Contemporary Epistemology*.

Selections from classic philosophical works relevant to this chapter can be found in John Cottingham, *Western Philosophy: An Anthology* (Blackwell, 1996). See part I section 3, Aristotle, 'Demonstrative Knowledge and its Starting-points', and part I section 5, John Locke 'The Senses as the Basis of Knowledge'.

3 Apriori Beliefs

1. Knowledge just by Thinking

Suppose you have three kittens and two baskets, and you are going to put some of the kittens in one basket and some in the other. How many ways are there of doing this? You could find out by trying all the ways and counting them. Or you could find out by thinking. You could reason as follows. Consider the first kitten; it could go in either the right basket or the left one. That gives two ways of starting. Each of them can be continued by putting the second kitten in either the right basket or the left basket. So that makes two times two, or four, ways of going on. Then the third kitten can be put in either the right basket or the left one, giving four times two, or eight, ways of distributing the kittens between the baskets.

This could be a fact about three particular real kittens and two particular real baskets. And you can see that it is true without having to collect evidence. You know in advance, prior to any evidence, what the answer has to be. Philosophers refer to knowledge that we can have in advance of any evidence as **apriori** knowledge. (The standard term is 'a priori'. It comes from two Latin words meaning prior to the evidence. Students find the term confusing, since it sounds like it is talking about a thing called a priori. So this book will join a small trend of writing 'apriori' as one word.) The opposite of apriori knowledge is **aposteriori** knowledge, knowledge which can be gained only after, posterior to, seeing the evidence. (Traditionally two words, 'a posteriori'.) Mathematics, as in the mini-proof about the kittens and the baskets, is one of the main sources of apriori knowledge. Or, to put it more carefully, mathematics gives many examples that philosophers use when explaining their theories about apriori knowledge. But there are many examples which do not come from mathematics.

Suppose, for example, that someone tells you that they have a moose in their pocket. You find this hard to believe, and challenge them to produce it. They reach into their pocket and bring out a pebble. When the person claims that this is a very unusual moose, you are more than sceptical. You know the person must be either joking, or lying, or crazy, or mean something very different by the word 'moose'. You do not need to consider any further evidence to know that a small piece of stone cannot be a large mammal. If you did not know things like that, you would not be able to understand any evidence.

Or suppose that you are mixing some paint in order to decorate a friend's kitchen. She is very particular about colours, and so you show her the yellow shade you plan to use. She says to you: 'It's not red enough yet.' You go to mix in some more red paint and by mistake mix in blue. So the result is a greenish yellow instead of an orangeish yellow. You apologize, but she says: 'No, that's great, the more blue you put in, the more orange it gets.' Here too you know immediately that something is drastically wrong with what she is saying: a yellow-coloured object cannot get redder (more orange) and bluer (more green) at the same time. Either this person is not serious, or she is very confused.

The issues here are in a way the opposite of those in the previous chapter. One main question there was: 'How many of our beliefs can we base on evidence from what we perceive?' The contrasting question here is: 'How many of our beliefs can we base on reasoning rather than on evidence from perception?' This chapter discusses some ideas about beliefs based on reasoning, involving the concepts of apriori, analytic and necessary beliefs. These ideas have a long history in philosophy, and contemporary philosophy is profoundly influenced by challenges to traditional views of them begun by W.V. Quine. The chapter ends with the conclusion that some of the traditional ideas survive the challenge, though with very significant changes.

2. Apriori, Analytic, Necessary

There are different ways in which a belief can be independent of perceptual evidence, and it is important not to confuse them. Apriori knowledge has already been mentioned. Consider now two similar, but different, kinds of belief.

Analyticity

Consider again the moose example of the previous section. You know that a moose is not a stone, just because you know that 'moose' means 'large North American mammal of the deer family', and you know that no stones are large mammals of the deer family. (A complete definition of 'moose' would have to say more: this is only part of the meaning of 'moose'.) So you can know that a moose is not a stone just by understanding the meaning of the words you use. Philosophers have considered many similar examples. 'All bachelors are unmarried', 'All sisters are female', 'Your mother's mother is your grandmother' are all examples that have been suggested. In all of these it is hard to see how someone can doubt the belief as long as they understand what the words mean. All these are **analytic** beliefs. (The sentences that express them are called analytic truths, or analytic propositions.) Analytic beliefs are apriori, because knowing how to speak a language makes it unnecessary to consider evidence for them. In the next section we consider whether all apriori beliefs are analytic.

A special case of analyticity is **logical truth**. Suppose you believe that it will either rain or snow and it will not snow, but do not believe that it will rain. Then there is something very wrong with your beliefs, because anyone who understands the meaning of the words 'and', 'not' and 'or' knows that if it will either rain or snow and it will not snow, then it will rain. This is a fact not about the weather but about logic. There are many similar examples. You can know that either all moose are chipmunks or there is a moose that is not a chipmunk, without ever having seen a moose or a chipmunk. In all these cases knowing the meaning of a few words, 'logical' words such as 'and', 'not', 'or' and 'all', allows you to know that very many beliefs must be true.

Another way of approaching logical truths is through the idea of a **deductively valid argument**. Consider the following argument: It will either rain or it will snow; and it will not snow, therefore it will rain. Logicians call arguments like this 'deductively valid'; their defining feature is that the conclusion of the argument ('it will rain') will always be true if the premises ('it will either rain or it will snow', 'it will not snow') are true. Any argument of this general form ('p or q, not q; therefore p') will lead reliably from true premises to true conclusions. Logicians study the many forms of deductively valid argument. For each such form of argument there is a whole class of logical truths. 'p or q, not q; therefore p' gives us 'if p or q and not q, then q'. 'All As are Bs; all Bs are Cs; therefore all As are Cs' gives us 'If all As are Bs and all Bs are Cs, then all As are Cs'. For example, this last class of logical truths includes 'If all cats eat mice and all mice are small mammals, then all cats eat small mammals'.

The result of the link between logical truths and deductively valid argument is that as long as a person can understand deductively valid arguments, he or she can know that logical truths are true. As long as you can reason from the assumptions 'All cats eat mice and all mice are small mammals' to the conclusion 'All cats eat small mammals' you know that if all cats eat mice and all mice are small mammals, then all cats eat small mammals. So to know logical truths, we can rely, it seems, not on evidence, but just on our ability to reason and argue.

Both analytic beliefs and apriori beliefs are often connected with the concept of **necessity**. This is not a central concept in the theory of knowledge; but it is worth saying something about it, since issues about apriori knowledge are closely connected to issues about necesssity. Necessary beliefs are beliefs that not only are true but have to be true. They could not be false. (Notice that the discussion of the moose example in section 1 said that you know that a small piece of stone *cannot* be a large mammal, and the discussion of the paint example said that something *cannot* get redder and bluer at the same time.) Many beliefs that are known apriori are also necessary. It is necessary that $2 + 2 = 4$, or that a set with three members has eight subsets. However the universe had been, from the very beginning, it could not have developed so that $2 + 2$ was anything other than 4, or that moose were pebbles, or orange was blue.

It is very easy to get confused here, though. When we say 'without consulting the evidence you can know that $2 + 2$ has to be 4', we can mean two things. We can mean that we *have to think* that $2 + 2 = 4$, or we can mean that $2 + 2$ *has to be* 4. These are only the same if the things that we have to think are things that could not have been false. And there are good reasons for doubting that this is so. Consider two examples.

The first example needs a single person who is known by two names, such as the writer Mark Twain (author of *Huckleberry Finn*) who was originally known as Samuel Clemens. Mark Twain could have lived a different life, so that he was never given the name 'Samuel Clemens'. But that person, Mark Twain, could not have ever been different from himself, Samuel Clemens. So the belief that Mark Twain is the same person as Samuel Clemens is necessary; the fact that it refers to could not have been otherwise. But it is not apriori; it is something that we have to learn, on the basis of evidence. (In fact, we could learn that all the books are wrong, and that Mark Twain was not Samuel Clemens.) So necessary truths are not all apriori.

Just as not all necessary truths are apriori, so not all apriori truths need be necessary. Or, at any rate, this can be argued quite strongly. Consider two cases. First, suppose that human beings come with an inbuilt idea of space which makes them think, without considering the evidence, that space has three dimensions and is organized in the way it is (so that, for example, if a region B is contained within a region A and a region C is contained within B, then A is *not* contained within C). Suppose now that although space is like this, it does not have to be. Perhaps events within the first millisecond after the Big Bang determined that space would have three dimensions and the kind of organization it does have, but that if those events had occurred differently, then space would have been different. Then our beliefs about space are apriori, but not necessary.

A second example comes from Descartes. Suppose that Descartes, wondering whether he could be wrong even about his own existence, reassures himself by reasoning: 'I'm wondering about this, so I am thinking, so I exist.' He can know just by thinking, without any evidence from perception, that he exists. So his belief that he exists is apriori. (It is apriori for him. *My* belief that Descartes existed is not apriori.) But it is certainly not necessary. Descartes could easily not have existed.

There are also analytic beliefs that are not necessary. Here is a simple, though rather artificial, example. Define the word 'pouce' to mean 'the length of my thumb today, 8 July 1996'. Then it is analytic that my thumb is one pouce long today. But it is not necessary: my thumb could easily have been a bit shorter, because of malnutrition or some accident.

Neither of these arguments, the argument that some apriori truths are not necessary or the argument that some necessary truths are not apriori, are accepted by all philosophers. There are some objections to them worth thinking seriously about. But they do show that it is not at all obvious that there is a connection between a belief being apriori and its being necessary. Later in this chapter we will have to wonder what the connection is between a belief being apriori and its being true.

3. Kant on the Synthetic Apriori

All analytic beliefs are apriori. But what about the other way round? One reason for thinking that all apriori beliefs are analytic comes from thinking, as empiricists do, that evidence from perception is the main source of knowledge. For suppose that we make the empiricist assumption that what perception does is to link our minds to the facts in the world that our beliefs are about, through the experiences that are evidence for those beliefs. Then it follows that no beliefs about anything in the world are apriori. For all of these beliefs depend on evidence from perception. The only apriori beliefs, then, would be beliefs that are not about anything in the world. Suppose that the only thing that beliefs can be about other than the world around us are the meanings that we give to words in our minds. Then it follows that apriori beliefs are based on the meanings of words – that is, are analytic.

This argument makes several big assumptions. It assumes that the only reasons we have for beliefs about the world come from perception. And it assumes that all beliefs are either about the world or about meanings. Neither of these assumptions is very convincing. (But this does not have to mean that the conclusion – that all apriori beliefs are analytic – is false. There might be a stronger argument for it.) To see how we might challenge these assumptions and the conclusion they lead to, consider three examples of beliefs which some philosophers have thought were apriori but not analytic.

First, consider beliefs about colour, such as the belief that as a yellow colour gets more reddish, it cannot also get more bluish; or the belief that if something is red it is not green. It is hard to see why these have to follow from the meaning of colour words. The belief that green is a colour might follow from the meaning of 'green' and 'colour', but the fact that when a yellow object becomes more orange, it becomes less greenish seems to be just a fact about colours. Yet it is a fact that we can know without considering any evidence. As long as we know what colours are, we know that it is true. Or so some philosophers have argued.

Next consider beliefs about mathematics. A good example is the belief that there are infinitely many natural numbers, that the series 1,2,3,4, . . . goes on for ever. (Or, another way of expressing it, that for every natural number, there is another one which is greater than it.) If we know that arithmetic is true, we know that this belief is true. But it is hard to see how it is part of the meaning of the word 'number'. However you define 'number', it does not seem to follow that there are infinitely many of them.

Thirdly, consider beliefs about cause and effect. Suppose some person thought that there was never a reason why things happened. One billiard-ball rolls into another and the second starts moving, he thinks, just for no reason, the fact that it is immediately after the collision being a pure coincidence. Plants that get no water die, but he just thinks: some plants die and some do not, there's no reason. If we ask this person to investigate why something happened, he does not even understand the question. Perhaps such a person could collect basic evidence from perception, though it is hard to see how he could survive long enough to perceive anything interesting; but he could not use the evidence to support or refute any beliefs about why events occur, since he does not think any such beliefs could be true. This points to the importance of beliefs about causes: beliefs that there are causes to be discovered in the world, that very often something that happens does so because of some other event, and that we can learn the connections between causes and their effects by considering evidence about them. These seem to be beliefs that we have to have before we start considering evidence about the causes of particular events.

None of these examples are completely convincing. Philosophers who believe that only analytic beliefs are apriori can find replies to them. But they do make the beginning of a case for non-analytic apriori beliefs. What is needed to make the case stronger is a general pattern which would show what the examples have in common. One such general pattern is found in the work of Immanuel Kant (1724–1804), especially in his *Critique of Pure Reason*. Kant pointed out that collecting evidence for or against our beliefs is something that itself needs to be guided by beliefs. For example, someone who had no beliefs about distances in space would not be able to begin to use a telescope, or interpret what she saw through it. And someone who had no beliefs about numbers and counting would not be able to make or use any measurements, and so would be unable to understand almost all scientific experiments. So, Kant reasoned, behind our ability to collect evidence through perception for our beliefs, there must be a body of fixed beliefs, which we have to assume in order to get the enterprise of finding and interpreting evidence started. Kant called these beliefs *synthetic apriori*.

Kant's own list of synthetic apriori beliefs included the propositions of arithmetic and geometry, the belief that events have causes, the belief that there are laws of nature that we can discover, and the belief that people and physical objects persist through time. We can see how these explain the examples about cause and arithmetic at the beginning of this section. It is not so clear how they fit the example about colours. One way of fitting that example into Kant's picture would be to argue that if we are to describe the endless variety of colours and shades in the world with a few fixed terms like 'red' and 'green', then we will have to think in terms of degrees of red and green (and other colours) so that we can capture all the in-between shades. But to do this, we will have to combine the colours into a single structure, which means making assumptions like 'more red is less green'. So here too the same Kantian idea can apply: before we can begin to describe the world, we have to make some assumptions.

Kant had a lot more to say about the assumptions we must make before we can begin to describe and understand the world. The central problem that he tried to answer was why these assumptions should be true. Why should the fact that we have to have some beliefs before we can begin to collect and consider evidence give us any confidence that these beliefs are true? His answer was that they are true because we make them so. They are not true because of the way the world around us is, but because of the way our minds are. Some later philosophers have thought that this was a very deep insight into the relation between thought and reality. Others have thought that it was mistaken. The important point for us is the claim, accepted by most philosophers now, that without some prior beliefs we could not even begin to describe what we perceive. We have to have some beliefs before we consider evidence.

4. Quine on the Analytic/Synthetic Distinction

W. V. Quine, writing in the 1960s, made a claim that at first seems the opposite of Kant's. Yet, when we consider Quine's full position, it turns out not to be so very different from Kant's. Quine's claim was that there is no fundamental difference between analytic and synthetic beliefs. No belief, according to Quine, is true simply because of the meaning of words. All beliefs are true or false because of the way the world is and the meaning words have, and we cannot separate these two components.

Consider some standard examples of analytic beliefs: the belief that all bachelors are unmarried, the belief that cats are animals, or the belief that people are born before they die. If these really were a special kind of beliefs, argues Quine, it would be impossible to find any evidence against them. But in fact we can imagine circumstances in which we might even begin to doubt whether they were true. Here is an example (not one of Quine's). Suppose that a sect of mad fanatics insists that all females over the age of 16 must be married. If they discover that any woman is not married, they kill her. In order to prevent this, every young woman at the age of 16 marries a young man of the same age. This is not a 'real' marriage; the couple do not live together or act as man and wife, and when either of them wants a 'real' marriage with someone else, they divorce and begin relationships more like marriage as we know it. Suppose now that young men in their twenties, looking for young women to share their lives with, describe themselves as 'bachelors' if they are only married in this 16-year-old fanatic-forestalling way. It would then be very natural to call these men married bachelors.

Someone might argue against this as follows: 'bachelor' means 'unmarried man', so if we ever come to think that there are married bachelors, we have simply changed the meaning of the words. Quine has a reply to this. There are many definitions we could give for 'bachelor' that fit the way we use the word equally well. For example, we could define it as 'man who is not in a relationship with a woman which late twentieth-century people would think of as marriage'. The differences between these definitions do not matter for us, but they would be significant differences for the people in the situation described. To think that we can tell definitely when a word's meaning has changed is the same kind of mistake, according to Quine, as to think that there is a definite distinction between analytic and synthetic beliefs.

It is important to see that Quine is not claiming that any belief can be abandoned at any time. To abandon the belief that bachelors are unmarried, or even to be in a position to think that there might be evidence against it, we would have to be in a very different position from the one we are in now. The example in the last but one paragraph above describes one such very different position. So Quine is not denying that it is reasonable to treat the standard examples of analytic beliefs as if they were apriori, believing them without considering evidence from perception, and using them when we consider evidence for other beliefs. He is just pointing out that the situation could change so that it no longer makes sense to treat some of them as apriori.

One particular kind of change of situation is particularly important, on Quine's way of thinking. That is change of our beliefs. Quine emphasizes that beliefs are linked to one another in a vast network, which he calls the 'web of belief'. For example, the belief that the earth is round is linked to the belief that compasses point north, to the belief that light travels in straight lines, to the belief that the same sun rises every day, and to many others. To consider evidence for or against any of these, we would have to take the others into account, either assuming them or at the same time considering whether the evidence told for or against them also. In this web of beliefs some beliefs are nearer the edge and some are nearer the centre. Perceptual beliefs are nearer the edge, in that they are linked very much to experience and comparatively little to other beliefs. These beliefs are fairly easy to change, given new evidence. Other beliefs are nearer the centre in that they are linked very much to other beliefs and only very indirectly, through long chains of other beliefs, to perception. These beliefs change very slowly as we get new evidence: they are insulated from evidence by the beliefs that surround them. Moreover, they can rarely be refuted by contrary evidence, since instead of abandoning such a belief, we can nearly always instead abandon some other belief to which it is linked. (For example, instead of abandoning the belief that bachelors are unmarried, the people in the story above could instead have abandoned the belief that everyone who had gone through a marriage ceremony was married.)

5. Conceptual Truths

Quine's conclusions and Kant's are different in an obvious way. Quine is saying that no belief is safe: it might be reasonable to abandon absolutely anything we believe; whereas Kant is saying that some specific beliefs have to be maintained in order to make any sense of our experience. But underneath this difference there are important ways in which Kant and Quine agree. Both philosophies agree that we cannot make sense of what we perceive without some beliefs that interpret and link perception to thought. So both break with the empiricist idea that we can get evidence for or against our beliefs simply by describing our experience. And both agree that it is structured patterns of beliefs, rather than single beliefs, that allow us to think, consider evidence, and explain the world around us. In the long run these similarities are more important than this difference.

One difference is very important, though. Kant's conclusion was that there are beliefs that everyone must have in order to make sense of their experiences, while Quine's conclusion was that that everyone must have some beliefs which are at the centre of their web of belief. To translate Kant into Quine's terms, he is saying that there are beliefs that must always be at the centre of the web of belief, whereas Quine is saying only that there must always be a centre, though different beliefs can be there. There are many subtle connections between these two positions, but both agree that for any person at any time the web of belief will always have a centre. There will always be beliefs that a person needs to make sense of what they perceive, and which are not for that person at that time supported or challenged by any evidence. So in what follows I shall investigate the consequences of this weaker conclusion.

At this point it is important to distinguish concepts from beliefs. In order to have a belief, you need to have the concepts involved in it: to believe that cats eat mice you have to have the concepts of 'cat', 'mouse' and 'eat'; to believe that no moose weighs more than six tons you have to have the concepts of 'moose', 'weight', 'six' and 'more than'. Nearly all simple apriori beliefs can be used as tests for having concepts. If you think that orange is more blue than yellow, you do not have the colour concepts that the rest of us have. If you think that cats are a kind of pebble, then something is unusual about your concept of cat or of pebble. (Note that these tests come by combining simple apriori beliefs: the belief that orange is redder than yellow; the belief that as a colour gets more red, it gets less blue; the belief that cats are animals; the belief that animals are not stone; the belief that pebbles are stone.)

So the web of beliefs is also a web of concepts. When someone has a belief – for example, that cats are generally smaller than moose – they will also have other beliefs involving the concepts involved in it, which give the beliefs meaning and allow there to be evidence for and against it. So the beliefs that cats are small carnivores and that moose are large herbivores allow explanations of why cats are smaller than moose, and beliefs about what cats and moose look like allow everyday perceptions of cats and – if you're lucky – moose to give evidence for the belief. A well-functioning web of beliefs will link all of its beliefs both with perception and with apriori beliefs, the first to provide evidence, the second to provide clarity.

There are many ways to have a well-functioning web of beliefs. Empiricism suggests that we should have a stock of concepts which are specifically for gathering evidence from perception. Call these **experiential concepts**; they would include concepts like those of colour and shape and sound. These would provide evidence for beliefs involving *theoretical concepts*, with which we explain and understand the world. Concepts such as those of mass, energy, gene, virus, and the structure of space and time would be theoretical concepts.

Most concepts are not purely theoretical or purely experiential. For example, one aspect of concepts of animal species, like the concepts of cat, moose and fish, consists in their links with perception, since we know what cats, moose and fish look like. But another aspect is theoretical, since we think of these animals as fitting into a complex system of classifying living creatures. As a result of this second aspect, we do not think that everything that looks like a cat, a moose or a fish really is one. There are fake moose, and it may not be easy to tell just by looking. And not everything that has fins and swims in the water is a fish. Whales and scuba divers are mammals, not fish. In our contemporary system of beliefs and concepts almost all concepts are linked both to perception and to theories.

One result of the-two way linkage of most concepts is that the beliefs that give us our understanding of concepts – the apriori beliefs – often change. Only a few centuries ago the concept of a fish was so closely linked to having fins and swimming in the water that whales were thought of as fish. Now we connect the concept of a fish to being cold-blooded, having gills, and being related to other fish by a common evolutionary history. So we do not think that whales are fish. While it may once have been an apriori belief that anything that has fins and spends most of its life under water is a fish, now we think that this is false. A clear example of this occurs when someone introduces a new word for a specific concept. Suppose that I invent the word 'infoCD' and define it as 'Compact Disk with a computer program on it'. Then the belief that infoCDs have computer programs on them is an apriori belief *when the concept is first introduced*. But after that other people may use the concept for their own purposes; the web of belief takes over; and anything can happen. Perhaps all the infoCDs have information stored on them in a different way to music CDs, and this is the same way as CDs with information that is not in the form of programs. So then people may take this as the defining characteristic, and it may no longer be apriori that infoCDs have computer programs. Or perhaps we cease to think of all programmable digital devices as computers, so that the very objects I originally named as infoCDs are no longer used to program what we then think of as computers. Anything can happen. The important conclusion is this: *we always have apriori beliefs, but at different times we treat different beliefs as apriori.*

6. The Uses of Reasoning

This chapter began with a mathematical example. It was meant to support the idea that simply by reasoning we can know facts. That question led us to a discussion of apriori knowledge which focused on beliefs which are needed in order to have particular concepts, beliefs without which we would not be able to communicate or consider evidence. Most of these beliefs were pretty simple, bordering on the trivial. This might make them uninteresting. But to think this would be to ignore one of the most basic and amazing features of human thought: that by reasoning from trivial assumptions, we can get to non-trivial conclusions. In fact, we can often get to non-trivial conclusions surprisingly quickly. Among the many ways we can reason from the trivial to the amazing, three stand out. Call them destruction, exploration and accumulation.

Destruction

Often a philosopher makes assumptions which at the time she is writing would be accepted by everyone as being so obvious that anyone who doubted them must be joking or confused, and from these assumptions derives very surprising conclusions. Very often the conclusion is something that is hard to believe, so that the result is a paradox. For example, the ancient Greek philosopher Zeno started with simple assumptions such as that 'in order to move from one point to another, you have to pass through all the points in-between' and that between any two points there is another point, and came to the paradoxical conclusion that motion is impossible. (For to get from A to B, one will have to pass through the infinitely many points between them in only a finite amount of time.)

Paradoxical conclusions like this can be used to argue that something is wrong with the apriori beliefs they assume. Obvious though they may seem, a little reasoning shows that some of them may be false. But when it begins to seem that apriori beliefs are false, we begin to loose our grasp of the concepts involved in them. For the philosopher who says, for example, that perhaps you can move from one point to another without passing through all the points in-between, is a bit like the fool or the confused person who simply does not have the concepts needed to grasp this belief, and does not understand what 'point' or 'move' mean. With an important difference, though. The philosopher is usually trying to show that there is something wrong with the concepts she is making trouble for. She is in effect saying: 'If this is what we mean by "motion" and "space" (for example), then we should consider using other concepts instead.' So within philosophy one important purpose of reasoning from apriori beliefs is to show problems and limitations of our concepts. The effect is not only destructive; very often the aim is to get clearer or better concepts, which will be linked to different sets of apriori beliefs.

Exploration

Sometimes we think something is obvious when a little reflection shows that it is not. Sometimes we think that anyone who has a particular belief must be confused, and then a little reflection shows that the belief is not so confused after all. For example, you might think it was obvious that the fairest way of dividing something between people is to give each person an equal share. Then you might think a bit further and wonder whether this was fair when some people had more to start with, or when some people would get more satisfaction from their share while others would have no interest in it. As a result, you might try to formulate a more subtle definition of fairness, in terms of the situations of the people before the distribution and the benefits they would get from it. In doing this, you would be formulating new apriori beliefs to define the concept of fairness. But they would not be entirely new. You would probably be trying to find beliefs which you and others had implicitly held all along, without being able to express them clearly. This too is a major philosophical activity: to find better ways of articulating beliefs which lie behind the concepts that we use all the time.

Accumulation

Instead of generating paradoxes or digging out implicit beliefs, reasoning can begin with apriori beliefs and lead to more apriori beliefs. Much of mathematics is like this. We can begin with assumptions so obvious that they seem completely uninteresting, like '$0 + 1 = 1$' and 'for every number there is another distinct number which is greater than it by one', and by deducing consequences from them we get to completely unexpected, interesting conclusions, such as that the sum of any sequence of consecutive numbers is the first plus the last multiplied by half the number of members in the sequence. The remarkable thing about mathematics is that when we deduce consequences from apparently apriori beliefs in this way, we do not very often get paradoxes or find we have to dig out further implicit beliefs. At any rate, this happens less often in mathematics than in the rest of our beliefs. Although paradoxes and problems about what assumptions are the right ones do crop up regularly, mathematicians seem to be able to handle them in such a way that the body of mathematical theorems keeps accumulating. Philosophers disagree about the best explanation of this. Some point to the special non-perceptual intuitions that are used in mathematics, whereby we can 'see' numbers and geometrical structures in our minds and reason about them. Some point to the rigorous nature of proofs in mathematics. Some point to the place of mathematics in the web of belief, as central as any beliefs could be. None of these explanations is completely convincing.

Reading Questions

1 Which of the following beliefs are apriori beliefs, and which are aposteriori? (All are Australian beliefs, for no particular reason.)
   (a) Australia is bigger than New Zealand.
   (b) Australia is in the southern hemisphere.
   (c) If you have two koalas and three kangaroos, you have five animals.
   (d) If Perth is west of Adelaide and Adelaide is west of Sydney, then Perth is west of Sydney.
   (e) Perth is west of Sydney.
2 Which of the following beliefs are analytic, which are logical truths, and which are necessary?
   (a) Kangaroos carry their babies in their pouches.
   (b) Kangaroos live in Australia.
   (c) Kangaroos are mammals.
   (d) If George is the brother of Sam and Sam is the father of Frederika, then George is the uncle of Frederika.

(e) If George is the uncle of Frederika and George is a kangaroo, then Frederika is a kangaroo.

3   Kant thought that 'There are infinitely many numbers' does not follow just from the meaning of the word 'number'. Consider the following definition of 'number': the number of any set of things is the result you get when you count them. Say why that claim of Kant's is plausible if we use this definition. Is it obvious that this is the right definition?

4   Tell a story in which people come to abandon the belief that cats are animals (similar to the story in section 4 in which people come to abandon the belief that bachelors are unmarried).

5   Near the beginning of section 5, Kant's and Quine's positions were contrasted by saying that Kant claims that there are beliefs that must always be at the centre of the web of belief, whereas Quine claims that there must always be a centre, though different beliefs can be at the centre. Which of the four claims below is a restatement of Kant's position, and which is a restatement of Quine's?

(a) Given a person and a time, there must be beliefs which are at the centre of that person's web of belief at that time.

(b) There are beliefs which at any time are at the centre of the web of belief of any person.

(c) Given a person and a time, there must be beliefs which are not only at the centre of that person's beliefs but of any other person's too.

(d) There are beliefs which are at the centre of any person's web of belief at a given time, and given a different time or a different person there are beliefs which are at the centre of the web for that person and that time too.

6   Which of the following are experiential concepts, which are theoretical concepts, and which are not clearly either: middle C, pain, causation, evolution, democracy, television, electromagnetic radiation, triangular?

7   Suppose that a philosopher is arguing that the right action for any person at any time is the one that causes the greatest amount of happiness for that same person. Suppose she argues for this by claiming that concepts of duty and obligation to others lead to conclusions we do not want to accept, such as that each person should give all their money to famine relief, and that even people who think they are committed to acting for the sake of others are

really trying to achieve selfish aims. To what extent is her project best described as destruction, exploration or accumulation?

Thinking Questions

8   In section 2 it was claimed that if someone says that a pebble is a moose, they must be joking, lying, crazy or mean something very different by 'moose'. Describe a situation in which a pebble could really be a moose. Suppose we came to think that this situation could actually occur, what other beliefs (besides 'No moose is a pebble') would we have to abandon?

9   To explain Kant's idea of synthetic apriori beliefs, three examples were used. The example about colours is in several ways unlike the other two. Suppose you are watching a sunset and have no words for colours, but a good understanding of physics. How will your description of what you see differ from the description a person with a normal colour vocabulary might give? How will your explanation of what is happening be different? How does this relate to the example in the text?

10 There is an example near the beginning of section 3 of a person who believes that there is never a reason why anything happens. The opposite of such a person is one who believes that for every event there is a cause which determines that exactly that event, and no other, has to happen. To the first person there is no regularity or system to the world; to the second person the world seems completely regulated by cause and effect. In section 4 it was argued that the first person would have such trouble understanding the world that they would not be able to gather or understand evidence that might show them they were wrong. But what about the second person? Might she not be locked into a mistake too? Consider how such a person might gather and consider evidence about coincidences (such as finding that four people at a party have the same birthday) or (if you have enough knowledge of them) about random physical events such as radio-active decay. What problems might come from the second person's convictions?

11 To support his picture of the web of belief, Quine uses an argument from the French philosopher Duhem. Duhem argued that

evidence never shows conclusively that any belief is true or false, since there is always some other belief that can be accepted or refuted instead. For example, if you believe that the earth is flat, you do not have to abandon your belief when you learn of people flying due west and eventually returning to their starting-point. Instead, you could conclude that following a compass does not lead to traveling in a straight line, or that at the western edge of the world there is a mirage of the eastern edge and a hyper-fast air current that takes one eastward. This idea can be used to argue that any belief could be abandoned, too. Suppose we discover that the things we take to be cats are the fruits of a kind of fungus that flourishes in cat-litter trays. We could use this as evidence for either (a) cats are not animals, or (b) some animals are fungi. What *other* beliefs might we have to consider abandoning in deciding to accept either (a) or (b)?

12   Section 5 said that nearly all simple apriori beliefs can be used as tests for having concepts. To see why only simple apriori beliefs can be used this way, give some examples of complicated but true apriori beliefs, which someone might deny without showing that they are confused, insane, or misunderstand the meaning of some word.

13   Suppose that someone is confused about whether a complicated apriori belief is true. For example, suppose someone thinks that 13 cubed is 2,199, when it is actually 2,197. Suppose that they have calculated this result very carefully but made a mistake. Should we describe this belief as reasonable or unreasonable, justified or unjustified? Discuss the difficulties of applying these labels to cases like this. (It may help to look back to question 15 of chapter 1.)

14   Suppose that someone's use of the word 'fish' is like that of most English speakers 300 years ago, so that she insists that whales are fish and argues with people who tell her that they are not. Is her belief unreasonable?

15   Suppose that instead of the definition of 'number' used in question 3 we use the following definition: one is a number, and two is a number, and anything that is got from a number by adding one is a number. Is the belief that there are infinitely many numbers now analytic?

Further Reading

Expositions of some basic ideas about apriori and analytic beliefs are found in chapter 4 of W. V. Quine and Joseph Ullian, *The Web of Belief* (Random House, 1978). Quine and Ullian make very few connections with standard philosophical ideas and terminology, though. Quine's exposition of his ideas in 'Two dogmas of empiricism' and other essays collected in *From a Logical Point of View* (Harvard University Press, 1955) is stimulating, though not always easy. Many of the papers in Paul Moser (ed.) *A Priori Knowledge* (Oxford University Press, 1987) are clear and helpful, especially Richard Swinburne's 'Analytical, necessary, and *a priori*'.

More advanced papers, including Saul Kripke's 'Identity and necessity', are in A. W. Moore (ed.) *Meaning and Reference* (Oxford University Press, 1993). A personal favourite is Marcus Giaquinto, 'Non-analytic conceptual knowledge', *Mind*, 105 (1996), 247–68. Kant's views are found in his *Prolegomena to any Future Metaphysics that can Qualify as a Science*, and in part I of his *Critique of Pure Reason*. Both are very difficult. Straightforward expositions of Kant are found in Stephan Körner, *Kant* (Penguin, 1955), and Ralph Walker, *Kant* (Routledge, 1978). For introductions to the philosophy of mathematics see Hugh Lehman, *Introduction to the Philosophy of Mathematics* (Blackwell, 1979), or S. F. Barker, *The Philosophy of Mathematics* (Prentice-Hall, 1964), or the introduction to the second edition of Paul Benacerraf and Hilary Putnam (eds), *Readings in the Philosophy of Mathematics* (Cambridge University Press, 1983). Hempel's paper and the symposium involving Carnap, Heyting and von Neumann, in Benacerraf and Putnam, are particularly suitable for beginners.

Selections from classic philosophical works relevant to this chapter can be found in John Cottingham, *Western Philosophy: An Anthology* (Blackwell, 1996). See part I section I, Plato, 'Innate Knowledge'; part I section 6, Gottfried Leibniz, 'Innate Knowledge Defended'; part I section 8, Immanuel Kant, 'Experience and Understanding'; and part VI section 7, Immanuel Kant, 'Causality and Our Experience of Events'.

4 Induction and Probability

1. Simple Induction

$$1100110110011011001101100110$$

There is a pattern to this sequence of zeros and ones. After a moment's thought, you can see the pattern and continue it. If the zeros and ones were data about some natural phenomena – for example, the number of accidents at some busy intersection on successive days – then when you saw the pattern, you might predict that it would continue in the same way, that the next four days would have 1, 1, 0 and 0 accidents.

Many philosophers have thought that a large proportion of our knowledge is obtained by a process rather like this. We observe patterns in the world around us; by understanding them we are able to predict how they will exhibit themselves in cases that have not yet been examined. Call this process 'simple induction'. Sometimes this term is applied to an even simpler kind of reasoning, in which all the observed instances are the same in some respect, and we conclude that all unobserved instances are the same in that respect. This comes to pretty much the same thing. For example, in the history of human observation night has been followed by day in every 24-hour period, so we expect night to be followed by day in the future (ignoring what happens in the Arctic and Antarctic). We can see this pattern as the constant repetition of the single phenomenon 'night and then day' or as a pattern of two phenomena 'night, day, night, day, . . .'. It isn't essential that the prediction be about the future: we predict data that we have not yet obtained, but the data can concern the past as well as the future. The term **induction**, without the 'simple', is used by some writers for reasoning that goes from a particular set of data to a general conclusion about future data (not necessarily asserting that some pattern found in the data will be repeated). Others use it for any reasoning that does not claim to be deductively valid. I will discuss only simple induction.

The idea that much of our knowledge can be obtained by starting with observations and reasoning by induction is attractive. For reasoning by induction is modest and careful; it does not seem like wild speculation. To put the point more carefully, the conclusion of a piece of inductive reasoning is meant to go as little as possible beyond the data on which it is based, while yet describing a general pattern which will allow us to predict more data. The conclusion contains no concepts not found in the description of the data, and asserts no more than that the pattern of observations will continue. In the example, you do not speculate why two days with accidents are always followed by a day without an accident, why this accident-free day is sometimes followed by another and sometimes by a day with an accident, or why there is never more than one accident per day. You just look at the data and see where they are going.

Unproblematic as induction may seem, there are troubling questions about it. Two of them are basic and very hard. The first is: What reasons do we have to believe that the conclusion of simple induction is true? The other is: What inductive inferences do we actually make and treat as supporting their conclusions? These two questions are closely connected. I shall discuss each, and then their connection.

2. Hume's Problem

David Hume first raised sharp, uncomfortable questions about whether it is reasonable to be influenced by inductive arguments.

Hume's argument is complicated and subtle, but the issues turn around a single simple fact about inductive reasoning.

The premisses of an inductive argument can always be expanded to include additional information. We can find out the number of accidents on the next few days; we can watch the sun rise yet another morning. The added evidence may strengthen the argument; it may give more reason to believe the conclusion. But it can also weaken it; it can produce an argument that gives one less reason to believe the conclusion. Sometimes, additional evidence can turn an inductive argument for a conclusion into one against it. Suppose that the sun does not rise tomorrow; if I add this to the evidence, I will have an argument showing that the sun does not always rise. Hume's point can now be put as follows: since additional evidence, not yet discovered, may weaken an inductive argument, or even establish the opposite conclusion, and since one cannot be sure that such additional evidence may not turn up, one can easily doubt that the conclusion is true. Some have supposed that Hume went on from this to the further assertion that an inductive argument gives one no reasons to believe in its conclusions. It is not at all clear that Hume believed anything like this. Just as well, for it is not at all clear that anything like this is true. (See question 10 for more on what Hume may have meant.)

The reason that the further assertion is more doubtful is that although Hume's argument shows that a conclusion obtained by induction can be doubted, it may yet be certain. That is, given the evidence, it may be perfectly reasonable to treat the conclusion as being true and to act accordingly, while remaining ready to suspend belief or even to believe the opposite if contrary evidence should be found. It could be reasonable to expect the accidents to continue according to the same pattern; it would be crazy not to expect the sun to rise.

Many particular instances of inductive reasoning are completely convincing. It would be irrational not to be convinced by them, to wait for some more powerful assurance that their conclusions are true. It would not be irrational, however, to wonder why inductive reasoning can be so compelling, to ask where its force comes from. (Why, after a million sunrises, do we expect more of the same, rather than thinking that the universe must soon be running out of them?) To think about this in any systematic way, we have to know which inductive inferences are the convincing ones. Nelson Goodman was the first to realize how hard it is to know this.

3. Goodman's Problem

Goodman made an important discovery about the inductions which we regard as reasonable. He discovered that we have very little idea about which they are. Goodman's argument rests on the fact that a finite sequence of events or observations or items of evidence can always be taken as conforming to a great many – in fact, infinitely many – different incompatible general patterns. It cannot be reasonable to believe that all these patterns are realized; the data cannot continue in accord with more than one of them. And it is very hard to see what makes one pattern more plausible than another.

The sequence of 0s and 1s at the beginning of the chapter could have been taken as exhibiting the pattern: blocks of two 1s and two 0s and blocks of two 1s and one 0, alternating. This may be the way most of would most easily think of it. But it is not the only way. We could have taken the series as consisting of blocks of ten digits, first 1100110110 then 0110110011, then 0110011000, then the first again, and so on. Then the series would continue 0011 instead of 1100. Or we could have taken it as consisting of 1100110110011011001101100110 followed by itself backward, then forward again, and so on. Then the next four digits would be 0110. There are an infinite number of possibilities.

Goodman pointed out that this fact about sequences applies to all simple inductions. A sequence of past sunrises is just as much in accordance with the pattern 'The sun rises every 24 hours until

22 April 2045, and then no more' or 'The sun rises every 24 hours until 22 April 2045, and then every 37.8 hours' as it is in accordance with the pattern 'The sun rises every 24 hours forever'. Evidently there can be no rule of simple induction which says: If you observe a large number of instances of a pattern, assume (until contrary evidence turns up) that the pattern will continue. For such a rule would lead to wild and contradictory results. (Quite how wild the results would be is shown by question 13 on the famous 'grue' example.)

Another example tending in the same direction is due to C. G. Hempel, and is known as the 'ravens paradox'. Sitting by my desk, looking around my study and seeing the books and the pictures, the cat and the curtains closed in front of the windows, I notice that many of these things are not black. Moreover, all the things which are not black are not ravens. I check to make sure of this, and yes, every single non-black thing is a non-raven. This makes me remember that every thing I have ever seen in my life that was not black was not a raven. So, reasoning by simple induction, I conclude that all, absolutely all, things that are not black are not ravens. Then I remember some logic: 'Everything that is not B is not R' is equivalent to 'Everything that is R is B'. So if I am concluding that everything that is not black is not a raven, I should also conclude that everything that is a raven is black. But this is an outrageous conclusion. It is not outrageous that all ravens are black, of course; but it is outrageous to think that I could find evidence for this belief by looking around my study, where there is not a single raven. Armchair ornithology, as Hempel puts it, should not give us beliefs about real birds in the wild.

The relation between the ravens paradox and Goodman's problem is this: In both cases we have a possible pattern 'All As are Bs' and a body of data which fits it, since it consists of As that are Bs, but which does not give us reason to believe that the pattern holds for all cases. Seeing the sun many times before 22 April 2045 does not make us believe that the sun will rise every day till 22 April 2045 and never thereafter, even though the data fit this pattern. Seeing many non-black things that are non-ravens (and no non-black things that are ravens) does not make us think that all non-black things are non-ravens. In both cases simple induction leads to conclusions that it should not. In fact, the close connections between Goodman's point and Hempel's can be seen by reflecting that all the days that you (or anyone) have experienced which have had a sunrise have been not after 22 April 2045. So reasoning by simple induction, you should conclude that all days with sunrises are not after 22 April 2045. But this is equivalent to concluding that all days that are after 22 April 2045 do not have a sunrise. Combine this with the conclusion, also coming from induction, that all days before 22 April 2045 do have a sunrise, and you have Goodman's problem.

We should *not* take these problems to show that induction is not a good way to reason. As Hume pointed out, an enormous proportion of our beliefs are supported by induction. Why else do most people believe that the sun will rise tomorrow? (Astronomers may have complex theories to back up their belief, but the rest of us expect a sunrise every day because that is the pattern we have always known. And the astronomers' theories themselves depend in part on reasoning by induction.) Why else do most people believe that bread nourishes, water quenches thirst, and fire burns? Instead, we should realize that inductive reasoning does not consist in taking any data that fit any regular pattern and supposing that the pattern holds generally. Induction consists in taking the right data and the right pattern, data and pattern that fit together in the right way, and in the absence of any contrary evidence supposing that the pattern holds generally.

What is the right way for data and pattern to fit together? You might think that all that is required is for the pattern not to be a peculiar and complicated one like 'The sun rises every 24 hours before 22 April 2045 and every 27 hours thereafter'. So the question may seem trivial, for it may seem perfectly clear which inductions are reasonable and which are not, hard as it may be to find a formula that exactly captures the distinction. But the question is far from trivial, and the distinction far from obvious.

Often there is a real practical problem in telling which features of the evidence should be used as a basis for inductive reasoning. Suppose that in the traffic accident example all the data refer to days on which the sun was shining. Should we use the data to predict the number of accidents on future rainy days? We might or might not, depending on all sorts of other factors. Philosophers have suggested ways of discovering irrelevant features of the evidence, in order to reveal the true pattern and the causal law behind it. (One of the most influential was J. S. Mill in the nineteenth century.) But none of these methods is obviously right, and none applies in all cases. Goodman's puzzle is a way of making one see how fundamental the problem is.

4. Solutions to Goodman's Problem

Philosophers have suggested many solutions to this problem. Nearly all of them have one feature in common: they point out that we do not do inductive reasoning in a void. Before we reason from any particular data to any particular general pattern, we already believe many general patterns, some of which we believe from earlier instances of inductive reasoning, and some for other reasons. Consider, for example, someone who sees many instances of sodium making an orange flame when it is burned, and concludes that sodium always burns with an orange flame. This person will already believe that sodium is a chemical substance with regular, predictable properties, and will probably already know of other substances that have the same colour flame whenever they are burned, about which there may be many more data than there are for sodium. So this person's beliefs will have described 'being sodium' as the kind of property that could fit into a general pattern – in particular, one about colour of burning – and will have described colours of flames as the kind of pattern that can be expected to continue.

There are many ways of elaborating on this point. For there are many features of the situations we find ourselves in that could be emphasized. Goodman emphasizes the fact that no instance of inductive reasoning is ever the first. So we can look at the terms in which the evidence is described and the pattern stated, and see how these have fitted into previous cases of induction. Suppose that we can describe the evidence as a large number of cases of objects of kind K (ravens or mornings) having some property P (like 'black' or 'having a sunrise'), where K and P are terms used in many earlier inductions, which have not led to false conclusions. Then, Goodman suggests, we may select the hypotheses 'All objects of kind K have property P' as stating a likely pattern, and take the hypothesis to be supported by inductive reasoning from this evidence. It is hard to evaluate this suggestion, for no one has ever made a thorough study of a large number of inductive inferences, to see if the natural ones can be differentiated from the unnatural ones by this criterion. Also, it is not clear how the idea is to be applied to hypotheses more complicated than those of the form 'All objects of kind K have property P'.

Another suggestion, found in the writings of Carnap, Jeffrey and others, is that even before considering any evidence, we are more inclined to believe some hypotheses than others, and that the extent to which a pattern or hypothesis is selected depends upon the extent to which we are inclined to believe it before taking account of the evidence. This suggestion, too, is hard to evaluate, and for similar reasons. A realistic analysis of actual inductive practice in terms of it has not been performed, although philosophers of science working in the Bayesian tradition (discussed in chapter 9) have done a lot of relevant work. But the suggested explanations of the degree to which a person is inclined to believe a hypothesis apply only to fairly simple hypotheses.

A third suggestion is a more general version of this second one. It is that when we make an inductive inference, we do so against a background of a large number of beliefs besides those about the evidence for the inference. Many of these beliefs are about the sorts of regular patterns that we can expect to find in the world. We believe such things as: objects left alone tend to remain in existence and change few of their characteristics; natural processes that occur with a regular periodicity tend to continue with that rhythm, and if interfered with gently, tend to change their periodicity rather than become non-periodic; animals of closely related species tend to have similar characteristics. Given the evidence for an inductive inference, those beliefs do not enable us to deduce the conclusion as something indubitable, but they do help us to select the hypothesis to be supported by the inference from among those which it does not support. The hypothesis selected is the one that describes a pattern of events, a uniformity in nature, of a kind which, according to one's general beliefs, is likely to exist.

Opinions about the possible causes of a body of evidence do affect how we are inclined to generalize from it, and provide some support for this position. Roughly, the harder we find it to imagine what kind of process could result in a general pattern of events, the less willing we are to look for, or believe, it. The fallacy of 'charting' the stock-market is an illustration of this. It is foolish to expect a stock to be worth $20 per share tomorrow just because it has been worth $14, $16, and $18 on the three preceding days. A wise investor knows that most of the factors that affect future stock prices are not represented in the graph of past prices. The pattern alone doesn't mean much. We can imagine the prices of a stock following some mysterious pattern so long and so consistently that we were forced to conclude that the pattern might continue, having no idea at all of how this pattern was produced. But the evidence would have to be mighty impressive. On the other hand, if you can see how business conditions and a company's reputation and the financial climate could easily produce such a pattern, you will soon expect it to continue, as long as these conditions remain. To do otherwise, to ignore the possible causes and use induction in a purely formal manner, would be pure superstition.

5. Justifying Induction

The first question about induction was: What reasons do we have to believe that the conclusions of simple inductions are true? I didn't answer this question. Some philosophers have tried to say why it is reasonable to believe the conclusions of inductive inferences, and some have argued that it is only out of confusion or misunderstanding that one could think that any such reasons were possible or necessary. I think that Goodman's problem about induction shows that it would be wrong to argue along either of these lines.

For how can we put forward an argument showing why we should believe the conclusions of inductive inferences when we do not know which inferences have the believable conclusions? No good argument could convince us that we should follow the general rule, 'On seeing a large number of instances of a general pattern, suppose that the pattern will continue', because, as we have seen, this rule is not one that anyone in their right mind would follow. Until we know more about what our habits of induction actually are, we cannot say very much about whether they are reasonable. But for the same reason it is not right to decide that they are all reasonable; if we knew which inductive inferences we actually make, we might find that some of them are rather less sensible than others.

For example, many people believe that if a coin has been tossed very often and always comes down heads, then it is very likely to come down tails the next time; such people also tend to believe that standing beside a tree that has been struck by lightning is safe, because lightning very rarely strikes twice in the same place. There is a general principle behind such inferences (sometimes it is misnamed the law of averages; philosophers often call it 'the gambler's fallacy'). It is something like: If you see a large number of instances of a pattern and you believe that the pattern is very improbable, then assume that it will not be continued. Now this principle is *not* rational; a little thought should convince one that a coin that has come down heads a large number of times is at least as likely to come down heads again the next time. This principle is not accepted by many people. Yet it is perfectly possible that among the inductive inferences we are accustomed to make is a group of inferences which can be seen to be unreasonable when considered in the light of the purposes of enquiry, of the other inferences we make, of our beliefs about the world, and of common sense.

There is one other fact that has to be mentioned here. Explanations of why induction is reasonable must be careful not to be too ambitious. They must not try to show that even the best kinds of inductive reasoning, using the right kind of evidence to support the right kind of general belief, will always give true conclusions. For, as Hume pointed out, this is wrong. The best inductive reasoning will sometimes give false conclusions. Tomorrow we might find some kind of water that does not quench thirst, some circumstances when sodium does not burn with an orange flame, even a lead weight that rises when released, or a free lunch. All that a justification of induction can do is to give reasons for how often some kinds of inductive reasoning will give true conclusions. Some philosophers, such as Hans Reichenbach and Wesley Salmon, have tried to argue that inductive reasoning gives true conclusions more often than other methods of reasoning from the known to the unknown. They have tried to show that induction is more reliable than believing the first thing that comes into your mind, or believing what fits the patterns in your tea-leaves. Other philosophers have tried to assess the reliability of induction in terms of facts about probability, some of which are discussed below in section 8. None of these attempts gives a complete and satisfying treatment of the question, but they are the kinds of theories that respect the two basic facts about induction: that it must go from the right kind of data to the right kind of generalization, and that however well-fitted data and generalization are, there can be no guarantee that the result is not a false conclusion.

6. The Safeness of Induction

How safe is induction? Much of what I have said suggests that induction is not as safe as it appears to be. I pointed out that many inferences that have the outward form of simple induction are totally unreasonable, and I suggested that when induction is reasonable, it is because of its congruence with a background of previous inductions, assignments of probability, and beliefs about nature. Presumably when these things are mistaken, an induction is not to be trusted.

But induction is safer than many other methods. Without getting into delicate issues about whether one can give a reason for trusting inductive reasoning, one can give reasons why inductive reasoning will less often result in false conclusions than various kinds of non-inductive reasoning. The safeness of induction lies in the fact that it does not risk speculating about the causes of the patterns it predicts. Compare the inductive generalization that the traffic accident data will continue to show the pattern one would naturally find in them with the following hypothesis about the causes of the data. The road in question is used only by trucks serving a construction project. On Monday the drivers drive enthusiastically, and there is an accident. This doesn't inhibit them, and there is another on Tuesday. However, the experience of two accidents makes them drive more carefully on Wednesday and Thursday, and there are no accidents. But by driving carefully for these two days, they are now behind schedule, and have to drive furiously on Friday and Saturday in order to have even one day's holiday, Sunday. So there are accidents on Friday and Saturday. There are never two accidents in a day, because after the first accident the drivers slow down for the rest of that day. Every week is the same.

This hypothesis might be right; it might be wrong too, and one can easily think of a number of rival hypotheses incompatible with it. It would be hard to choose between the hypothesis and some of its rivals on the basis of evidence one would be likely to have. Yet many of these rival hypotheses would also predict that the accidents will continue in the 1100110 pattern. The inductive generalization asserts only what these bolder, farther-reaching, more interesting hypotheses have in common; it is true as long as any one of them is true.

Induction is modest; it makes no guesses about the causes of events. It is therefore less risky than other parts of the enterprise of hypothesizing about the nature of nature (and less interesting, too). We could not reason inductively, I think, unless we also made hypotheses about causes, and our choice of inductive generalizations may depend on the causal hypotheses that we make. But the truth of induction's conclusions does not require that our causal hypotheses be true. We can be right about the patterns found in the data, and wrong about the reasons why they are found there.

7. Probability

In discussing inductive reasoning, we have considered cases where someone has seen a number of instances of a pattern, has seen no counter-examples, and has to decide whether or not to believe that the pattern holds in all cases. (You have seen *n* moose that can swim, and you have to accept or reject the hypothesis that all moose can swim.) But in many – perhaps most – circumstances in which we reason from particular instances to a general pattern, things are not this simple. For example, you want to know whether you should take your raincoat when you go to town. You listen to a weather forecast which says 'overcast but dry'. You think: 'Most of the time the forecast has been right – about eight times out of ten in recent months – but it has sometimes been wrong, and there was that time a month ago when it forecast a bright cloudless day and, trusting it, I went out in my shorts and T-shirt and got drenched.' Or you are a doctor advising someone about their prognosis if they undergo a certain treatment. You say: 'In 98 per cent of cases the treatment has been very successful, and the patient recovers, with no side-effects, but in 1.5 per cent of cases there have been side-effects on the road to recovery, sometimes quite severe, and in 0.5 per cent of cases the patient has died.'

There are two important features of these more complicated kinds of inductive reasoning. The first is that the evidence is not all one-sided: there are instances where the weather forecast has been reliable, and those where it has not. The second is that the conclusion that we have to draw is more subtle than simply Yes or No in all cases. You want to know whether rain is so unlikely that you can forget your raincoat or whether you should bring it just in case. The patient wants to know whether the likelihood of death or severe side-effects is great enough to outweigh the likelihood of being cured of the disease.

In these cases it is natural to think in terms of probability. We want to ask questions like: 'Given that n objects of kind K, out of m observed, have had property P, what is the probability that all cases have P?' Or: 'Given that n objects out of m have had P, what is the probability that a randomly selected object will have P?' It is easy to see that inductive reasoning is a special case of this kind of reasoning, applying when all of the objects that have been sampled have had the property in question. Even when this is the case, we still often want to ask questions about probability. For example, suppose that you are testing a new drug for effectiveness against a certain disease. Trials with humans are just beginning, and you administer it to fifty human volunteers with the disease. All of them recover, with no side-effects. Reasoning by simple induction, you might conclude that the drug is safe and effective in all cases. But that would be hasty. Fifty is really a very small number of cases, and you need to ask questions about how they were selected, whether they included cases distributed evenly between men and women, between different ethnic groups, and between old and young. Once you know the answers to these questions, you may be able to say, not whether you believe that the drug is safe and effective, but how confident you are that it is. (Given the terrible effects that drugs which were believed to be safe have sometimes had, we may never want to say that we are completely sure that a drug is safe.) Probability gives you a way of expressing degrees of confidence.

The basic use of probability is to tone down a conclusion so that one can be more sure of it. Instead of arguing for a simple, and risky, conclusion, one makes a more guarded assertion which states that the simple conclusion has a certain probability. This more guarded assertion tends to be more certain than the original. It is nearer to the premisses in certainty. A weather forecast, that it will rain the next day, often does not make it certain that it will rain; but most often a forecast about the probability of rain is certain. Or consider a die about to fall: one cannot be sure that it will not fall on the six, but one can be sure, usually, that the probability of its not falling on the six is 5/6.

The basic examples of reasoning about probability can be derived from non-probabilistic arguments like the following:

First premiss: Sam is 23 years old, has just passed a physical, and has never spent a day in hospital.
Second premiss: 99 per cent of all 23-year-olds who have recently passed physicals and who have never been hospitalized live to be 24.
Conclusion: (a) Sam will live to be 24.

The argument is pretty compelling; Sam seems to qualify for cheap life insurance. The conclusion is not completely assured; Sam could die in spite of both premisses being true. But given the truth of the premisses, it is very probable that he will not die in the next year. Thus we can transform the argument into the following:

First premiss: Same as above.
Second premiss: Same as above.
Conclusion: (b) Sam will probably live to be 24.

Or we can transform it into an argument with the same premisses and the conclusion:

Conclusion: (c) The probability that Sam will live to be 24 is x.

Many have argued that x should be 0.99. Each of these conclusions is clearly more certain than the conclusion that Sam will live to be 24.

Things are never as simple as one first thinks. Let me tell you some more facts about Sam, in the form of an argument:

First premiss: Sam has advanced heart disease, cancer and tuberculosis, which were not detected by the doctor, who had advanced stupidity.

Second premiss: 99 per cent of all those with advanced heart disease, cancer and tuberculosis die within six months.

Conclusions: (a) Sam will die within six months. (b) Sam will probably die within six months. (c) The probability that Sam will die within six months is x. (Let us take x to be 0.99.)

Now if the first set of arguments about Sam is acceptable, then so is the second set. Sam thus seems to be at once a good and a poor insurance risk. Yet each conclusion seems to be warranted by the premisses, and the premisses are all true. Thinking of arguments involving probability as like inductive reasoning, this should not be very surprising. It is just another version of Hume's discovery that more evidence can always change the conclusions of inductive reasoning. Both simple induction and reasoning from statistical data to conclusions about probability are subject to a *total evidence requirement*: it is only reasonable to believe the conclusion on the basis of the evidence if it is all the evidence available to you that is relevant. The fact that a total evidence requirement applies just means: this is induction, not deduction; more evidence can always change the picture.

8. Probability and Hume's Problem

Hume pointed out that induction is not deduction. He also set philosophers wondering whether we have good reasons for believing in the conclusions of inductive reasoning. Attempts to show why we should believe the conclusions of inductive reasoning often try to transfer the certainty of deductive reasoning in some diluted form to induction. Thinking in terms of probability gives us ways of doing this.

Consider again the arguments of the last section. They are all subject to the total evidence requirement, and are thus not deductively valid. But the conclusions marked (b) and (c) seem to be much more certain consequences of the premisses than those marked (a). This suggests that we might try building the total evidence requirement into the premisses to get arguments like the following:

First premiss: Sam is a randomly selected human being with advanced heart disease, cancer and tuberculosis.
Second premiss: 99 per cent of all those with advanced heart disease, cancer and tuberculosis die within six months.
Conclusions: (b) Sam will probably die within six months. (c) The probability that Sam will die within six months is 0.99.

It now seems much more plausible that (b) and (c) are deductive consequences of the premisses. Or, to be a bit more cautious, it seems to be an apriori truth that the probability of death within six months of an individual randomly selected from a population 99 per cent of whom will die in six months is 0.99. That seems to be what we mean by probability. And this might look like a kind of solution to Hume's problem. If, given this evidence, the conclusion is 99 per cent probable, then although there is a small chance that the conclusion could be false, we can see why it would be reasonable to believe it.

But this is not a solution to Hume's problem. The reason lies in the second premiss. It describes not what proportion of observed people with cancer, heart disease and tuberculosis have died within six months, but what proportion of *all* people with these diseases have died within this period. In the language of statistics, it is an assertion about a population, not about a sample. It is an assertion that we cannot know except by reasoning from samples of observed people, and thus from induction. So in order to conclude from observations about individual people that the probability of Sam's dying within six months is 0.99, we would need a rule of inductive reasoning of the following form:

Premiss: In a sample of n people with advanced heart disease, cancer and tuberculosis, 99 per cent died within six months.
Conclusion: The proportion of people in the whole population with advanced heart disease, cancer and tuberculosis who die within six months is 99 per cent.

A large part of the science of statistics studies inferences such as these. Many of the issues that we have seen concerning simple induction arise again here. For example, the reasoning above is clearly not valid unless the sample is a randomly chosen one, which can be taken to be representative of the whole population. This has close connections with the issues raised by the ravens paradox and Goodman's problem. If we want a random sample of sunrises, we should not deliberately select them so that they all fall before 22 April 2045. If we want a random sample of bird colours, we should not deliberately select non-black non-ravens from my study. So it should not be surprising that conclusions drawn from these very skewed samples do not hold of the larger populations.

Statisticians have produced a large and complex doctrine about inferences from samples to populations. Some of it is highly mathematical, and some of it is simple practical advice. Most of the insights of philosophers such as Hume, Mill and Carnap about simple induction have been absorbed into statistics, and can now be seen as special cases of more general rules and problems. In fact, it is in statistics that we find the detailed working out of our inductive practices that solutions to Goodman's problem, discussed at the end of section 4, need.

In statistics we find solutions to Hume's problem, in that we find apriori principles relating the proportions of objects in a sample having some property to the proportions that we can expect to find – with various degrees of probability and confidence – in a larger population. You'll have to study statistics to learn these principles, but they do share a basic feature that is of profound importance for the theory of knowledge. It is that no inference is possible from a sample to a population without some information about the population. If you want to know what proportion of a population has some property P, given the proportion in a sample, you need to know either what kind of probability distribution describes P in the population, or some important features of this distribution, or some other similar information. Given suitable information, statistics will give you an apriori rule that will tell you how confident you can be in projecting from the sample to the population. (For different kinds of information it will give you different rules. See question 14 for a warning note here, though.) But it will never give you a rule for inferring from a sample to a population about which you know nothing. If *that* is Hume's problem, then it can have no solution. If you want to have conclusions that talk about probability, you will need some premisses that talk about probability too.

Reading Questions

1 Which of the following are instances of reasoning by simple induction?

    (a) Mary likes chocolate, Sally likes chocolate, Rosanne likes chocolate; all the women I have ever met liked chocolate; therefore all women like chocolate.

    (b) All human beings die; for example, Socrates died, Joan of Arc died, Bertrand Russell died; therefore I too will die.

    (c) When this ball is dropped, it accelerates downwards; when a bird stops flying, it falls; if you lose your balance at the top of the stairs, you end up at the bottom; therefore there must be a force of gravity.

2 The following are both features of deductive argument:

(a) When B follows deductively from A and C follows deductively from B, then C follows deductively from A.

(b) When B follows deductively from A, then B follows deductively from A & C, for any C.

One of them is not true when 'follows deductively' is replaced with 'follows by simple induction', and this is an important difference between deduction and induction. Which?

3 Find another two ways of continuing the series of 1s and 0s, at the beginning of the chapter, besides the three mentioned in section 3.

4 Astronomers, according to section 3, may have reasons for believing that the sun will continue to rise besides reasoning from simple induction. Why? Who besides astronomers could have non-inductive reasons for believing this? Why does section 3 say that 'most people' believe that bread nourishes, water quenches thirst, and fire burns on the basis of inductive reasoning, instead of 'all people'?

5 Describe a situation in which someone predicting the stock-market solely from the pattern of the data, ignoring all information about the causes of the data, could lose a lot of money.

6 Suppose that two people are betting on the tosses of a coin. Theodora sees it land heads six times in a row, and then bets all her money that it will land tails the next time. Elena sees it land heads six times in a row, and then bets all her money that it will land heads the next time. Explain who is more likely to be the richer afterwards. How does this relate to the issues in section 5?

7 Suppose you decide that the weather forecast is more often right than wrong. In fact, since it is right 80 per cent of the time and the forecast is for sunny weather, you put the chances of rain at less than 20 per cent. Does it follow that you should not bring your raincoat?

8 In the arguments discussed in section 7, which conclusion is most certain, of (a), (b), (c), and which least certain?

9 Suppose you have a population of people all of whom have advanced heart disease, cancer and tuberculosis. Describe a non-random way of selecting an individual from this population, so that the probability of that individual dying within six months is much less than 0.99.

Thinking Questions

10   Read Hume's discussion of induction in his *Enquiry Concerning Human Understanding*, chapters 4 and 5 (or his *Treatise on Human Nature*, book I, part 3 (sections 2, 3, 4)). Hume may be taken as arguing for any of the following: (a) induction does not have the force of deduction, since the conclusion of an inductive argument can be false though the premises are true; (b) when we reason inductively, we are assuming that the future will resemble the past, and we can never justify this assumption; and (c) when we reason inductively, we are blindly following a way of thinking that cannot be shown to be reliable. Produce evidence for at least one of these interpretations of Hume. Can you find evidence for more than one?

11   Consider the following reasoning: All the evidence that has ever been produced has been consistent with the theory that objects fall because there is a gravitational force between them and the earth. Therefore all future evidence is likely to be consistent with this theory. Therefore we should accept it. How does reasoning like this complicate the contrast between inductive reasoning and reasoning to the causes of phenomena described in this chapter?

12   John Stuart Mill, in chapter 8 of book III of *A System of Logic* (first published in 1843) describes four methods for determining what the causes of a phenomenon are. For example, his 'first canon' is: 'If two or more instances of the phenomenon under investigation have only one circumstance in common, the circumstance in which alone all the instances agree is the cause (or effect) of the given phenomenon.' By this Mill means that if you observe that P occurs under many conditions which always include a factor F, and you observe that when F occurs without any other factors, P is also observed, then you can conclude that 'P whenever F' is a law of nature. Find examples like those of section 3 to show that this rule is too simple.

13   Nelson Goodman's example to illustrate his point was the following: Define an object to be *grue* if it is either green and we see it before 22 April 2045 or blue and we see it after that time. Now we have seen many samples of green emeralds, and none that was not green. But they were all grue, since they were seen before 22 April

2045. So all the emeralds we have ever seen have been grue. So, reasoning by simple induction, we may conclude that all emeralds are grue. But this means that emeralds seen after 22 April 2045 will be blue, which is crazy.

The advantage of making the point with a special word like 'grue' is that the weird general principle 'All emeralds are grue' is then expressed in language that is just as simple as the non-weird principle 'all emeralds are green'. What are the important differences between 'green' and 'grue'? Here are three possibilities:

(a) 'Grue' refers to a specific point of time, and 'green' does not.
(b) We can tell by looking whether something is green, but we cannot tell whether something is grue just by looking.
(c) 'Green' is a word of ordinary English, and 'grue' is not.

For each of these, show that there are words which have the characteristic of 'grue' which can be used to make general principles which can be supported by simple induction. What is the relevance of this to Goodman's problem?

14 Suppose that you have bought a ticket in a lottery, and you know that 999,999 other people have also each bought a ticket, and only one will win. You know that the probability of your winning is very, very small; it is equal to 0.000001. And the probability of your losing is very, very high, 0.999999. But you cannot conclude that you will lose; you cannot be certain of it. If you could, you would also conclude of each of the other 999,999 people that they will lose. If you concluded that each person would lose, then you would conclude that no person will win, and this is absurd. So the assertion that you will not win the lottery, although extremely probable, is not one that you should believe.

This is known as the 'lottery paradox'. It shows that the relation between the probability of a proposition and whether one should believe it is not simple. How does this complicate the conclusions of section 8?

Further Reading

Simple introductions to issues about induction are in chapter 9 of Robert M. Martin, *There are Two Errors in the Title of this Book* (Broadview, 1992); chapter 5 of Adam Morton, *Philosophy in Practice* (Blackwell, 1996); chapter 8 of W. V.

Quine and Joseph Ullian, *The Web of Belief* (Random House, 1978); and chapters 2 and 3 of Merilee H. Salmon, *Introduction to Logic and Critical Thinking* (Harcourt Brace Jovanovich, 1984).

The relation between probability and induction is explored in chapters 1 and 2 of Brian Skyrms, *Choice and Chance* (Dickenson, 1966). More advanced topics are developed in chapter 13 of Jonathan Dancy, *An Introduction to Contemporary Epistemology* (Blackwell, 1985). The best way to learn about Goodman's problem is by reading chapters 3 and 4 of Nelson Goodman, *Fact, Fiction, and Forecast* (Bobbs-Merrill, 3rd edn, 1973).

Personal favourites are R. C. Jeffrey, 'Goodman's query', *Journal of Philosophy*, 63 (1966), 281–8; Mary Hesse, 'Ramifications of grue', *British Journal for the Philosophy of Science*, 20 (1969), 13–25; and David Johnson, 'Induction and modality', *Philosophical Review*, 50 (1991), 399–430.

Selections from classic philosophical works relevant to this chapter can be found in John Cottingham, *Western Philosophy: An Anthology* (Blackwell, 1996). See part VI section 5, David Hume, 'The Problem of Induction'; part VI section 8, John Stuart Mill, 'The Uniformity of Nature'; and part VI section 6, David Hume, 'The Relation between Cause and Effect'.

5 Middleword: Fallibilism

We are now half-way through. This is the middle chapter of the book, and marks the point where the most fundamental distinctions and ideas of epistemology have been introduced. The topics in the second half of the book are more specific, and in preparation for them this chapter draws together some threads from the first half. The general thread-drawing theme is that of **fallibilism**, the idea that anything we believe, however good our reasons for believing it, could be wrong. This is a controversial idea, and before seeing the reasons for and against it, we must think carefully about what it really means. Some versions of fallibilism are wild implausible positions, verging on lunacy. Others are safe and responsible positions, verging on platitude. I shall try to describe an intermediate fallibilism, strong enough to be interesting, but weak enough to be believable. In doing this I shall allow my own views to show more explicitly than in any other chapter except chapter 10. You should read this chapter warily, not accepting what it says unless it really convinces you.

1. Error versus Ignorance

In the first four chapters the topic of risk kept recurring. In chapter 1 truth was listed as a basic desirable quality of beliefs, but with the worry that there might be a price to pay for aiming only at true beliefs. Chapter 2 asked whether reasoning from perceptual beliefs meant taking a risk of arriving at false conclusions, and discussed the empiricist aim of gaining true beliefs without running any risk of acquiring false beliefs along with them. In chapter 3 we asked whether there were any beliefs – apriori beliefs – which ran no risk of falsity. And in chapter 4 induction was described as a method of reasoning which went minimally beyond the evidence, giving novel beliefs at a minimal risk of falsity.

The risk in all of these is risk of falsity. The reason is that the ideas in these chapters all come ultimately from the philosophies of the seventeenth and eighteenth centuries, when philosophers and scientists were searching for a method of acquiring beliefs which would replace what they saw as the ramshackle falsity-ridden edifice of traditional beliefs with a more reliable, more confidence-inspiring structure. Philosophers were looking for a method that was guaranteed to produce truths, and so the danger of getting false beliefs was foremost in their minds.

But falsity is only one possible danger. Call the danger here **error**. Fear of error is fear of having false beliefs. Consider another danger, which we can call **ignorance**. Ignorance is the danger that we will not have the beliefs we need to understand the world and live our lives. Ignorance and error are not the same. For example, if someone has no beliefs at all, they run no risk of error, but their ignorance is total. And if someone believes only certain or apriori beliefs, such as the belief that $38 - 12 = 26$ or that moose are animals, they run a very small risk of error, but their ignorance is still very large. So we should ask what the important kinds of risk are. Here are six possibilities, which are closely related and easily confused:

(a) Risk that there will be many falsehoods among the beliefs we acquire now.

(a′) Risk that there will be many falsehoods among the beliefs we acquire in the long run.

(b) Risk of too many false beliefs.

(b′) Risk of not enough true beliefs.

(c) Risk of too many irrational and useless beliefs.
(c′) Risk of not enough rational and useful beliefs.

There are three independent dimensions of risk here: long term/ short term, excess of falsity/deficiency of truth, and truth/useful- ness. It would not be unreasonable to want to minimize risk along all three dimensions: to have beliefs which are true in the short and the long term, to have few falsehoods and many truths, and to have beliefs which are both true and useful. But we would have to be very optimistic to think that we could maximize along all these dimensions at once. The early rationalists and empiricists were extremely optimistic; they hoped for a way of acquiring beliefs which would give us as many true beliefs as we can get on any topic we consider. Now philosophy is older and wiser, and we suspect that there is no such method. When you realize you can't have everything, you begin to consider trade-offs between the things you can get.

2. Foundationalism versus Holism

Consider two extreme ways of setting priorities among these kinds of risk. The first would be extreme error-avoidance, mak- ing (a) above a priority and avoiding at all costs acquiring any false beliefs at any stage of trying to understand the world. The other would be the choice that contrasts most dramatically with this: extreme ignorance-avoidance, making (c′) a priority, and avoiding at all costs having a shortage of the beliefs we need to live with one another and have comfortable lives. No doubt anyone who made either of these extreme choices would try to argue that other kinds of risk were not as risky as they might seem. Someone who prioritizes (a) would argue that if we build our beliefs up carefully, avoiding getting any false ones, we will eventually get true and useful beliefs on any topic we investigate. And someone who prioritizes (c′) would argue that beliefs that contradict the evidence are not going to be useful, so that in trying for useful beliefs, we will end up with beliefs that are as near to true as makes no practical difference.

Extreme error-avoidance has been very influential in philosophy, though few contemporary philosophers would agree with it. It is most clearly shown in a family of epistemological theories called **foundationalism**. Foundationalist theories assert that there is a class of beliefs called **basic beliefs**, which do not require any evidence. A person is justified in holding a basic belief just by having and understanding it. For many foundationalist theories, beliefs about what one is perceiving and some kinds of apriori beliefs are basic. A foundationalist theory will also describe ways of reasoning it approves of, which, when used to reason from basic beliefs, will give true conclusions as often as possible. By reasoning from basic beliefs, we can justify non-basic beliefs. So all beliefs are justified when (and only when) they can be obtained by approved reasoning from basic beliefs.

Different foundationalist theories suggest different basic beliefs and different kinds of approved reasoning. The most influential foundationalist theory is classical empiricism (as discussed in chapter 2). It suggests as basic beliefs each person's beliefs about his or her own perceptual appearances, plus analytic beliefs (as discussed in chapter 3). And it suggests as approved reasoning simple induction (as discussed in chapter 4). Other foundationalist theories can suggest other candidates for basic beliefs and approved reasoning, but the important point for our purposes is the strategy that all such theories share of beginning with beliefs which are taken to present a minimal risk of falsity and then adding new beliefs to them by reasoning which increases this risk as little as possible.

In extreme contrast to foundationalist theories are *holist* or *coherentist* theories. ('Holism' is the more common word, but 'coherentism' is becoming increasingly common as a clearer alternative to it.) According to **holism**, a person is justified in changing their overall pattern of beliefs when the change results in a simple, unified pattern, leaving a minimum of beliefs which contradict or cannot be explained by others. Thus, when a person acquires new beliefs by perception, they are justified, according to holism, in changing their other beliefs so as to provide explanations of what has been perceived and reject beliefs which the perceptions show to be wrong. Changes in belief should make our beliefs more coherent with one another.

The point to note about holistic theories is that they do not propose any basic beliefs or any particular ways of reasoning from evidence to beliefs that the evidence supports. (Deductive reasoning plays an important role in most holist theories; but they do not propose any specific kinds of non-deductive inference.) Instead, they propose ideals of coherence that we should try to make our beliefs approach. One holist theory might have a simple ideal that there should be no logical contradictions between any beliefs; a more plausible holist theory might have a more complicated ideal that as many beliefs as possible should have explanations, so that there are few mysteries or exceptions. (This more plausible theory has a cost, though; it makes it necessary to say what we mean by 'explanation'.)

Holistic theories are the natural means to express extreme ignorance-avoidance. There are two main reasons for this. Most fundamentally, the kinds of consideration that justify holding beliefs according to holism are exactly the features that make them practically and socially useful. Suppose that a scientific theory predicts that medical or technological innovations will produce certain effects under certain conditions. Then the belief that the theory is true will be coherent with the belief that these effects happen under these conditions. So belief in nuclear physics, or in the molecular biology of viruses, will be justified. The beliefs are justified because they work. Or, for a very different example, the beliefs all people have about the emotions and characters of other people, and the actions that other people perform, are essential both to the coherence of each person's system of beliefs and to human social life. We would be lost without these beliefs, both socially and intellectually. And here again the coherence of beliefs and their use in practical life are very closely related.

A related reason for connecting holism and ignorance-avoidance is that they share a conservative attitude to change of belief. That is, when a belief is coherent with other beliefs, then, according to holism, we are justified in continuing to believe it even if we do not have specific evidence that that particular belief is true. But many beliefs which we hold for their practical or social consequences are like this: we do not know if other beliefs could work just as well as a basis for technology or medicine or everyday life, but we know that these beliefs taken together with others which we also hold work well enough for these purposes, and so we hold on to them. Both holism and ignorance-avoidance satisfy the slogan 'If it ain't broke, don't fix it'.

3. Fallibilisms

Foundationalism comes from fearing falsehood above all else. Holism accepts the likelihood of falsehood in order to obtain beliefs that will allow us to understand the natural and human world around us. Holist epistemologies accept the likelihood of falsehood in another sense too. True to their alternative name of **coherentism**, they take the reasons for accepting or rejecting a belief depend entirely on the way that it coheres with other beliefs. So whenever a person comes to acquire a new belief, or loses a belief that they had, their system of beliefs changes. Over time, as new beliefs enter and old ones leave, the whole pattern changes, so that beliefs which were once essential to the coherence of the whole come to be unnecessary. As a result, holist epistemologies usually claim that any belief could, in time, come to be abandoned. We could in the future come to think that anything we now believe, however firmly, is false. (This is not to say that any belief could *now* be abandoned. The sequence of changes that would be necessary for us to abandon, say, the belief that a million is bigger than ten, or that the parts of the parts of a thing are parts of a thing, might take centuries.)

This claim that any belief could be abandoned raises many questions, though. What kinds of evidence or change of belief would suggest abandoning beliefs that we now consider certain? How many other beliefs would have to change first? Would beliefs be abandoned as a compulsory or optional matter? That is, is the claim that for any belief there is a situation in which abandoning it is one rational option, or that for any belief there is a situation in which not abandoning it would be irrational? Different answers to these and other questions can determine whether the claim that any belief could be abandoned is a wild, radical suggestion or a harmless platitude masquerading as a bold idea. Here are arguments defending three possible versions of the claim. Each considers the status of three apparently certain beliefs: the belief that moose are animals, the belief that the earth revolves around the sun, and the belief that 65 + 14 is greater than 67.

Jungle fallibilism

We might have to abandon any of our beliefs at any time. For we can never know what evidence might appear tomorrow. We might discover that there are tiny radio transmitters buried inside the brains of moose transmitting instructions to them from extraterrestrial controllers, and also find out that moose calves are not born from mother moose but are beamed down from alien spacecraft. (Have you ever seen a moose being born? Do you know anyone who has?) Then we would be forced to conclude that moose are not animals, but machines. Or we might send up a probe into space which collided with a sphere surrounding the earth on which lights move in exactly the patterns they would if there were stars and a sun moving in the way that astronomy claims they do. Or we might discover a new kind of particle in atomic physics such that any apparatus we design to count them gives the result that if you count 33 pairs of them you get the answer 66, but if you count two sets of 33 you get the answer 0.

On this view, the universe is a jungle in which wild discoveries lie in wait for us. We can never tell what is around the corner or hiding in the trees. All we can do is to say: this is what the evidence suggests so far, and tomorrow's evidence might be anything at all.

Boring fallibilism

Any belief could be abandoned, in that for any belief there might arise a situation in which we could reasonably choose to say No to the words which now express that belief. Suppose, for example, that we find it confusing that 'moose' and 'mouse' sound alike. (People very often say 'mice' when they mean 'mooses', moreover, the Danish and Latin words for mouse sound like 'moose'.) So we decide to avoid confusion by calling moose 'woodland elk'. This confusion arose because 'moose' and 'mouse' both refer to kinds of animals, so it would not be confusing to use the word 'moose' to refer, for example, to a kind of knot which has large antler-like bows but gets very tight when one end is pulled. (Be careful, never put your head in a moose.) Then, of course, people would deny that a moose is an animal. A moose would be a kind of knot. As for the belief that the earth goes round the sun, we are already in a position to deny it, in that we realize that the sun itself is moving in a complex path through the galaxy, so that if we plot the paths of the earth and the sun relative to the nearby stars we find that they do not have the pattern of a single location for the sun and an elliptical path around it. The belief that $65 + 14$ is greater than 67 is similarly already false if we understand '$=$' to mean what it does in some mathematical theories. An example is modular arithmetic, in which two numbers are identical if they leave the same remainder when divided by some 'modulus', such as 13. Then $65 + 14 = 1$ (since 13 divides into 79 six times, leaving a remainder of 1) and $67 = 2$, (since 13 divides into 67 five times leaving a remainder of 2). But 1 is not greater than 2, so, understanding equality and greater than in this special way, 65 + 14 is not greater than 67.

Informed fallibilism

We could be forced to abandon any belief, though the route that would take us to this would in some cases be a very long one. Sometimes a rather shorter route would take us to a situation in which abandoning a belief would be a rational option. There are two important ways in which we could come to abandon beliefs which now seem to us obviously true. Call them 'observation-refining' and 'concept-splitting'. Observation-refining occurs when we find ways of making new observations, either by perceiving things we could not perceive before or by classifying our perceptions in new ways. For example, the invention of telescopes and microscopes allowed scientists to observe many things that had been invisible before, and more recently electron microscopes and brain-scan equipment allow completely new observations. An example of new ways of describing perception is when mathematical analysis of patterns in the output of a microscope or telescope allows us to describe it in completely different terms from the ones that we would naturally use (for example, in terms of 'spatial frequencies'). As our theories of the world become more complex, they open up new ways of making and classifying observations, and thus make available new kinds of evidence, which may, paradoxically, cause problems for the theories that made them possible.

Concept-splitting occurs when we come to accept a belief which shows that we have been running together ideas that are actually different in important ways. An example of this is when we discovered that the animals we had been calling 'fish' were really of several different kinds. There are normal fish which have gills, are cold-blooded, and whose young develop from eggs usually outside their bodies; there are whales, which have lungs, are warm-blooded, and whose young develop inside their bodies separated from their mothers' bodies by a placenta; and there are squid, and also other kinds of water creatures. The fact that these differences are very basic and important became clear only when biological theory developed to a point where it could classify animals in more basic and less-obvious terms than the shapes of their bodies and the way they move.

Both these processes describe important ways in which we can come to abandon beliefs in which we had felt confident. Suppose we discover that the chemical that carries genetic information from an animal to its descendants, DNA, comes in two fundamentally different kinds. Most animals have one of these kinds, but a few have the other kind, which shares important features with the DNA of fungi. Among the creatures of this unusual kind are moose. Then it might be reasonable to say that moose are not animals but fungi-like creatures. Or suppose that we create a new kind of radio telescope by mounting one receiver on the earth and one on the moon, and then by treating them as two parts of one fragmented aerial, we manage to relate the positions of the earth and the sun with respect to radio signals coming from the stars. Suppose that when we do this, we find that the earth is indeed tracing out an elliptical orbit through space, but the sun is not at a focus of this ellipse. Instead, the motions of both the earth and the sun are determined by the gravitational field of an invisible massive object, perhaps a black hole.

Lastly, consider how on this account the belief that $65 + 14$ is greater than 67 could be abandoned. Addition of numbers is a feature of the union of sets. To say that $2 + 1$ is 3 is to say that if we have a set A and distinct objects s and t in A, and a set B and an object u in B, and nothing is in both A and B, then there are distinct objects a, b, c in the union of A and B. In other words, adding is counting the objects formed by the union of sets. Now suppose we learn that the union of sets is not the simple thing we naively take it to be. Suppose we learn that there are some kinds of sets which do not have unions with other kinds. If there is a set of the first kind and a set of the second kind, then there is no set which is the union of these two sets.

Then many basic principles of arithmetic will be challenged. It may no longer be clear that we can say anything in general about 65 + 14, because sometimes there will be no such thing as the sum of these numbers. (But 65 dogs and 14 cats will still be more dogs-or-cats than 67 dogs-or-cats.)

4. How the Web Changes

Which of these fallibilisms is right? In a way they all are. The processes that each of them describes can and do happen. But there is also a way in which jungle fallibilism and boring fallibilism are very misleading and suggest that our beliefs change in ways that they in general they do not.

Let us begin with boring fallibilism. Although it is true that we could come to mean something else by 'moose', and as a result come to deny the sentence 'Moose are animals', this would not really mean that our beliefs had changed. We would not have lost the belief that moose are animals. We would still have that belief, but we would express it with the words 'Forest elk are animals'. Similarly for the beliefs that the earth goes round the sun and that 65 + 14 is greater than 67. In each case we would not have changed our beliefs, only the words that we used to express them.

Jungle fallibilism is more subtly misleading. It is true that we cannot completely rule out the possibility that, for example, we will discover that moose are machines sent to earth by aliens. But this does not show that this possibility is one that we should take seriously. It is not one that we should prepare for or await. It is not even a kind of possibility that we should expect, although we should expect that there will be really astounding surprises in the future evidence. (Surprises are by definition surprising; but some surprises, even astoundingly surprising surprises, are of kinds that we expect. We expect, for example, that occasionally a tossed coin will land heads twenty times in a row, although it is extremely surprising when one does.) If we know anything about the world, we know that the unexpected refutations of our beliefs will not occur completely at random.

This point can be made in terms of questions about method in the theory of knowledge. Since the theory of knowledge is concerned with understanding and evaluating our reasons for our beliefs, we might think that we should not assume any of these beliefs when trying to gain this understanding. The most we should assume in epistemology is pure logic and an understanding of the meaning of the words we are using. Then perhaps we could add more assumptions when we succeeded in showing that there are doubt-proof reasons for believing them. This would be like Descartes's project in his *Meditations*, and it would commit us to some sort of foundationalist theory of knowledge. The problem with this is that it does not work; we end up with no theory of knowledge at all, because in fact we cannot find enough doubt-proof assumptions to gain any real understanding of how human beings gain knowledge and where their attempts to know the world are likely to succeed or fail. So one result is likely to be jungle fallibilism: we have no assurance that any belief is more secure than any other, or that evidence against our beliefs is more likely to take one form than another.

An alternative approach to understanding our beliefs is to allow ourselves to make the same kinds of assumptions as we would in any other kind of investigation. We can use results from psychology, physics and biology, and of course common sense, in order to describe both human beings and the world around them in ways that help us to see the possibilities and limitations of human attempts to understand this world. Of course it makes sense in doing this to take account of the strength of the evidence for the assumptions we are using, to see that there is a lot more evidence for the assumption that, for example, people see with their eyes and hear with their ears than there is for the theory of evolution. Still, you can't do a job without tools, and the tools needed for making a theory of human knowledge have to be put together out of that knowledge itself. (See also the discussion of naturalism in chapter 9, sections 5, 6 and 7.)

If we take this second attitude to epistemological method, we are inclined towards informed fallibilism, or something much like it. For in evaluating the ways in which our beliefs are likely to be wrong, in stating the serious expectations we should have of surprising developments in our understanding of the world, we have to rely on what we know about the way our beliefs have been supported and refuted by evidence in the past, and what we know about the strengths and weaknesses of our capacities for gathering evidence, reasoning and making theories. And when we combine the history of knowledge with a little psychology in this way, what we learn is that when beliefs that we had thought were certain come to be abandoned, it is often either because we have found new ways of obtaining and evaluating evidence or because our theories have given us new concepts which allow us to see that these beliefs were fundamentally ambiguous. And these are the two patterns described by informed fallibilism.

Informed fallibilism can be seen as an aspect of a familiar idea, the web of belief. As chapter 3, sections 4 and 5, explained, Quine and others have argued that our beliefs are connected to each other in a complex structure in which some beliefs have a very central position, so that evidence is relevant to them only very indirectly. Other beliefs are at the outside, affected more directly by evidence and thus more amenable to change. The usual candidates for the centre are beliefs about mathematics and other apriori beliefs, and the usual candidates for the outside are perceptual beliefs. (See question 19 for relations between this picture and holism.) On this picture, we should not expect beliefs near the centre to change very often, and we should expect situations in which we were forced to abandon such a belief (rather than simply having abandoning the belief among our reasonable options) to be extremely rare. We should expect that changes that reach well into the web of belief occur when the structure of the web itself changes, as when beliefs at the edges are augmented with new kinds of perceptual beliefs or when beliefs further in split and are replaced with several new beliefs. But these, again, are the suggestions of informed fallibilism.

Informed fallibilism tries to show how the web of belief could change while keeping its power to give us understanding of the world. It describes how, as our knowledge grows, we may have to discard many of the beliefs with which we began, even though we keep much of the understanding they gave us. We might abandon beliefs like 'moose are animals' because of a richer biological classification system that includes the one we use today as a special case; we might abandon the belief that the earth orbits round the sun as a result of observations which rely on the physics we have been building up over centuries; we might abandon the belief that 65 + 14 is greater than 67 while keeping all the rules for counting animals, money and so on that we need in everyday life. Informed fallibilism thus retains some of the optimism about our capacities to increase our understanding that is seen in old foundationalist views. (But with an important difference: unlike foundationalism, this view allows that while our understanding may accumulate, our beliefs do not.)

Jungle fallibilism, on the other hand, focuses on cases in which the web of belief disintegrates or shrinks, rather than grows. And boring fallibilism focuses on cases in which the web hardly changes at all. The cases described by all three of them occur. But it is informed fallibilism, I am convinced, which points to important facts about the ways in which the structure of our beliefs can change.

Reading Questions

1 Section 1 begins with a contrast between risk of falsity and risk of ignorance. It then continues with six kinds of risks, (a) to (c'). Which of these are risks of falsity, and which are risks of ignorance?

2 We can define 'ignorance' so that either (b') or (c') becomes a risk of ignorance. How do the two definitions differ?

3 Why would someone who thought they had a method which would give them all and only true beliefs not be concerned about the difference between falsity and ignorance?

4 Why is foundationalism motivated by error-avoidance?

5 Section 2 said that one holist theory might claim that there should be no logical contradictions between beliefs, while another might claim that as many beliefs as possible should have explanations. Which of these is the more demanding ideal, in the sense of being harder to achieve? Can you give an example of a set of beliefs which satisfies the first ideal but not the second?

6 In section 2 it is claimed that the usefulness of beliefs about people's characters and emotions is the same as their coherence. Coherence with what other beliefs?

7 Explain the difference, appealed to in section 3, between a situation in which abandoning a belief is a rational option and a situation in which it would be irrational not to abandon a belief. Give an example.

8 What is the connection between jungle fallibilism, discussed in section 3, and Hume's discovery about induction, discussed in chapter 4, section 2?

9 Here is an old philosophical puzzle: 'Suppose that ostriches were called "horses" and horses were called "ostriches". How many legs would a horse have?' What does this have to do with boring fallibilism?

10 Informed fallibilism, discussed in section 3, postulates two processes which underlie the abandonment of well-established beliefs, observation-refining and concept-splitting. Which of these processes is involved in which of the examples of how, from the point of view of informed fallibilism, a well-established belief could be abandoned?

11 In section 4 an objection is made to boring fallibilism's account of how we could come to abandon the belief that moose are animals. Describe similar objections to its account of how the belief that the earth revolves around the sun and the belief that 65 + 14 is greater than 67 could be abandoned.

12 In section 4 it is said that we expect that a tossed coin will occasionally land heads twenty times in a row, though it is extremely surprising when it does. How can an event be extremely surprising although expected? Explain why this is an analogy for the ways in which evidence against our theories tends to occur.

13 Why might someone think that in order to evaluate our reasons for our beliefs, it would be best not to assume any of them?

14   Why, if we think in terms of the web of belief, should we expect very few situations in which we were forced to abandon a belief near the centre of the web?

Thinking Questions

15   In our attempts to understand the world, there are virtues and vices, just as there are in our attempts to live with one another. Consider the following virtues: *patience, imagination, tolerance, carefulness, hesitation, enthusiasm.* Which of these are likely to play a role in an error-avoiding approach to knowledge, and which in an ignorance-avoiding approach? Describe a central epistemic virtue for the strategy of avoiding each of the six kinds of risk (a) to (c').

16   Jungle fallibilism may, as argued in the text, suggest a misleading picture of the ways in which evidence against our beliefs is likely to appear, but is it not still *true*?

17   At the beginning of the chapter it was claimed that some forms of fallibilism are 'verging on lunacy'. The wildest fallibilism discussed in the chapter is jungle fallibilism. But it does not seem to be exactly lunatic. How can it be modified so as to bring out its truly wild possibilities?

18   The criticism of boring fallibilism in section 4 interpreted it as saying that we could abandon any belief simply by deciding to use the words to mean something else. Can the statement of boring fallibilism in section 3 be understood so as to make a less boring claim?

19   The web of belief is usually thought of as an image of holism. For the threads of the web connect each belief ultimately to every other belief. But holism should allow no basic beliefs, no beliefs which need no support from any other beliefs. So what about the beliefs at the edge of the web? These are usually thought of as beliefs about evidence from perception. What puts them at the edge is the fact that they respond to factors outside the web itself: namely, perception. So are they not in effect basic beliefs? And is this holist picture not really a foundationalist picture in disguise?

Further Reading

Simple expositions of fallibilism are found in chapter 5, section F, of John Cottingham, *Rationalism* (Oxford University Press, 1988); chapter 3 of Martin Hollis, *Invitation to Philosophy* (Blackwell, 1985); and chapter 11 (especially section 6) of Adam Morton, *Philosophy in Practice* (Blackwell, 1996). More advanced treatments are in chapter 15 of Jonathan Dancy, *An Introduction to Contemporary Epistemology* (Blackwell, 1985), and chapter 10 of Donald Gillies, *Philosophy of Science in the Twentieth Century* (Blackwell, 1993). The crucial distinction between avoiding falsity and avoiding error is made in chapter 1 of Alvin Goldman, *Epistemology and Cognition* (Harvard University Press, 1986). For the contrast between foundationalism and holism (coherentism) see Laurence Bonjour, *The Structure of Empirical Knowledge* (Harvard University Press, 1985).

Selections from classic philosophical works relevant to this chapter can be found in John Cottingham, *Western Philosophy: An Anthology* (Blackwell, 1996). See part I section 4, René Descartes, 'New Foundations for Knowledge', and part II section 1, Plato, 'The Allegory of the Cave'.

6 Defining Knowledge

1. Top-grade Belief

Consider three cases in which a person does not have knowledge.

A weather forecaster, McA, is preparing to make a radio report on the weather to be expected the next day. He finds, five minutes before he must go on air, that he has lost all the data on which the report was to be based. So he tosses a coin. Heads for rain, tails for dry. Heads for winds under five miles per hour, tails for winds over five miles per hour. And so on. After five minutes he has his report, and he goes on air and predicts a hurricane, though the sky is blue, the barometer is steady, and the breezes are gentle.

McA does not *know* that there will be a hurricane the next day. Suppose that by some freak of the weather there is a hurricane the next day. That does not turn his report into knowledge; it was just guesswork, and only turned out accurate by chance.

A detective, FitzB, is investigating a murder. Near the victim's body she finds a wallet containing a driver's license in the name of Z. She goes to interview Z and finds that he has left town in a hurry. Z is tracked down and found to have traces of the victim's blood under his fingernails. Moreover, his fingerprints are all over the scene of the crime. A little investigation reveals that Z had a long-standing grudge against the victim and stood to gain a lot of money from the victim's death. There are no other suspects. FitzB concludes that she has solved the crime: Z is the killer.

But Z is not the killer. Z was framed by a very clever enemy of the victim who managed to plant all the evidence while leaving no traces of her activities. Z is convicted and executed, and the real killer is never brought to justice. So FitzB did not know that Z was the killer. She thought she knew, and she had very good reasons for so thinking. But in fact her belief was false, so it cannot have been knowledge.

A scientist, Dr O'C, is testing a drug, magicillin, which she thinks may be a good treatment for cancer of the liver. Suppose that her suspicion is right, and magicillin does cure liver cancer in a large proportion of human cases. Suppose, moreover, that she performs experiments on both human and animal subjects, designed to measure the rate of recovery when the drug is administered and to rule out alternative explanations. Suppose that her reasoning from these experiments is faultless, so that when she publishes her results in a research paper, they provide very good reasons to believe that magicillin will save the lives of a large proportion of people with cancer of the liver. Suppose now that, although Dr O'C does not know it, one of her lab assistants has falsified part of an experiment by replacing one experimental animal which looked as if it might be diseased with a healthy animal that had not previously been part of the experiment.

When Dr O'C finds out, she will be furious and dismayed: her research has been ruined. After she learns that the experiment has been tampered with, she can no longer maintain to her colleagues that she knows that magicillin cures liver cancer. She does not know it; she did not know it even before she discovered what her assistant had done, and thereby discovered that what she had thought was knowledge was not. Yet her belief is true – magicillin does cure liver cancer – and her reasoning is perfect – her belief is justified.

In all three cases we have a belief that fails to be knowledge. But the reasons for this are different. McA does not know that there will be a hurricane the next day, because what he passes off as reasoning is so feeble. You cannot predict the weather by tossing coins. So the fault here lies in him. FitzB does not know that Z is the killer, because her belief is false. As it happens, Z is not the killer, although FitzB's reasoning is fine. The fault here lies in the relation between her beliefs and the facts.

Looking at the McA and FitzB cases, we might think that it is obvious what knowledge is. To have knowledge, you have to have a belief which is both true and justified. Both the facts and your reasoning have to be right. But the O'C case shows that things are not that simple. Dr O'C's belief is true, and her reasoning is fine, but she does not have knowledge. The O'C case is one of many examples – known as Gettier examples after Edmund Gettier, who first pointed out their significance – which show that we cannot take 'know' to mean simply 'true and justified'. When we say that someone knows something, we are saying more than that they believe it and their belief is true and they are justified in believing it. What more?

This is a controversial question. There is very little agreement about what the right answer to it is, or even whether it is an important question. In this chapter I shall describe several approaches to the question which have been defended by philosophers since the 1970s. The chapter is thus an introduction to a part of the theory of knowledge with a very distinctive flavour of its own. Some people find the questions and approaches here fascinating; others have trouble seeing the point of them. My aim is to make a case for thinking that there are important and central questions here. But before entering this controversy, it is worth stating some simpler, uncontroversial facts about the concept of knowledge, to give us something definite to hold on to.

A belief qualifies as knowledge if, in acquiring it, one has achieved the basic aim in the enquiry that led to it. In other words, we use the term 'knowledge' as a kind of stamp of high quality for beliefs: if a belief fails to be knowledge, it is because it falls short of some expectation we might reasonably have of it. Thus McA's belief that there would be a hurricane the next day, and the beliefs of the people who believed what he said on the radio, were not knowledge, because we expect weather forecasters to pay more attention to the evidence than he did. FitzB's belief that Z is the killer is not knowledge, because we want beliefs to be true – that is one of the most basic aims of having beliefs – and it was not. Dr O'C's belief that magicillin cures liver cancer is not knowledge, partly because we cannot take the evidence and reasoning she presents as grounds for believing it ourselves: once we know that some of the data have been tampered with, we know that the experiments are flawed and will have to be rerun and reanalysed.

This general picture holds in many ordinary cases where we say that someone knows something, too. When we classify a belief as knowledge, we are saying that it has the good qualities that a belief should have. When we say that a student knows the answers on a test, we mean that the answers she gives are true and that she is not just guessing. (We mean more than this, but at least this.) When you are asked what the capital of Colombia is and you say 'I don't know, but I think it's Bogota', you are saying that we should not treat your belief that Bogota is the capital as a completely safe basis for our beliefs. When we say that the police know that a certain person has committed a certain crime, we mean that the police have done their job successfully; they have the right person, and they have discovered him by sensible detective work. Moving on to rather different ways of talking, when we say that someone knows about marathon running, we are saying that he has beliefs which make him a good source of information for us to base our beliefs about marathons on. And when we say that someone knows which the best restaurants in town are, we are saying that she can supply descriptions of the restaurants which can both help us to get a good meal and help us to find them. Moving on even further, when we say that someone knows how to recognize a good restaurant when she sees it, we mean that in the presence of good restaurants she will form the belief that they are good. Her skills are ones that she and others can base reliable beliefs on.

These are only some of the good qualities that beliefs can have. One way of understanding the definitions of knowledge that are discussed in the rest of the chapter is as ways of classifying and organizing all these desirable features of beliefs. Which are the most fundamental and most important of them?

2. Lehrer's Principle

Dr O'C's reasoning, though correct, began with a false premiss, that the animals with which the experiment ended were those with which it began. Perhaps knowledge is true belief that lies at the end of a chain of reasoning which begins with true premisses.

This suggestion is not right either. For suppose that Dr O'C does other experiments. This time her experiments don't get fouled up. But unfortunately they don't directly indicate that magicillin cures liver cancer; instead, they indicate that it inhibits cell division in a certain complicated way. From this result she infers that it will be effective against cancer. Now as a matter of fact (in this story) magicillin is effective against liver cancer, but it does not inhibit cell division in the way that the experiments indicated. Again things have gone wrong; again Dr O'C has not got knowledge, though this time her belief is not only true, and obtained by good reasoning, but also proceeds from true premisses.

It seems, then, that for a chain of reasoning to lead to knowledge, it must not only start with true premisses but must also not have any false steps at any point along the way. It should have no detour through falsity. We have here a fairly simple principle that does seem to correspond to something important about knowledge. Let me call it **Lehrer's principle** and state it more carefully: if a belief is based on reasoning, then it qualifies as knowledge if, and only if, it does not depend on any chain of reasoning that has a false step at middle, beginning or end.

A number of philosophers have accepted Lehrer's principle. But, like many valuable philosophical ideas, it contains an enormous fudge. For it says that knowledge cannot *depend on* any reasoning that proceeds through falsity. What does 'depend on' mean?

A belief does not necessarily depend on the reasoning by which it was originally acquired. One can first acquire a belief for some reasons (perhaps bad), and later obtain other reasons (perhaps good) for holding it. For example, a person may hold a belief just because someone he dislikes believes the opposite; later he makes some investigations and finds some strong evidence for the belief he already has. Now he may have knowledge, although his first reasons were bad. (Another example is the case of Harvey's belief in the circulation of the blood, mentioned in chapter 1, section 3.)

Nor does a belief depend on just any reasoning which *could* support it, whether or not the person holding the belief uses or is aware of the reasoning. For often something that one clearly knows can be obtained as the conclusion of reasoning which has the fatal characteristics that it is logically correct, one believes each of its steps, but some step is false. This false step should not cause one's belief not to be knowledge if one does not actually use the fatal reasoning to get or support it. For example, Dr O'C may have the false belief that magicillin inhibits cell division; but suppose that, although this might be used in a persuasive argument to conclude that it cures liver cancer, she does not base her belief upon this reasoning. She bases her belief instead on a line of reasoning which does not involve any false step. She then knows that magicillin cures liver cancer; her knowledge is not undermined by the faults of the reasoning she does not use.

We must take 'depends on' to mean roughly the following: A person's belief depends on a chain of reasoning when the reasoning is used by the person, publicly or privately, to show why he should hold the belief; if the reasoning is refuted, if the person stops thinking that it is correct or that all its stages are true, then the person will either find some other reasoning to support the belief or cease to consider it as one of his well-supported opinions.

3. Knowledge not Based on Reasoning

Lehrer's principle applies to beliefs which depend on reasoning. When I tried to explain what 'depends on' must mean, it turned out that the reasoning had to be fairly explicit; the person must be able to formulate it to himself. Many beliefs are not based on any such reasoning, and most beliefs result in part from processes that are not explicit reasoning. Perception, for example, though it is far from a simple unstructured process, does not consist in reasoning that the perceiver can express. So all our beliefs based partly on perception rest partly on processes that are not explicit reasoning.

Moreover, it is rational to hold many beliefs not because they are supported by any reasoning, but because they explain, unify or predict one's experience and opinions. This is the case with many systematic or theoretical beliefs and with much of the knowledge that we get by learning from others. Consider, for example, the knowledge that the earth is round or that germs cause certain diseases. Such knowledge is useful, and one would be foolish to give it up just because one does not have at hand an argument that would convince someone who thinks that the earth is flat or that all diseases are caused by lack of faith. (See the discussion of ignorance-avoidance in chapter 5.)

No doubt in many cases one could invent an argument which would do part of the job, if one thought hard enough. It would probably be some version of the 'inference to the best explanation', discussed in chapter 10. It would run roughly: this hypothesis explains the following facts, and fits in with these other facts in the following nice way; the alternative hypotheses for explaining these things won't do, for the following reasons, so it seems to be true. (I say that such an argument might do 'part of the job' because someone who believes, say, that the earth is flat, is likely to have enough other strange beliefs about the way the world is and what a scientific hypothesis should do that he will not be much affected by any such argument.) It has often been taken as one of the functions of philosophers to provide such sophisticated arguments for things most people believe without an argument. But in any case we saw that Lehrer's principle is not concerned with reasoning that could be used to support a belief, but rather with reasoning that is actually used; and it is clear that although most people know that the earth is round and that typhoid is caused by a bacillus, very few people can make convincing arguments for these statements.

4. Reliability

Beliefs to which Lehrer's principle cannot be easily applied are also obtained from theories which give reliable predictions although they are in fact partly false. Here is an example. Before the discovery and acceptance of the idea that the earth revolves around the sun, rather than the other way around, sailors used to compute their latitude from the position of the sun and other heavenly bodies by using a theory which falsely assumed that the earth was stationary. As a matter of fact, sailors got the right navigational results this way. Consider now an old sea captain who computes his latitude (how far north or south of the equator he is) from observations of the heavens, and imagine him to have enough astronomical lore to think things through in terms of the old false astronomy. Surely, if he gets the right answer, if he makes no mistakes and concludes that his latitude is what it really is, then he knows what his latitude is. But his reasoning involves many false assumptions. Lehrer's principle seems wrong here.

The important thing about this case is that the captain has obtained his result by a method that is reliable – it always works – and that could have been based on true assumptions, though it was not. For the captain's calculations could have been derived from the true astronomical facts, or even on the non-committal assumption 'If the apparent positions of the stars in the sky are such and such, then the latitude is the following'. It is important that it is a whole method that can be given a true foundation, and not just a single belief. For if the captain had obtained his estimate of his latitude from the horoscopes of the crew, and by pure luck had come up with the right answer, then the fact that he could have derived his latitude from sound navigational principles does nothing to confer the status of knowledge on his guess. What is special about the captain's case is that his method is reliable, and it is no accident that it is reliable; given the way things really are, it is inevitable that the method will give true results.

The case of the old sea captain is important because it leads to another side of the concept of knowledge, as basic as the side expressed by Lehrer's principle. The captain knows where he is because his method of discovery is *reliable*: there is a good reason why it gives the right answers. However rational or irrational he is in using his method, others can rely on his results; seen as a source for other people's reasoning or as part of a larger scientific project, his method is just as it should be.

The reliability of methods is a subtle business. Another story: in this story, unlike the earlier one, Dr O'C has discovered that magicillin works against all cancers in rats, mice, gerbils and squirrels; so she concludes that it works against cancer in all rodents, and therefore will be effective in chipmunks. This reasoning is sound, and, as it happens, magicillin is effective against cancer in chipmunks. But the way that it cures cancer in most rodents is completely different from the way it works in chipmunks; by some freak of chipmunk metabolism, it is the substance in which the normally active ingredient of magicillin is dissolved, rather than that ingredient itself, that is effective against cancer in chipmunks. Dr O'C does not know that the drug works in chipmunks, although her reasoning does not violate Lehrer's principle and is trustworthy, in that it leads, and will usually lead, to a true conclusion. What is wrong with her belief is that its truth is a sort of accident: the reasons why her roughly inductive reasoning usually works do not explain why it worked this time.

'Reliable' is a word that can be interpreted in several different ways. One way is statistical: a reliable method is one that gives true beliefs a high proportion of the time. (So we could speak of 75 per cent or 98 per cent reliability.) Statistical reliability is probably not the right way to think about knowledge. For suppose you have a ticket in a lottery and 999,999 other people have also bought tickets. (See chapter 4, question 14.) If your method of getting beliefs is to believe everything that has a more than 99 per cent chance of being true, then you should believe that you will not win the lottery. Suppose you do not win. Although this was the almost certain outcome, it does not seem right to say that you knew in advance that you would not win.

Another way is causal: a belief is reliably acquired if the laws of nature and mind explain why the process that resulted in the belief resulted in a true belief. So reliability requires a firm connection between the fact and the belief, as a result of the ways in which information is transmitted and processed and the effects of any disturbing factors. In fact, a process can be reliable, in this way, even if it operates only once and cannot be repeated. For example, I may have been blind since infancy (after a brief sighted period in which my visual system developed somewhat); then, late in life, the injection of a powerful drug allows me to see for a few moments, before it utterly rots away my retinas. During those few moments I know that there are people about me, what their movements are, and the colours of their clothes.

The idea is still vague. A belief is reliably acquired if there is an explanation of why the process that resulted in it resulted in truth. What process? Does Dr O'C's belief result from thinking, from scientific method, from the particular experimental design she used, or what? Any way of spelling out what the relevant process is will appeal to conditionals: that is, if-statements. Suppose we say that Dr O'C's belief is reliably acquired if the actual experimental design she used was reliable. This means that (given the way human minds and the rest of the world work) if that design had been used in various circumstances, the result would have been a true belief. A reliable method is one that, when used in the right circumstances, will not give a false belief. (Perhaps in many circumstances, it gives no belief at all.) So a more precise way of talking about reliability would specify a range of circumstances and of beliefs, and then say that if the person was in those circumstances, then those beliefs would be true.

One specific form of this idea is the concept of *tracking*. Consider the most basic kind of knowledge: perception. Suppose that you are watching a bird fly across your garden and land in a tree. As the position of the bird changes, so does your perception, and thus your perceptual belief. If the bird had followed a different path, your sequence of beliefs would have been different. Your beliefs therefore track the position of the bird, much as the eyes of a predator track the position of potential prey, or a blip on a radar screen tracks the position of a plane.

Tracking can be defined in terms of conditionals, if-sentences. If the bird had followed a different course, your beliefs would have been different. And before the bird flew the way it did, it would have been true to say that if it were to fly in the way it did, then you would believe that it was flying that way. Generalizing, we can turn this into a definition:

A person's belief *tracks* a fact when two conditions are met: (1) if that fact had occurred (perhaps under slightly different circumstances), then the person would have believed that it occurred; (2) if the fact had not occurred, the person would not have had the belief.

This definition is essentially due to Fred Dretske and Robert Nozick. They suggested that we can define knowledge in terms of tracking: a person's belief counts as knowledge when it tracks the fact that makes it true. So, for example, you know that the bird is half-way to the tree when your belief that it is half-way there tracks the fact that it is half-way there. And this will be so when, if the bird had only been a quarter of the way there, you would have believed that it was a quarter of the way there, and if it had been three-quarters of the way there, you would have believed that it was three-quarters of the way there.

This approach to knowledge is clearly a version of the reliability approach. Reliability, remember, depends on whether there are good reasons, in the workings of the mind and the routes by which information comes to it, why true beliefs should result. So if a belief is based on a reliable process, then the process should give the belief only when it is true, and should give different beliefs in different situations. In other words, the belief should track the fact that makes it true.

There is something intuitively very right and appealing about this approach. It captures the feeling that when someone knows something, then it is no accident that their belief is true: it is true because it tracks the facts. It captures the feeling that a person who has knowledge can be used by others as a reliable source of information: for if you know that the person's beliefs track the facts, then you know that if you trust what they say, your own beliefs will be true. And it captures the feeling that beliefs based on irrational reasoning or mistakes are not knowledge, even if they happen to be true. For such deviations from correct thinking usually introduce factors which make the belief independent of the facts: even if the facts had been different, the person would still have held the belief.

5. Missing Information

But there are still problems, more tricky examples. One family of problem cases involves beliefs which track the facts but do so because of an accident. Suppose, for example, that you are in a psychological experiment like one of those described in chapter 2. You are given eyeglasses which make everything look upside-down. But you do not know that this is what they are; you do not even know you are in a psychology experiment. (Perhaps the experimenters tell you that they are comparing different glasses' frames for comfort.) The glasses are put on you in the dark, and when the light comes on, you see a scene through a window. By mistake a mirror has been left by the window which inverts the scene, exactly cancelling the effect of the glasses. In the scene a balloon is floating, and you are asked if it is rising or falling. You say that it is rising, as it in fact is. Your belief is true, and tracks the facts: if the balloon had been falling, you would have said that it was falling; if it was stationary, you would have said it was stationary, and so on. But the set-up that allowed your belief to track the fact was a fluke; all the subjects in the experiment before and after you believed that the balloon's motions were the opposite of what they in fact were. Many people when they think about this case will conclude that you do not know that the balloon is rising. Although your belief tracks the fact that it is rising, you could too easily have had a false belief. Knowledge should be more secure than this.

One feature of this case is very significant. Suppose that you had been given the true information that you were being fitted with inverting glasses. Then, when the balloon appeared to rise, you would not have believed that it was rising. You would have thought: 'I am in an experiment, and they are doing weird things to my vision; who knows what may really be happening?' So there is true information you do not have which would have prevented your having the belief, even though the belief was true. This fact is closely linked to the accidental way that the belief tracks the truth. For although there is a variety of circum-stances in which it is true that if they held you would have true beliefs about them, there is also a slightly larger variety of circum-stances in which you would not have true beliefs. In many cases in which tracking is the result of an accident, information about the accidental features of the situation can create circumstances in which the person's beliefs would be false.

The failure of a belief to be knowledge is often connected with the fact that it would not have survived exposure to some true information. For example, suppose that you are walking around central London thinking about the troubles of the British royal family. Around the corner walks a woman whose appearance you have often seen on television and in newspapers; you go back to your hotel to tell your friends, 'I just saw Princess Diana'. But there are facts that you do not know. On that day anti-royalist protesters have flooded the streets with Diana look-alikes. There are hundreds of them in the area. Moreover, this fact has been well publicized; if you had been reading serious newspapers instead of tabloids, you would have realized it. Now, as a matter of fact, the woman you saw was (surprise surprise) Princess Diana. But, according to most people who reflect on cases like this, you do not know that it was her. For you could as easily have encountered one of the look-alikes, and then you would have been fooled.

Or consider a more tangled version of the same example. Again you are walking around London, and again you see the princess. But this time there are not hundreds of look-alikes out and about. Instead, there are newspaper headlines visible all over the place saying, falsely, that there are hundreds of Diana look-alikes wandering the streets. If you had seen any of these head-lines, you would not have believed that the person you saw was the princess. And it is a pure accident that you do not see any of these many headlines. In this case too people's reactions are usually that you do not know that the person you are seeing is the princess. And one explanation of this reaction is that the fact that if you had seen the headlines you would not have believed that the woman you saw was the princess shows that your belief did not rest on a reliable process. Although it gives a true belief in this case, there are very similar circumstances in which it does not.

It is interesting to make two contrasts here. On the one hand contrast your situation – seeing the princess but in the unseen presence of look-alikes or misleading headlines – with that of a close friend of the princess, who could tell her from all the look-alikes. The friend would know the princess on sight, even if he knew about the look-alikes or had seen the misleading headlines. On the other hand, contrast your situation with that of someone who knows the princess no better than you do, but just happens to see her coming out of an expensive London shop, when there are no look-alikes about or misleading headlines to be glimpsed. This person knows that it is the princess before her, just by using her ordinary powers of perception and recognition. So the concept of knowledge has a really subtle and interesting combination of strictness and tolerance. It is tolerant in that we can often know things by use of our ordinary capacities to perceive, reason and remember, even though these capacities sometimes lead to false beliefs. It is strict in that it does not allow that every use of these capacities which leads to a true belief results in knowledge. Sometimes we have to consider a much more specific process operating in a much more specific context, and ask: 'Is this reliable?'

There are many examples along these lines, in which people's beliefs are not knowledge not because of any false or irrational belief they have but because there are true beliefs they lack. Such examples are particularly troublesome for accounts of knowledge based on reliability or tracking. What they show is that if we want to define knowledge in terms of the conditions under which the process behind the belief results in truth, we are going to have a delicate job specifying the right process. If we define it too narrowly, as tracking analyses do, then a belief can fail to be knowledge because there are wider circumstances in which the person would have had a false belief. (For example, we ignore the effect of the look-alikes or misleading headlines in the Diana cases.) If we define it too widely – for example, by counting reason or perception as belief-giving processes – then we will run into the problem that these processes often give false beliefs. (So then we wrongly fail to count as knowledge the belief of a normal person under normal circumstances who sees and recognizes the princess.) We will need a definition narrow enough that the facts of the case can explain why this belief obtained by this process in these circumstances is true, and wide enough that the belief can be seen as a special case of a general truth-producing process. The right balance has not yet been found.

6. Internalism/Externalism

The many examples that philosophers have produced to support and refute definitions of knowledge have not resulted in a completely correct definition. Not yet, anyway. But they have brought out a large number of important qualities of beliefs. We want beliefs to have these qualities, and will withhold the label 'knowledge' if they are absent. We want beliefs to have all of the following qualities:

truth	justification
reliability	coherence
fact-tracking	reasonability
usability by others	not undermined by others' beliefs

There is a fundamental contrast between the qualities on the left and those on the right. The qualities on the right are *internal* qualities. They describe ways in which beliefs relate to the functioning of the individual, aspects of the individual's reasoning and perceptual processes. The qualities on the left are *external* qualities. They describe ways in which beliefs relate to the world around the individual. Some theories of knowledge, **internalist** theories, emphasize internal aspects and qualities, while others, **externalist** theories, emphasize external aspects and qualities. (See the discussion of radical externalism in section 5 of chapter 1.) The more a theory emphasizes justification, evidence and reasoning, the more internalist it will be, and the more it emphasizes reliability and the objective conditions under which a person's belief will be true, the more externalist it will be. One fundamental question is: Is knowledge basically a matter of the internal or the external qualities of a belief?

The obvious answer to this question is: Both. The old definition of knowledge as justified true belief was in agreement with this answer, since it emphasized one external quality (truth) and one internal quality (justification). Yet this may not be a promising way to answer the question; it may duck important issues. Some considerations about scepticism will make clear why this might be. Consider two sceptical possibilities.

First, suppose that our powers to reason are not nearly as reliable as we think they are. This is easiest to imagine with inductive reasoning: suppose that very many of the generalizations that we think we have conclusive inductive evidence for are in fact false, and that the true generalizations are too subtle and complicated for humans to understand. But a similar story is on the edge of imaginability for deductive reasoning. The reason, let us suppose, why our powers of reasoning have not failed us very often in the past is that we have been exposed to only a small part of the universe. If we were to explore just a little further out in time or space, or if some simple fact about the environment were to change, we would suddenly find that our attempts at reasoning consistently produced false results.

Would this show that very few of our true beliefs – our beliefs about the little part of reality where reason is effective – are knowledge? No, according to internalists. For our beliefs are reasonable, and they result from our best possible attempts to understand the world. To claim that they are not knowledge would be like claiming that kindness and fairness are wrong just because the world is cruel and unfair. But Yes, according to externalists. These facts, if they really were so, would show that the truths among our beliefs have come about by lucky chance, not because we are well equipped to understand the world.

Now consider another improbable story. Suppose that in some part of our lives our rational explanations about how our beliefs are obtained are completely mistaken, but many of our beliefs are true all the same. For example, suppose that many of each person's beliefs about other people's minds – whether other people are angry or disappointed or in love and so on – are true, but that our beliefs that we understand these things by reasoning in a rational way from other people's behaviour and facial expressions are wrong. In fact, suppose we gain these beliefs in a purely instinctive way based in part on how people smell and the rhythms of their body movements. Does this mean that we do not have knowledge about these things (about other people's minds)? Internalist theories allow a sceptical Yes. Although many of our beliefs on this topic may be true, they are irrational and amount to lucky hunches. Externalist theories, on the other hand, allow a more comforting No. Irrational though they may be, our methods for obtaining such beliefs work. They give us reliable truths.

So internalist and externalist approaches to knowledge can lead to sceptical conclusions, given different assumptions. Internalist approaches emphasize the proper working of our capacities to reason and process information. When these capacities are working properly, internalism will count the result as knowledge, and when they are not, it will tend to scepticism. Externalist approaches, on the other hand, emphasize the connection between belief and the world. If these are operating reliably, externalism will be ready to ascribe knowledge, and if they are not, its attitude is likely to be sceptical.

Internalism and externalism are thus fundamentally opposed attitudes to knowledge. They differ in the kinds of analysis of the concept that they present, the qualities of beliefs which they consider centrally important, and the conditions under which they will allow drastic sceptical conclusions. They are too different to be easily reconciled; a bland acknowledgement that each of them has an angle on the truth does not do justice to the conflict.

7. Knowledge and Trust

To end this chapter, I shall briefly describe some very basic qualities of beliefs that underlie the qualities in both columns of the list in the previous section. These do not lead to a definition of knowledge. But they do allow us to pull together some of the ideas of the chapter, and see why the concept of knowledge is so subtle. These ideas are controversial, though; they are more one person's suggestions than a report of the consensus among philosophers.

People rely on others for information. An isolated individual using the evidence and ways of thinking available to us could know very very little. There are two ways of using a person as a source of information. The simple way is to trust what they say. If someone says that she saw a moose walking down the street at two in the morning, then you believe that at two in the morning a moose walked down the street. The other way is to take what someone says as evidence about their state of mind. You conclude that she believes a moose walked down the street at two in the morning, or perhaps that she believed she could get you to think that a moose had walked down the street. On the first of these ways, you assume that she knows what she is saying. On the second, you simply talk about her beliefs. So one thing we can mean when we say that what someone has is knowledge is: you can trust what they say.

Now consider a rather different use of knowledge. We build our beliefs on other beliefs, using what we already believe as evidence and as background for new beliefs. We do not use all our beliefs in the same way here. We treat some of our beliefs as definite facts about the world, safe to use as guides for future beliefs, and we treat others as conjectures, which we are prepared to revise when more information comes in. (Notice that safety is not the same as certainty or as being apriori. We can treat a scientific theory – for example, the theory of evolution – as a basis for evaluating later beliefs, although there is more evidence to consider for or against it, and although we can see that possible evidence could refute it.) The difference between the two kinds of beliefs becomes particularly clear when evidence against a belief appears, and we have to think out how to react. You believe that all mammals have live young and then you discover the platypus, which has the appearance and metabolism of a mammal but lays eggs. In reconsidering your beliefs, you think: perhaps the platypus is not a mammal, or perhaps some mammals lay eggs, but at any rate we know that all mammals in Europe and the Americas have live young, and that the placenta appeared very early in the evolution of mammals. When you think 'at any rate we know', the concept of knowledge is being used to set aside some beliefs which you do not take to be threatened by the evidence at hand. So another thing you can mean by saying that something is knowledge is: we can take this for granted in evaluating the evidence for and against other beliefs.

The most interesting aspect of these two implications of the concept of knowledge is that they are essentially the same. If we treat someone as an authority on a subject-matter, taking them as someone who has knowledge about that subject, then we will take what they say on the subject as definite fact rather than conjecture. (You are wondering what to believe about the platypus, so you consult a biologist. If you treat her as a source of knowledge, then you revise your beliefs in ways that do not challenge what she says.) And, the other way round, if we treat some of our beliefs as definite facts, then we are taking ourselves to be authorities with respect to those facts. (In the morning you seem to remember a moose walking down the street at 2 a.m. If you wonder whether you were dreaming or hallucinating, but subsequently decide to accept your own memory-beliefs as facts, you are in effect saying: I know what happened to me last night, so I'll trust what I believe.)

I suspect that this is the core of the concept of knowledge. Knowledge is based on those properties which beliefs have when we can treat them as authorities in evaluating other beliefs, holding them constant as new evidence accumulates and new arguments are considered. This feature of knowledge explains why in many cases we allow or withhold the label. For example, Lehrer's principle generally applies because when we learn that a belief is based on false evidence, then even if we do not come to doubt the belief, we cannot take it for granted in further reasoning. The evidence is flawed, so the belief cannot be trusted. Sometimes, though, we can see how false assumptions on which a person's belief is based will not make it dangerous for us to use this belief ourselves. For example, in the case of the old sea captain the false astronomy that he uses does not make his beliefs about his latitude unreliable. We can see that as long as we stick to beliefs about navigation, the falsity of his beliefs about astronomy are not going to matter. So we say that he knows where he is. (We say this because we understand enough about both navigation and astronomy to see that he will get the same answer if he uses his false beliefs or the truth. But if it is explained to him that all his beliefs about the movements of the earth, sun and stars are wrong, he may conclude that he does not have knowledge.)

Reliability theories of knowledge fit into this picture in an obvious way. When we think that someone's belief is based on a reliable process, we think that they can be used as an authority on which to base our beliefs. We can trust what they say. We can do this as long as their beliefs are on the topic about which they are reliable. (What exactly the extent of this topic is, is a hard question, as we saw in sections 5 and 6.) The misleading true information problems for reliability theories also now make sense. Although if you are an ordinary person under ordinary circumstances, your belief that a certain very famous person is walking down the street can be used by yourself and others as authoritative, if there is misleading information around, then someone else using your beliefs as a basis for her own would have to be sure that you had much better than average recognition skills, the kind that only a really good friend of the famous person would have, before trusting your report. In fact, you yourself, when you later learn about the misleading information, will want to reconsider your report, and will wonder whether you could have distinguished the celebrity from the look-alikes.

So we have a formula: to take a belief as knowledge is to take it as something that you can trust when forming other beliefs. But this is not a definition of knowledge. It is much too vague, for one thing. In addition, it is a formula not about what actually *is* knowledge, but about which of a person's beliefs that person or another will *treat as* knowledge. The nearest it brings us to a definition is this: it is reasonable for one person, A, to take another person, B, to know something if from what A knows of

B's situation it is reasonable for A to share B's belief. Or, another way of saying the same thing, A should take B to know something when A can take B to be a reliable source of beliefs like the one in question, where what counts as 'like' is determined by B's purposes.

Notice that these definitions refer to the purposes of the person who classifies another person's beliefs as knowledge. (Or, very similar, to what it would be reasonable for that person to think.) This element of purpose is often quite clear when we attribute knowledge. Suppose, for example, one bank robber says to another: 'The police know it was us who pulled the Chase Manhattan job.' The force of 'know' here is that the police have information about their identity of a nature and reliability that is relevant to tracking them down. (Compare the examples of special knowledge about police work, restaurants and other topics towards the end of section 1.) When we try to make a general abstract definition of 'person P knows fact F', one of the problems we are tackling is that of finding a single, core purpose for having beliefs. Is there a unified aim of enquiry in terms of which we can say what counts as a top-quality belief?

Reading Questions

1   The McA case contrasts with the FitzB case. One case shows that truth is required for knowledge, and one shows that justification is required. Which is which?
2   The O'C case shows that truth and justification are not enough for knowledge. Why is Dr O'C's belief justified?
3   Suppose that a person is listening to the radio and hears McA's weather forecast. As a result she prepares for a hurricane. And a hurricane arrives. How does Lehrer's principle apply to her belief?
4   A father believes that his son is wonderful. He defends his belief with good school reports and his son's large number of friends. He also believes that any son of his has to be wonderful. How could we discover whether his belief that his son is wonderful depends (in the sense described in section 2) on the school reports and

friendships, on his belief that his son must be wonderful, on both, or on neither?

5   If the old sea captain had derived his estimate of his latitude from the horoscopes of the crew, would this method have been more or less reliable than his use of old-fashioned astronomy?

6   Why is my belief that I will not win the lottery (see section 4) statistically reliable? What reliable method is being used in this case?

7   An officer is using a radar device to measure the speeds of cars on a road. The device registers the speed of car A as 100 mph. Which of the following are relevant to the question of whether the use of the device tracks the speed of car A?

   (a) If the previous car had gone 60 mph slower, the radar would have registered 100 mph.
   (b) If the car after car A goes 100 mph, the radar will register 100 mph.
   (c) If car A goes 100 mph, the radar will register 100 mph.
   (d) The car is going 100 mph.
   (e) If car A goes 60 mph, the radar will register 60 mph.
   (f) If the car goes 60 mph, the radar will register 100 mph.

   Which of these are relevant to the question of whether the officer knows that car A is going 100 mph?

8   Does McA's belief that there will be a hurricane track the fact that there will be a hurricane?

9   Which of these are externalist properties of beliefs, and which internalist: falsity, causes, simplicity, being more or less perceptual, being apriori, being necessary?

Thinking Questions

10   Are all desirable features of belief relevant to whether a belief is knowledge? What about unoffensiveness, simplicity, comfort-ingness?

11   Newspaper quotation: 'The trekkies who follow the voyages of the *USS Enterprise* have known for years that there are planets of all kinds orbiting practically every star in the galaxy.' The author of this clearly does not think that the trekkies' belief is true. But he

or she still says that they 'know' it. Does this show that knowledge does not have to be true?

12   How does Lehrer's principle relate to cases like the Princess Diana example in which there are relevant true beliefs which the person does not have?

13   We might try defining knowledge as belief which is true and justified and would remain justified whatever true beliefs were added to the believer's stock of beliefs. What problems would this definition run into?

14   Internalist properties might reduce to externalist ones. For example, a reasonable belief might be one that is produced by a method that most often gives true conclusions. How might an internalist object to this?

15   Externalist properties might reduce to internalist ones. For example, a true belief might be one which a reasonable person who had access to all the evidence would hold. How might an externalist object to this?

Further Reading

Good surveys of work on defining knowledge are Robert K. Shope, *The Analysis of Knowing* (Princeton University Press, 1983), and chapters 2 and 3 of Jonathan Dancy, *An Introduction to Contemporary Epistemology* (Blackwell, 1985). Dancy is probably the simpler of these.

Part 2 of Robert Nozick's *Philosophical Explanations* (Oxford University Press, 1981) is a standard source for reliability and conditional theories of knowledge. Personal favourites are Fred Dretske, 'Conclusive reasons', *Australasian Journal of Philosophy*, 66 (1971), 1–22, and Edward Craig, *Knowledge and the State of Nature* (Oxford University Press, 1990). For an extremely stimulating, unorthodox approach to knowledge, read Peter Unger, *Ignorance: A Case for Scepticism* (Oxford University Press, 1975).

The philosophical text which started the debates reported in this chapter can be found in Part I section 2 of John Cottingham, *Western Philosophy: An Anthology* (Blackwell, 1996), Plato, 'Knowledge versus Opinion'.

7 Knowledge of Minds

1. Psychological Beliefs

Many of our beliefs are about our thoughts, characters and feelings. These beliefs are central to our social and practical lives: without beliefs about what we and other people want and think, we could not co-operate with one another in any sort of practical, scientific or social activity. These are **psychological beliefs**: they include beliefs about what we think, know, hope, want, love, hate, remember, and all the other activities of our minds. Human beings could not live human social lives if they did not attribute belief, desire, emotion and other states of mind to one another.

Psychological beliefs are needed for almost all other beliefs. Scientific beliefs, for example, are based on evidence and reasoning that is shared among many people. Some people do experiments and gather data by observation. Other people search for theories to explain the data. Still other people organize the data and theories and write textbooks making sense of them for students and other scientists. None of this could happen if scientists were not operating socially, using their beliefs about one another's minds to transmit, criticize, modify and organize information which eventually emerges as scientific knowledge. One-person science would not be science as we know it. So here too our psychological beliefs are an essential background to the way we get and justify other beliefs.

Because psychological beliefs are so central to our lives, we rarely even notice them. Most of the time we take it for granted that what people tell us, and what we read in books and newspapers, is true. So we accept without realizing it the belief that other people have beliefs, and that most of these beliefs are true. Similarly, we accept without realizing it the belief that most people's actions are motivated by desires, and that most of these desires are for things we can sympathize with. We believe that other people have beliefs and desires, and that we understand what they are. Because this is so central to our lives, we feel very confident about many of our psychological beliefs. We act as if they were certain.

Yet it is not so obvious that this confidence is justified. We are sometimes very mistaken about one another's minds. (We are sometimes mistaken about our own minds.) When someone lies to you, or tricks you, or acts in a way that you do not expect, you realize that your beliefs about that person's mind were not true. You had misunderstood their beliefs or desires or feelings. If this happens often enough, or if you simply begin to notice how often you are wrong in your beliefs about other people's minds, you may begin to suspect that the confidence we have in our beliefs about one another may be a mass delusion. You may become a sceptic about our psychological beliefs, thinking that however useful to us they are, we do not have good reasons for thinking that they are true.

There are deep philosophical issues here. One of them is known as the **other minds problem**. That is the problem for each person of finding good reasons to believe that the other people around them have minds like theirs, with similar beliefs, desires and feelings. Might not other people be robots, or have mental states completely unlike yours? This is much more far-reaching than the doubt that is possible every time you assume that you know what someone is thinking or feeling, but on reflection realize that your reasons for assuming this are not very convincing.

There are many connections between these issues and general positions in the theory of knowledge. One important connection is with the contrast between foundationalist and holist (or coherentist) theories of knowledge, described in chapter 5, section 2. As we shall see, on foundationalist accounts the other minds problem is much harder to solve than on holist accounts. Another important connection is with the contrast between error and ignorance, described in chapter 5, section 1. If we choose to minimize error, and take very few risks of having false beliefs, then we will be very suspicious of our psychological beliefs. But if we choose to minimize ignorance, and take few risks of not having beliefs that we need to understand the world and live our lives, then we will be more willing to accept them even at the risk that some of them may be false.

Very intuitive and very abstract issues are closely linked here. On the one hand, the possibility that beliefs about ourselves and about other people on which we rely in everyday life may not be certain – in fact, that some of them may not be true – is a disturbing one. On the other hand, the philosophical project of separating the reasonable beliefs from those which we believe only because they are familiar or convenient is deeply threatened by problems about psychological beliefs. If we cannot give a good account of our beliefs in our own and other people's minds, then an enormous hole appears in our account of all our other beliefs.

Philosophers have often reacted to this situation by simplifying. They try to show that large classes of psychological beliefs are certain, and that we can base the less certain ones on them. In this chapter we will look at three such attempts: self-centred, behavioural and materialist. The conclusion of the chapter will be that the truth about psychological beliefs cannot be simplified. Each of the simplifying theories makes some important points, but in the end there remain deep and difficult questions which we should not pretend to have simple answers to.

2. Self-centred Theories

There is a tradition in philosophy, dating back at least to Descartes, which divides a person's psychological beliefs into three kinds. The first kind are a person's beliefs about their own experience: that is, their beliefs about what they are perceiving and feeling, and about the thoughts, desires and memories that pass through their consciousness. It is assumed that a person has very little difficulty knowing what they are feeling or thinking, so these beliefs are taken to be certain. The second kind of psychological beliefs are beliefs about action: that is, beliefs about what behaviour this person and others have performed under various circumstances. This too is taken to be fairly easy to know: to know whether someone is, for example, tying their shoe-laces, you just have to look and see what they are doing with their hands. The third kind of psychological beliefs are beliefs about other people's experience: that is, about the perceptions, feelings, beliefs, desires and memories of others. These beliefs are much less certain, according to this tradition. They present us with the other minds problem, which is understood as the problem of justifying the third kind of belief in terms of beliefs of the first two kinds.

One attempt to solve the problem, found in empiricist philosophers such as Locke and John Stuart Mill, is the **argument from analogy**. The idea is to use inductive reasoning (as described in chapter 4) to get from beliefs of the first two kinds (about your own experiences and about behaviour, in this case just your own behaviour) to beliefs of the third kind (about other people's experiences). The argument runs as follows. You know what experiences you have, and you can observe your own behaviour. As a result, you can notice correlations between your own behaviour and your own experiences. For example, you can notice a pattern of bringing a hammer down on your thumb, followed by the sensation of pain, followed by waving the thumb in the air and producing interesting language. So you can reason by simple induction to the conclusion that whenever you bring a hammer down on your thumb, this will be followed first by pain and then by a waving of the thumb and violent language. Then you can observe that other people sometimes hit their thumbs with hammers and then wave their thumbs in the air while cursing. So you extend your inductive generalization to conclude that in all people the pattern is: hammer-on-thumb, pain, cursing. So you have reason to believe that other people feel pain just as you do.

This is not a very convincing argument. If someone *really* believed that other people did not have experiences like their own, they would not find their belief seriously challenged by it. Think first of the two stages of inductive reasoning. Each of them has problems. To get to the first conclusion, that simple patterns connecting behaviour and sensation are found in your own experience, you have to be able to find such patterns, without exceptions, in your own experience. But in fact such simple patterns are pretty rare. Sometimes the hammer hurts a lot, and sometimes hardly at all. Sometimes you jump up and down and curse, and sometimes you just hit the next nail extra hard. The second bit of inductive reasoning – from a generalization about your own experience to one about other people – is just as bad. It too is affected by the variability of behaviour. In addition, it involves an enormous leap from one small class of events – your own behaviour and sensations – to another very different class – those of someone else. What reason is there for believing that the same generalizations hold among these different events? It is like discovering, say, how much iron expands when heated, and then concluding that copper will expand by the same amount. Or like discovering that all fish can swim and concluding that all animals can.

3. Behavioural Theories

Some twentieth-century philosophers have responded to the inadequacies of the argument from analogy by reasoning in the opposite direction, starting with beliefs about people's behaviour and ending with conclusions about their experiences. The basic thought of these theories is that, in order to have beliefs about people's experiences, we have to learn words for those experiences. To believe that someone is in pain, you have to know what pain is; to know that someone wants to hunt moose, you have to know not only what moose are, but what wanting is. We learn what pain is or what wanting is when we are children and adults describe other people or ourselves as being in pain or wanting things. So we learn to use words like 'pain' and 'wants' to describe people, on the basis of their behaviour. If someone is holding their finger tightly while moving in an agonized way and moaning, we think that their finger must hurt, and if some-one is trying with force and persistence to get a coin into a drinks-dispenser, we think that she wants a drink.

Assume for the moment that these considerations show that we can be reasonably certain in our beliefs about other people's states of mind (their beliefs, desires, feelings and so on). Assume, that is, that by observing what people do and then applying what we have been taught about how people behave in various states, we can often enough give a correct description of their minds. Then, according to behavioural theories, we can reason to conclusions about *our own* minds. A person can reason: when other people exhibit this behaviour, they are in pain (or angry, or sad, etc.), so, since I am exhibiting this behaviour, I must be in pain (or angry, or sad).

At first sight, this reasoning may seem completely pointless. Why should anyone need to consider their own behaviour to know what they are feeling or thinking? If you are angry or sad, do you not know it immediately, with no need to observe your actions? These reactions show the hold that the self-centred view of psychological beliefs has on us. But if we reflect, we can find many cases where this behavioural reasoning makes a lot of sense. Consider three.

A person, A, finds that he feels very strange in the presence of another person, B. He speaks much less than usual when B is around, and when he starts to speak, he often stops because he finds what he was going to say stupid or embarrassing. He often finds himself acting in a way that might suggest anger, resentment or sullenness after meeting B. This puzzles A until he reads a love-story and finds the behaviour of a character falling in love described in exactly these terms. He thinks: perhaps I love B, though that is not the kind of person I ever expected to be attracted to.

Another person, C, has recently been widowed. She had given up her career as a painter to support her husband's life-work of writing books about Mexican history, and then to nurse him through his illness. But there is still work to do; his last book needs to be edited and published, and there are always letters from younger scholars about his work that need answering. C finds herself often tired and depressed, and sometimes reacts very irritably when people make perfectly reasonable requests. She is discussing with a friend the depression of a mutual friend who has been abandoned by her no-good husband. C thinks: 'I'm behaving in just the same way. I think I'm angry at my husband, first because I abandoned my painting for the sake of his books, and then because he died and left me with all this work to do alone.'

A third person, D, is stung on the back by a wasp. 'Does that hurt?', asks a friend. 'No,' says D, 'stings never affect me much.' An hour later D is driving home, and twice narrowly avoids an accident. Wondering why this happened, D realizes that he has been frequently taking his hand off the wheel to reach around and rub his back. 'That must hurt more than I admitted,' he concludes.

These three cases are typical of many everyday situations in which people learn important facts or possibilities about themselves by observing their own behaviour and thinking what states of mind it might indicate. One important conclusion to draw is that this is something that actually does happen: we do reason from our behaviour to our minds. Another conclusion is that sometimes a good way to understand yourself is to consider your behaviour in the way you would someone else's, and ask yourself what conclusions you would draw. A third conclusion is that sometimes people have false beliefs about their own minds, when they are relying just on their convictions about themselves and not paying attention to their behaviour, seen objectively.

The behavioural point of view is not as absurd as it might at first seem, then. It points out that people can have mistaken beliefs about themselves, and that the assumption built into self-centred theories that people can be certain in their beliefs about their own minds is not obviously true. In fact, it makes us ask difficult questions about a person's beliefs about their own mind. To what extent are these beliefs based on a capacity to 'look into' our own minds, and to what extent on beliefs about our own behaviour?

Although the behavioural point of view is not absurd, serious problems arise if we try to use it to give a simple theory of psychological beliefs. The simplest such theory is *crude behaviourism*. Crude behaviourism assumes that each person can observe their own behaviour and that of others, and then classify it into a number of simple categories, such as 'angry behaviour', 'frustrated behaviour', 'pain behaviour' and so on. Then, in terms of these categories, each person can define the words for states of mind. 'Pain', for example, might be 'producing pain behaviour and not producing faking-pain behaviour', and 'seeing' might be 'having open eyes pointed in the direction of an object and reacting to changes in that object'. Beliefs about people's behaviour are supported by simple observation of what people are doing. Beliefs about people's states of mind are less certain, but are based on beliefs about their behaviour, in accordance with their definitions. So, for example, if you want to know if someone is in pain, you have to see if they are producing pain behaviour and whether there is also evidence that they are producing behaviour typical of someone who is faking pain. Faking behaviour may be harder to observe than pain behaviour, but there is nothing mysterious or invisible about it. So when you have observed the person's behaviour enough, you should be able to conclude with some probability either that they are in pain or that they are not.

The most basic problem of crude behaviourism is the assumption that for each state of mind there is a kind of behaviour which indicates it. This does not seem to be true even of simple states of mind like being in pain. A person may be in severe pain but not wince or groan or writhe, because, for example, he does not want some other person to think that he is ill. And one person's responses to pain may be very different from another's: one person may scream when another would grit their teeth or even joke.

Another problem with crude behaviourism is the assumption that all states of mind reveal themselves in behaviour at all. This is a much more subtle and controversial issue. Suppose that two people are listening to an opera singer. One person likes and appreciates opera, and the other usually listens to nothing but rock music. They both hear the singer hit the same note. Does the note sound the same to both of them? Suppose it does not. Then each one is in a different state of mind: the states of hearing a sound which sounds the way it does to each of them. (They have different 'qualia', as contemporary philosophers of mind say.) But the two people may behave in exactly the same way. Both may say: 'Wow, that was really high', or 'She really wobbled on that one'; and both may smile or wince.

More subtle theories which take beliefs about behaviour to be certain, and define states of mind in terms of behaviour, face similar problems. The problems they face can be compared to those facing a radical empiricism. They want to base our beliefs about things that cannot be observed on our beliefs about what we can observe, and they run into difficulties when we describe unobservables in terms which are hard to translate into the language of observations. How do you define 'atom' or 'justice' without referring to anything you cannot see or touch or hear? How do you define 'pain' or 'love' or 'believing that there is life on Mars'?

4. Folk Psychology

Neither self-centred nor behavioural theories give adequate ac-counts of our psychological beliefs. Both give oversimplified pictures of how to distinguish the sure from the unsure among our beliefs about our own and other people's minds. In fact, the consensus among contemporary philosophers and psychologists is that no theory as simple as either of these can be right. We are often wrong about our own minds, and often right about the minds of others. Yet some of our beliefs about our own minds are very reliable. And there are patterns in this, useful things to say about which of a person's beliefs about themselves and about others tend to be reliable, and which not. This section and the next explain some recent work by philosophers and psychologists, in terms of which part of this pattern can be described.

To begin, accept that not only are many of the facts about our own and other people's minds uncertain, but that many of them are mysterious. It is clear that other people's behaviour is often mysterious: you often have no idea why some other person did what they did. Moreover, your own behaviour and your own thoughts and feelings may be in some ways as puzzling to you as those of others: very often you may ask, 'Why did I do (or think, or feel) that?'

The basic fact is that all human behaviour can be pretty mysterious. And trying to understand why people do things is a basic human aim, partly because we need to know what people are likely to do next, and partly because we need to know people's character and trustworthiness. (And partly just because otherwise we would be so puzzled by each other.) We lessen the mystery by learning to explain what people do. As children learn how to get along with others, they learn a lot of rules, principles and theories about how people work. They learn when people are likely to get angry, what kinds of things people are likely to notice or overlook, what kinds of things people try very hard to get, and so on. You wouldn't survive kindergarten without knowing a lot of this. And as children learn these things, they find that they understand some of their own feelings and behaviour.

An example: You are walking across a room with a coin in your hand, approaching a coffee machine. A friend is watching you. Someone asks her: 'Why is that person walking across the room?' Your friend says: 'To get a coffee'. This prediction is based partly on knowing what people usually do and partly on knowing that you like coffee. If this explanation is doubted, they may ask you: 'Why are you going over there?' And your reply is: 'I want a cup of coffee, and I'm going to get it from the machine.'

What your friend says about you in this example is the same as what you say about yourself. And the reasons you have for what you say are very similar to the reasons your friend has. You too know that the most likely reason why you are walking in the direction of the coffee machine, digging a coin out of your pocket, is that you want a cup of coffee. You too have noticed that you often want a cup of coffee at that time of day. So when you are asked why you are walking across the room, you may answer so quickly that you do not even notice what your reasons are. It is true that you may have some information that your friend does not. You may be aware of sensations of thirst and caffeine withdrawal. But your friend may have some information that you do not have. Your regular craving for coffee at that time of day may be something which is obvious to your friends, but something that you find it hard to acknowledge, perhaps because you do not want to admit how much coffee you drink.

What examples like this suggest, together with facts about how children and adults ascribe states of mind to themselves and others, is that we make sense of what people do by comparing their actions to standard patterns we have learned. These standard patterns are like outlines of stories – for example, stories about how someone gets angry when they don't get what they want and then works off their anger on someone else. And they are also like rough theories: for example, the theory that people deceive themselves about many of their motives. Philosophers call this mixture of stories, theories and rules **folk psychology**. People use folk psychology in everyday life to explain why other people do things. They also use it to explain why they themselves do things. In both cases we often do not notice that we are using folk psychology. We just say: 'He is angry with me because I took his parking space' or 'I am upset because I didn't get the job I applied for', as if these things were perfectly obvious.

The folk psychology account of psychological beliefs includes aspects of both self-centred and behavioural theories. It is like self-centred theories in that it allows that people often have to go through complex reasoning to discover what other people's thoughts and feelings are. It is unlike self-centred theories, though, in that the reasoning it describes is not inductive reasoning, but instead a variety of more complex uses of the theories and rules of folk psychology. (Central here is the reasoning called 'inference to the best explanation'. See chapter 10.)

The folk psychology account is like behavioural theories in that it allows a person to reason from their own behaviour to conclusions about their own mind. But it is unlike behavioural theories in that it does not base all of a person's beliefs about their mind on observations of their behaviour. Another basic difference with behavioural theories is that instead of using a few fixed connections between states of mind and behaviour, the folk psychology approach allows an infinite variety of behaviour to correspond to any state of mind. For instead of assuming that we understand states of mind by defining them in terms of behaviour, it assumes that we understand them by the way they explain behaviour. So we can reasonably attribute any states of mind at all to a person, as long as we can use them to explain why the person acts as they do.

The most important difference between the folk psychology approach and both these previous approaches, though, consists in the account it gives of why it is reasonable to attribute states of mind to people. Both the self-centred and the behavioural approach try to base our beliefs about other people's minds on evidence we can get from our senses, and that means our observations of their behaviour plus our sensations of our own minds. But it turns out that it is very hard to justify these beliefs in terms of just this evidence. It isn't enough. The folk psychology approach accepts that it is not enough, and suggests that in everyday life we observe a person's behaviour, interpret it in terms of folk psychology plus our own experience, and then use folk psychology to find the best explanation of the behaviour.

When we use folk psychology, we explain people's actions in terms of their beliefs, desires, emotions and other states of mind. We suppose that people really do have all these states of mind, because we have no other way of explaining what they do. If we did not think that they cry because they are sad, get angry because they are frustrated or offended, make friends because they want co-operation and affection, and so on, we would find their behaviour completely mystifying. But this obviously does not prove that the states of mind we ascribe to people are always, or even often, correct. It does not even prove that the whole business of describing people in terms of beliefs, desires, memories, fears, pains and all the rest captures the way we really are. It just says: if you want to understand what people do and feel, and if you are living in our time, in our culture, then these are the beliefs you have to have. We do not have any better way of explaining human actions; so, for all its faults, folk psychology is what we have to assume if we want to be able to predict and explain our actions.

Note the ifs. The folk psychology line is definitely based on avoiding ignorance rather than avoiding falsity. If you want to take absolutely no risk that any of your beliefs are false, then the conclusion to draw, from the problems of the self-centred and behavioural theories and the advantages of the folk psychology approach, is that you should keep your beliefs about both other people's minds and your own mind to a minimum. Since nearly all your beliefs depend to some extent on trusting your own and other people's memories, and on relating your beliefs to those of others, the result will be that you will have very few beliefs. So considerations about psychological beliefs suggest that extreme falsity-avoidance might be a crippling strategy.

5. Materialist Theories

One of the big ifs in the justification of folk psychology was 'if you are living in our time, in our culture'. We do not now have any better ways of understanding one another than in terms of beliefs, desires, sensations, emotions and other psychological concepts. But this may change. We may find other, perhaps better, ways. Since the mind and the brain are very closely related, it is natural to wonder whether when we learn more about the human brain, we may discover facts and create concepts which can replace some or even all of our present psychological concepts. The most extreme such position is that of **eliminative materialism**.

According to eliminative materialism, folk psychology is a fairly useful account of human action, with a long history and some success. But it is false. It supposes that there are such things as beliefs and desires, which cause people to do what they do. But when we investigate the human brain, we find no evidence of such things. In fact, we find evidence that the aspects of mind that folk psychology groups together as 'belief', 'desire', 'memory' and the like have no real unity. There are a large number of brain functions which correspond loosely to 'memory', for example, and they work in very different ways: it is misleading to think of them as being all of the same kind. As a result, folk psychology leaves us unable to explain how children develop, how learning occurs, what happens in mental breakdown, and other equally fundamental aspects of human life. Our best attitude to folk psychology, according to eliminative materialism, is to think of it as a temporary, but very inadequate, crutch, which we must depend on until we understand the brain well enough to find a more adequate substitute for it.

Eliminative materialism is a programme, rather than an analysis. It does not tell us how to understand our present psychological beliefs, or how to separate the reasonable ones from the unreasonable ones. Instead, it tells us to wait for something better. One reaction is to agree: wait and see if something better than folk psychology emerges. But don't hold your breath! There are important points to make even in the absence of a concrete suggestion about what might replace folk psychology, though.

One very important point is that eliminative materialism assumes that folk psychology is a theory, basically like a theory in physics or biology or any other science. Like any theory, it should be accepted if it does a good job of explaining the available evidence, and rejected otherwise. Critics of eliminative materialism argue that this assumption is quite dubious. Unlike a scientific theory, no one ever created folk psychology; the reasons we believe it are not because we have evaluated the evidence for it, but because it is deeply embedded in our everyday lives. And we do not use folk psychology simply to explain people's behaviour in an objective scientific manner: instead, we use it as part of our attempt to love, co-operate, deceive and judge one another. Its uses are as rich and varied as human social life. So, some critics argue, we should ask about folk psychology and any proposed substitute for it not just 'Is it true?' or 'How strong is the evidence for it?', but also 'What kind of a social and emotional life could it be part of?' Perhaps in deciding whether we should believe something, these latter questions are at least as important.

A second basic point to make about eliminative materialism is more positive. The problem of other minds is often presented as if we had to find evidence against beliefs that no one could actually hold: that all human beings are mindless robots, or that human behaviour is caused by mysterious factors that we can never understand. Eliminative materialism provides instead a much more concrete sceptical possibility, with some basis in scientific theory. Perhaps, it suggests, human life forces on us an attitude to one another which, when we consider the evidence objectively, we can see to be flawed and, in fact, inferior to a conceivable alternative.

6. Errors of Self-attribution

Behavioural theories and materialist theories both suggest that our beliefs about our own minds may be less accurate than we suppose. On behavioural theories, this is because we can make as many mistakes reasoning from our own behaviour as reasoning from that of others. On materialist theories, it is because the real facts lie in our own brains, which are no more available to us than the brains of others. However much or little truth there is to either of these positions, they are in the spirit of much of the philosophy and psychology of the twentieth century, which have eroded our confidence in our ability to know ourselves.

The work of Sigmund Freud, the founder of psychoanalysis, is the most famous example of this. Although few people believe everything that psychoanalysis claims, almost everyone accepts that repression and self-deception are real. We believe, now, that people often hide their real desires and beliefs and feelings, even from themselves, so that they do not act on them directly, and are not aware that they have them. For example, a parent may believe that his or her child is a little angel, in spite of the evidence that the child bullies other children and tortures animals. Philosophers studying self-deception try to understand what sounds impossible, that a person can believe something (for example, that their child is sweet and good) while seeming to a understand the evidence that the belief is false well enough to have a strategy for evading it. (For example, the person may find reasons to ignore what other parents say, or reasons to think that the neighbour's cat must have brought in all those dead birds.) How can a person have a strategy to avoid evidence that they believe does not exist? One answer is that the person is subconsciously aware of strong evidence against something that they consciously believe.

Another example of how we have come to doubt self-knowledge is provided by recent cognitive and social psychology. A large number of experiments show pretty clearly that even when people are aware of their beliefs and desires, they are often wrong about which ones are causing their actions. Even when people are accurate about what they think and want, they may be mistaken about why they think and want them. A typical (but imaginary) experiment might divide a sample of teenagers into two groups. Group A is simply asked to arrange a list of rock bands in order of desirability (which band you would go 100 miles to hear, which ones you would go 1 mile to hear, and so on). People in group B are first given CDs by a band on the list, and only then asked to rank the bands in order of desirability. Then people in both groups are asked why they ranked the bands the way they did; in addition, people in group B are asked whether their rankings were affected by the fact that they had been given CDs of some bands. The result is that the two groups have very different rankings of the bands, but very similar explanations of their reasons. For people in group B deny that being given the CDs affected their judgements, though it is clear by comparing them with group A that it did affect them. (So a person is given a CD by the Depraved Moose but not given one by the Perfect Crystals, and rates the Depraved Moose high and the Perfect Crystals low, though people who have not been given a CD rate them in the reverse order.)

There are many such studies, and they point to systematic errors in our beliefs about our own minds. They show in particular that people are very often wrong about their reasons for believing and wanting things, and wrong in their predictions about what they will believe or want in future circumstances. There is a connection with folk psychology here. People base their explanations and predictions of their choices on folk psychology, and folk psychology does not give true explanations and predictions in these cases. Moreover, psychologists studying how children learn folk psychology find that at some stages they make mistakes about what they are thinking which seem very strange to adults. So, learning to use folk psychology in a way that gives accurate predictions of our actions is not an easy task.

7. Dispositions, Occurrences and Reliability

We have a confusing mass of facts and possibilities here. It certainly does not seem that we can find large simple classes of psychological beliefs which we can be sure are true. Nor are there large simple classes which we can be sure are false. But the considerations of the preceding three sections simplify the confusion in one particular way. They allow us to see a pattern in the psychological beliefs which are most relevant to the theory of knowledge: that is, the ones that we have to assume when we are acquiring or evaluating all our other beliefs.

One clear conclusion about the unreliability of our psychological beliefs is that we are often wrong about the causes of our actions and states of mind. Some states of mind are by their nature causes of actions and other states. These are known as **dispositional states of mind**, or simply *dispositions*. Dispositions are causes of general patterns of behaviour. For example, states of character like being cruel or being generous are dispositions. So are moods like depression and elation. So are unconscious beliefs like information a self-deceived person has but will not admit to having. All these are states of a person's mind over a period of time – from a few minutes to years – which are revealed in their effects on a person's actions during that time.

We show both remarkable insight and remarkable fallibility about one another's dispositions. For example, people sometimes have intuitive convictions that other people have dangerous character dispositions ('I can't put my finger on it, but I just have a feeling that he is not to be trusted'), and sometimes these convictions are true. But sometimes they are false, too. And people are often deeply mistaken about their own moods and character. There is no clean separation here between the states we can attribute reliably to ourselves and the states about which we are more fallible.

Contrast dispositions with *occurrences*, or **occurrent states of mind**. A mental occurrence – sometimes called a mental event or an occurrent mental state – is something that happens in your mind at a particular moment in time. If it causes actions or other states of mind, they too will have to occur near that particular moment. Two important examples of mental occurrences are perceptions and conscious thoughts. Suppose you look out of the window and see a ginger cat climbing a pine tree. Then you have visual sensations of orange, brown and green, and you perceive the cat in the tree. You also have the thought that there is a cat in the tree. At that moment these sensations, the state of perception and the thought are occurrences. The perception that there is a cat in the tree and the thought that there is a cat in the tree are different occurrences, since someone could have the thought without having the perception. But they have the same *content*: they both describe the world the same way. (Similarly, a sensation of red, brown and orange and a dream–image of red, brown and orange would have the same content.)

A person usually does not have more accurate beliefs about another person's mental occurrences than about their dispositions. Someone watching you looking out of the window may not know what you see or that you are thinking that there is a cat in the tree, even if they also see it. But a person usually has accurate beliefs about their own mental occurrences.

They are accurate in a very special way. First, if a person believes that they are in a certain occurrent state, then that belief is usually true. Second, if a person's belief that they are in a certain occurrent state is false, then the reason is more often that the person is wrong about what kind of state it is than that they are wrong about the content of the state. A person can think that she is perceiving a green and orange scene when actually she is dreaming about a green and orange scene, but it will still be true that she is having green and orange sensations. A person can think that he is thinking that the cat is going to fall out of the tree when actually he is just hoping that the cat will fall; but it will still be true that he had the thought that the cat was about to fall, whether the thought was a belief or a hope. (People often deceive themselves about what state they are in, while having a correct understanding of the content of the state. For example, someone can think that he fears that the plane carrying his wife will crash, though in fact he hopes it will crash. Or a person can think she believes in reincarnation, when actually her attitude is one of wanting reincarnation to be true.)

The knowledge people have of the content of their occurrent states can be partially explained in terms of a process called an **ascent routine**. To see how an ascent routine works, suppose that you are looking out of the window, where there may be a ginger cat climbing a pine tree. (A moment ago you saw something that may have been the cat, but it might also have been a shadow.) Someone asks you if you think there is a cat in the tree. To answer this question, you do not have to search your mind to find your beliefs about cats and trees. You look out, not in: you take another look out of the window, and if you think there is a cat in the tree, you say that you think there is a cat in the tree. Or, to put the point differently, in order to answer the question 'Do you think (believe) that there is a cat in the tree?', you first answer the question 'Is there a cat in the tree?' If the answer to this question is Yes, then you say Yes also to the question about your belief; otherwise you answer it No.

Ascent routines will nearly always allow a person to know the contents of their own beliefs. If you are trying to find out whether you believe something, you first ask yourself whether that something is true. If your answer is that it is, then you conclude that you do. Otherwise you conclude that you do not. There are limitations, however. Ascent routines are less effective at giving a person answers to questions like 'Do you have any beliefs which are inconsistent with this idea?' or 'What do you believe about moose that could be relevant in this situation?' And they are not completely reliable for distinguishing belief from hope or conjecture or other similar states. To tell belief from hope or conjecture, you might try asking yourself, for example, 'Is there a cat in the tree?' and then seeing whether your answer seemed to you to be a straightforward statement or wishful or suspicious. The trouble with this is that you might just not know whether your answer was wishful or suspicious. Or you might be wrong about this.

Ascent routines will therefore allow people to know whether a particular thought is passing through their mind at a particular moment. They will not allow people the same access to all the dispositions that lie behind the thoughts of the moment. But knowledge of the thoughts of the moment is a more substantial kind of knowledge than it might at first seem. If you think that you believe something, then you know two things for sure: that *that* is what you believe, and that *you* are the person who believes it. You can be confident of the content and of your identity. Both these factors apply to a wide range of states of mind. People's knowledge of their own states of mind is fairly immune to error from misidentifying either the content or their own identity. So when you perceive an orange, green and black scene, you can be sure that however deluded you are, it is you that is having some perceptual experience involving orange, green and black.

When you move beyond knowing who you are and the content of your thoughts, reliability suffers. People do have a variety of powerful ways of attributing states of mind to themselves and to others, though these ways are far from infallible. Some of them are part of human nature; some are learned as part of socialization into a particular society. And some are individual tricks which individual people find to work for them. For example, I have found that my own judgements of my day-to-day moods are based in part on how hard I find it to think about philosophical issues. (Melancholy stills the philosophical imagination; excitement makes it irresponsible.) These are surely improvisations of my own, rather than a universal means of self-knowledge. I imagine that such improvisation is widespread, and that each person has a collection of thoroughly personal methods for keeping in touch with the dispositions of his mind and for intuiting the dispositions of others.

8. Conclusions

We have beliefs about minds, our own and others', because of the lives we lead. We are psychological beings, and the adaptation each one of us makes to living with others equips us with skills and beliefs which we can use to attribute mental states to ourselves and to others, sometimes with considerable certainty. We can augment these with psychological theories, if we have the knowledge and the patience. Both the skills and the beliefs that we use in ascribing mental states can result in truths and in falsehoods. In some circumstances we are justified in trusting them, because in some circumstances they work.

Roughly, they work in those circumstances for which the processes that developed them, in the species or the individual, have prepared them. Thus people are pretty good at telling what thoughts are running through their minds as they prepare to speak, for the co-ordination of speech and thought is a primary function of consciousness. And people can tell fairly well when others are angry or affectionate toward them, as one of the basic purposes of being able to read another's face is to know whether to approach or to flee. For similar reasons people are not very good at judging their own characters or telling what thoughts are running through other people's minds. (You usually know what you are thinking and whether someone else is evincing hostility; you often don't know what the other is thinking, and whether you are showing hostility.)

In the theory of knowledge one particular use of psychological beliefs is most important. That is the attribution of beliefs and knowledge to one another when information is passed from one person to another. We think that we know what beliefs other people have and (to a lesser extent) what kinds of reasons they have for their beliefs. As a result, we are able to draw on the experience of previous generations and the discoveries of others in the present. Without this capacity, human knowledge would be a much feebler thing. To have this kind of knowledge of one another, on which almost all of our other knowledge relies, we do not have to make the full range of attributions that are found in everyday life. In fact, some of the less reliable kinds of psychological beliefs, such as those concerning people's moods and characters and the reasons for their actions, do not play a large role here. That is not to say that the assumptions about our minds that we make in transmitting information from one person to another are beyond doubt. We have to trust that human memory is largely correct, that humans make only limited errors in reasoning, and that people generally believe what they assert. These beliefs could be false. But if we do not assume them, we find that we have reasons for very few of our other beliefs. This gives beliefs in the general reliability of human testimony a kind of apriori status: if we were forced to revise these beliefs, we would be forced to doubt almost everything else we believe.

Reading Questions

1   Which of the following are psychological beliefs?
  (a) Your belief that you are looking at a book.
  (b) Romeo's belief that he loves Juliet.
  (c) Romeo's belief that Juliet loves him.
  (d) Romeo's belief that Juliet is a woman.
  (e) Romeo's belief that Juliet has a brain.
  (f) Romeo's belief that Romeo has a brain.
  (g) Romeo's belief that Juliet wants him to love her.
  (h) Romeo's desire that Juliet believe he loves her.

2   Could you doubt whether someone else has the beliefs, desires and feelings they seem to, without doubting that they have a mind?

3   Why is the second stage of the argument from analogy, described in section 2, an inductive argument? Why is it, like the first stage, affected by the variability of behaviour?

4   An advantage claimed for the behavioural point of view in section 3 is that it shows how we can have false beliefs about ourselves which can be corrected by looking at our behaviour objectively. In the three examples of that section, what are the false beliefs that A, C and D have?

5   In section 4 there is an example in which one person says: 'he is angry with me because I took his parking space.' How could this be an application of folk psychology? (What behaviour might be

explained, and what common-sense principle might be being used to explain it?)

6 What is it in the behaviour of a self-deceived person that makes it possible to describe them as acting as if they were subconsciously aware of the evidence against their conscious belief?

7 Why in the example of the Depraved Moose and the Perfect Crystals do the subjects have false beliefs about the causes of their desires?

8 Describe how by using an ascent routine you can tell whether you believe that $35 + 76 = 116$.

9 If a person believes that they are in a certain occurrent state, then that belief is usually true. Consider the reverse claim, that if a person is in a certain occurrent state, then they usually have a true belief that they are in that state. Is this claim true?

10 Why is it that an ascent routine cannot answer the question 'What do you believe about moose that is relevant to this situation?'

Thinking Questions

11 In section 1 it is claimed that one-person science would not be science as we know it. Does this mean that one-person science would be impossible? Consider how much of our science – physics, chemistry and biology in particular – one intelligent but uneducated person alone on a desert island would be able to develop in a normal lifetime. What about a super-intelligent being with a life span of several centuries?

12 The inductive reasoning in the argument from analogy, discussed in section 2, is implausible partly because it assumes that the causes of other people's behaviour must be similar to the causes of one's own behaviour. Could there be more plausible inductive arguments to the conclusion that all people have similar experiences, based on the similarity of all human nervous systems?

13 Do the examples in section 3 show that people can know facts about themselves on the basis of considering *only* their behaviour?

14 In section 4 one advantage claimed for the folk psychology approach over the behavioural approach is that it allows us to attribute any states of mind that will explain a person's behaviour.

But given perfectly ordinary behaviour, such as drinking a cup of coffee, we can think up completely bizarre explanations. For example, we can explain it by saying the person thinks that drinking coffee is a signal to aliens that one has a polluted body and thus is not worth kidnapping. How could a folk psychology approach find a difference between our everyday explanations of what people do and these bizarre explanations?

15   Experiments such as the imaginary one in section 6 with the teenagers and the rock groups are sometimes interpreted as showing that people interpret their choices as being more rational than they in fact are. Why might this example be interpreted in that way?

16   Are beliefs dispositions or occurrences? Consider your belief that
    (a) the sky is above the earth,
    (b) that you are reading a book,
    (c) that $2 + 9 = 11$.

17   What might ascent routines for knowing what your desires are be like?

18   Rewrite section 8 from the point of view of deep scepticism. (See chapter 1, section 5.)

Further Reading

Basic distinctions in the philosophy of mind are explained in Peter Smith and O. R. Jones, *The Philosophy of Mind: An Introduction* (Cambridge University Press, 1986), and Peter Carruthers, *Introducing Persons* (Croom Helm, 1986). More advanced, but still readable, philosophical papers on self-knowledge and its problems are in Quassim Cassam (ed.), *Self-knowledge* (Oxford University Press, 1994). For a very clear and interesting discussion of psychological work on failures of self-knowledge, see Richard Nisbett and Lee Ross, *Human Inference: Strategies and Shortcomings of Social Judgment* (Prentice-Hall, 1980).

  Ideas about self-deception are developed in the papers in Amelie Rorty (ed.), *Perspectives on Self-deception* (University of California Press, 1988), and in David Pears, *Motivated Irrationality* (Oxford University Press, 1984). Personal favourites are Paul Ziff, 'The simplicity of other minds', *Journal of Philosophy*, 62 (1965), 575–84 (reprinted in his *Philosophic Turnings* (Cornell University Press, 1966)), and Hilary Putnam, 'Other minds', *Philosophical Investigations*, 2 (1979), 71–2 (reprinted in his *Mind, Language, and Reality* (Cambridge University Press, 1975)). The best exposition and defence of eliminative materialism is chapter 4 of Paul Churchland, *Scientific Realism and the Plasticity of Mind* (Cambridge

University Press, 1979). Further more experimental ideas are found in Paul Churchland, 'Reduction, qualia, and the direct introspection of brain states', *Journal of Philosophy*, 81 (1985), 8–27. For criticisms of eliminative materialism see Patricia Kitcher, 'In defence of intentional psychology', *Journal of Philosophy*, 81 (1984), 89–106.

Selections from classic philosophical works relevant to this chapter can be found in John Cottingham, *Western Philosophy: An Anthology* (Blackwell, 1996). See part III section 4, René Descartes, 'The Incorporeal Mind'; part II section 8, John Stuart Mill, 'The Problem of Other Minds'; part II section 10, Gilbert Ryle, 'The Myth of the "Ghost in the Machine"'; and part IV section 4, Sigmund Freud, 'The Partly Hidden Self'.

8 Moral Knowledge

1. Knowing Right from Wrong

Children are sometimes said to be responsible for their actions when they are old enough to know the difference between right and wrong. But studying philosophy can make you uncertain that anyone of any age knows the difference between right and wrong. Moral philosophy is a confusing subject, and anyone exposed to it might conclude that no one knows the difference between right and wrong. After all, so many philosophers, religious thinkers and political theorists have come up with such a welter of contradictory ideas about right and wrong. If these brilliant thinkers cannot agree on what the difference is, how can the rest of us have a hope of knowing it?

In recent years philosophers have produced a number of interesting ideas about our moral beliefs: beliefs about right and wrong, justice and injustice, kindness and cruelty. One consequence of these ideas is to make it much easier to see how a simple common-sense idea about moral knowledge could be right. In spite of all the clever confusions of the philosophers, and in spite of the fact that we may not know which philosophical view of morality is right, we may be capable of knowing that acts are right or wrong, that societies are just or unjust, that people are kind, brave or horrible. The aim of this chapter is to explain these ideas, and to connect them with general themes in the theory of knowledge.

2. Thick and Thin Moral Beliefs

It is not necessary to have a general philosophical theory about morality to know that a particular act is wrong or that a particular person is morally admirable. There are two reasons for this. First, throughout our experience we find that we can often make reliable judgements without being able to give an intellectual description of what we are distinguishing and what criteria we are using. Almost everyone can tell the sound of a flute from the sound of a saxophone, but very few people can say what the difference between the sounds is. Almost everyone can recognize the faces of famous people, but no one can say precisely what it is about a particular person's face that distinguishes it from all others. We are sure that we know that the instrument we hear is a saxophone and not a flute, or that the face we see is one person rather than another. So why should we not consider ourselves to know that, for example, rape is wrong, or that a society without slavery is more just than one with slavery, even if we cannot give clear, uncontroversial explanations of why this is so?

These beliefs could not be knowledge if they were not true. According to one philosophical theory of morality, **emotivism**, assertions about morality are not true or false sentences, but just expressive noise. According to emotivism, to say that rape is wrong is something like saying 'rape: ugh'. According to another theory, assertions of morality are not statements but commands, so that to say that rape is wrong is to say: 'Do not rape.' Few philosophers now believe any such crude theories of morality. Yet more sophisticated theories can have similar consequences. The **error theory** of morality, due to John Mackie and refined by others, holds that our beliefs about morality are a kind of a myth. We find it useful to act as if there were a real difference between right and wrong, and so we invent words for moral qualities and use them to make complex judgements, while in reality these words do not describe any objective facts. According to the error theory, saying that rape is wrong is like saying that

Hamlet killed Polonius or that the wolf ate Little Red Riding Hood's grandmother: we all agree to these and think of them as the 'right' thing to say, but there is nothing in the world that makes them true.

Even if an error theory of morality were right, many moral beliefs could still count as knowledge. Consider, for example, beliefs about people's character. Suppose someone borrows money from you to pay for an operation for his sick cat, and tells you with apparent sincerity that he will repay you next week. When paying-up time come, he has no money, and gives as an excuse that he has had to buy a plane ticket to go to his mother's funeral. You learn later that he spent the money at a casino, boasting to friends that he could always get more money by telling you a sad story. You know then that he is a liar, and untrustworthy. That is something about his moral character that you have plenty of evidence for, and which no subtle moral theory could undermine.

Consider a very different kind of example. Suppose that a political candidate proposes to abolish all the laws against fraud. The idea is that if companies do not have to worry about avoiding lawsuits, they will be able to carry out their business more efficiently, and the economy will thrive. After thinking about the proposal for a while, you see the problems with it. Unscrupulous companies would be able to make false claims to their customers without being discovered until after money had been paid. The main victims would be individual members of the public, especially poor people, without the resources to check the claims made on behalf of goods and services. But companies would also suffer, and since they would often be doubtful that their suppliers' descriptions were true or that contracts would be honoured, they would be very reluctant to do business with any company that they had not been long associated with. So the trust which commerce requires would be eroded. Summing this all up, you say: 'It would be a disaster. The result would be exploitation and mistrust. And injustice: the poor and ignorant would be victims of the rich and well-informed.'

When you say that the person in the first example is an unreliable liar, and when you say that the proposal in the second example would result in exploitation and injustice, you are making definite claims for which you have strong evidence. If the evidence is not misleading, and other knowledge-defeating factors are not present, then your claim is knowledge. You know that the person is a liar; you know that the proposal would result in injustice. These are moral beliefs, and they are knowledge: they are moral beliefs because they are about the way that we think that people and societies should be, and they are knowledge because they are related in the right way to the facts.

Not all moral beliefs are like this. If you tell the liar that he is a liar, he will probably be offended and try to defend himself against your description of him. For he will probably agree with you that it is not a good thing to be a liar. But suppose that instead he grins and says: 'Sure, I'm a liar; and you're a sucker, but you've realized it a bit too late.' He shares your belief about his character, but for him it does not have the same moral force. It may be that he has very few moral convictions, and does not care whether or not he is a liar. Or it may be that he has different moral convictions from you, and will go on to say: 'I admire a good liar; I don't respect anyone who has to stick to the feeble truth. A good person can tell a good lie.' So beliefs about whether someone is a good person are different from beliefs about whether someone is a liar. This suggests that the kinds of moral beliefs for which there can be such straightforward evidence are also kinds which do not have direct consequences for what a person ought to do.

Two somewhat opposite conclusions emerge: first, that many moral beliefs can be known in the same ways that other beliefs about the world around us can be; second, that not all moral beliefs can be known in these ways. Beliefs such as that someone is a liar, or that a social measure would lead to exploitation of poor people, are sometime known as 'thick' moral beliefs. So now we have to ask in what ways non-thick, or thin moral beliefs can be known. One way to answer this question would be to run through the standard theories in ethics. What is the answer according to utilitarianism? What is the answer according to Kantian ethics? And so on. But that is a potentially misleading way, since it gives the impression that we have to decide which of these theories is right before we can say anything about how basic moral beliefs can be known. A different tactic is to describe some other kinds of beliefs that can be compared to thick and thin moral beliefs. This is the purpose of the next section. Then we will be ready to return to the main question, and for the appearance of some standard moral theories.

3. Analogies: Humour, Colour and Witches

Some other kinds of beliefs resemble moral beliefs in interesting ways. There are resemblances to beliefs about humour, beliefs about colours, and beliefs about personality, which bring out important aspects of our moral beliefs, and allow us a perspective on philosophical theories about them.

Humour

Humour may seem very different from morality. After all, morality is a serious business. But consider some similarities.

You cannot explain a joke. If someone does not see why something is funny, then making it more explicit may make the person understand why others laugh, but it will not make her join in herself. Imagine someone who is completely immune to humour, who never finds anything even mildly amusing, and who is puzzled when other people laugh at stories and pictures. (I think I know a couple of people like this; but perhaps they are playing a very straight-faced joke on me.) It might be possible to explain to such a person the psychology of humour, so that they could predict what kinds of things people will laugh at. (Perhaps – although the best laughs are the ones that take you completely by surprise.) But all the explanation in the world would not produce a chuckle. If you don't get it, you don't get it!

Now imagine someone who had no sense of morality. Such a person need not be a monster: they might treat others decently, keep promises, and co-operate reliably in social activities. They might do this in order to get others to treat them well and co-operate with them, or out of a fear of punishment. But the person would not feel revulsion at examples of evil, and would not feel admiration at examples of heroism or self-sacrifice. Most fundamentally, if the person was considering an action and came to see how it would be dishonest or cruel, the person would not feel a shiver of realization that what they were considering was wrong. Explaining that most people feel guilt, remorse and moral admiration, and explaining when they feel these things, might help such a person to understand how normal human beings act. But it would not enable the person to experience these emotions. If you don't feel it, you don't feel it.

Colour

For the next example consider our beliefs about colour. Human beings can judge fairly reliably when objects are red, green, blue and so on. Under similar conditions of illumination, most people describe objects using the same colour words. (Except for a few well-known cases: the boundary between blue and green is a mess; no two people seem to see it in exactly the same way.) As a result, people have long tended to suppose that colours are simple properties of objects, like their masses or shapes or locations. But physics and physiology teach us that this is not so. We call things green, for example, when they reflect several different patterns of wavelengths to our eyes. It is hard to describe these patterns so that they seem like basic features of objects. Instead, we find ourselves saying something like: an object is green when normal human beings seeing it in normal illumination call it 'green'.

Colour is therefore in some ways like humour. It is hard, perhaps impossible, to specify what all green things have in common without referring to the ways human beings will react to them. And a colour-blind person could know a lot of physics and psychology, understanding how light works and how the eye works, and still be unable to say what objects other people will call red, green and purple. So when a person knows what colour an object is, their knowledge is in part about what reactions other people will have to it.

Witches

Now a third and last example. This example is semi-imaginary, though. Imagine a culture in which there is a concept of a 'witch'. These people often call a woman a 'witch' and then burn her at the stake. The process that results in being called a witch begins with rumours. Perhaps a child fell ill, or perhaps a farmer's crops were blighted. Someone must be blamed, and it is suggested that a witch may be involved, so gossips wonder who the witch may be. If a woman's name is mentioned often enough in such gossip, it is said publicly that she is a witch. She is then tried – for example, by being tied up and thrown into a river. (If she floats, she is a witch, since the river has rejected her; if she sinks, she is acquitted, lucky woman.) If the trial 'proves' that she is a witch, she is burned.

Do people in this culture know that the people they have burned are witches? Do they know that there are witches? In a sense they do. They know that particular women have been convicted of witchcraft. They know that there are women who, if tested, will turn out to qualify as witches. And in a sense they do not. They do not know that there is any real or objective difference between the women they have burned and anyone else. They do not know that there are people who have a special property which will cause them to fail the witch tests. Their lack of knowledge turns on their misunderstanding of their concept of a witch. They do not know that being a witch consists almost entirely in other people deciding that the person is a witch.

The three examples – humour, colour and witches – are different in many ways. What they have in common is that in all of them people have beliefs which concern their own and other people's reactions. They all concern beliefs which have more of a human-specific content than people may realize. In all three cases a sceptical person can find grounds for saying that the beliefs are not objectively true. They can seem just made up, true because we decide that they are to be. The last example, witches, is the most extreme. In it people have beliefs which, unbeknownst to them, are almost entirely about what judgements other people will make. The least extreme is the second, colour. For although the limits of what gets called 'green' are determined by the way human beings react to light, at least the light is real, and objects that are called by different colour names do reflect different wavelengths of light. In terms of objectivity, humour lies between witches and colour. Humour is very human, and it might be argued that if there were no humans, nothing would be funny. On the other hand, some jokes are funny, and some are not, and some people have definitely false beliefs about which jokes (particularly their own) are funny. So we do not simply make up the facts about humour.

Are moral beliefs more like beliefs about witches, humour or colour? Different philosophies of morals will give different answers. Some philosophies make morality a completely objective matter, more objective than beliefs about colour. For example, if you think that what is right is what God commands, then you will think that an action's being right is as objective a feature of it as its location or date. Likewise if you think, as utilitarians do, that right actions are those which produce the maximum amount of happiness among all people. On the other hand, if you think, as emotivists do, that to say that something is wrong is just to express an emotion of disapproval of it, then you will think that calling something wrong is a lot like calling someone a witch. It is an expression more of subjective attitude than of objective fact.

The most important fact here is that we do not have to choose between these extremes. Morality does not have to be either as objective as the mass and shape of an object or as subjective as the quality of being a witch (as described in the third example above.) There are many positions in between. Morality may be like humour or like colour.

A strong case can be made for beliefs about morality being rather like beliefs about colour or humour. Beliefs about the moral character of individual people or about the fairness of particular institutions are much like beliefs about colour, in so far as they describe aspects of the world which a person lacking certain basic capacities might be incapable of understanding, but which are caused by real psychological features of people and real structural facts of institutions. Some people really are difficult to co-operate with, or in other ways do not fit well into the attempts of others to live satisfactory lives together. And although the exact ways in which, for example, being untrustworthy differs from being a cheat may not be possible to describe except by using moral concepts, the fact that someone is untrustworthy or a cheat is a fact about something very real: namely, the ways in which that person will fit into co-operative activities with others.

Beliefs about 'thin' moral topics, such as what a person ought to do, or whether a given act is wrong, may also be like beliefs about colour. Or they may be like beliefs about humour: rather less objective, rather more closely tied to human reactions, but still capable of being true and false in ways that are independent of our judgements. Different moral beliefs may be at different places on this spectrum. (For example, beliefs about what general kinds of acts are right or wrong may be different from beliefs about what people should do in particular real-life moral dilemmas.) To get a general picture of the precise degrees of objectivity of moral beliefs, we need a general theory of morality. And here the standard philosophical theories are relevant. For example, a moral theory based on God's commands will give some moral beliefs a very high degree of objectivity, as high as any fact about the natural world. And the effect of utilitarianism will be similar.

In spite of the radical differences between a morality based on God and a morality based on bringing happiness to other people, in both cases there is a completely objective answer to questions about what a person should do. On the other hand, on theories according to which morality is a matter of social convention or, as in existentialism, arbitrary choice, moral beliefs have a much lesser degree of objectivity, more like beliefs about humour than like beliefs about the solar system.

The important point here is not that some moral theories make morality very objective and others much less so. Instead, the point is that nearly all moral theories make morality at least as objective as humour, and most of them make it as objective as colour. And these are fairly objective domains. We do not hesitate to say that one person knows what colour his socks are, or that another knows that the joke she has told is really not very funny. We have no problem saying that there is no evidence that red roses turn green when nobody is looking at them, or that there are good reasons for thinking that racist jokes will not often be extremely funny. Beliefs about humour and about colour often qualify as knowledge; there can be evidence for and against them; they can be supported or undermined by other beliefs. And this should make us more willing to accept the obvious interpretation of the fact that we say exactly similar things about moral beliefs. We certainly use the language of knowledge, justification and reasons about moral beliefs. We say that one person knows that she really should confess that she was the one who put the dent in the car, or that there are good reasons for doubting that eating apples is wrong. If someone wants to argue that all these things we say are wrong, she had better have some pretty strong arguments.

4. Cognitivism

One argument for thinking that moral beliefs cannot be known or justified comes from the moral theory called 'non-cognitivism'. This claims that what we call moral beliefs are not really beliefs at all. For they cannot be true or false. The best-known version of this theory is emotivism, referred to at the beginning of this chapter, the theory that when people say things like 'Slavery is wrong', they are not making statements of fact, but expressing feelings. If emotivism or some other non-cognitivist theory were right, then one could no more know that slavery was wrong than one could know a scream.

There are very few non-cognitivists among contemporary philosophers. The main arguments against non-cognitivism depend on the fact that we use our moral beliefs in all the ways we use our other beliefs. We can deny them: one person says 'Slavery is wrong', and another says: 'No, slavery is not wrong.' We can deduce consequences from them; we can reason: 'If slavery is wrong, and working for no wage is slavery, then working for no wage is wrong.' We can worry about consistency between moral and non-moral beliefs: for example, we can worry about whether the moral belief that individuals should be judged as good or bad in terms of the acts they perform is consistent with the scientific belief that events have causes and many of the actions of human beings are caused by facts over which they have no control. And we can make distinctions between different moral concepts: one person can say 'Slavery is wrong', and another can reply: 'Slavery is unjust, as an institution, but people who live in slave-owning societies are not all evil.' These are all ways of using moral beliefs that are hard to explain except by saying that moral beliefs are real beliefs, like any others, involving a rich body of concepts and building on our capacity for logic and reasoning.

The problem for non-cognitivists here is that they have to explain what moral beliefs are if they are not real beliefs. And most of the explanations they give suggest, falsely, that we cannot reason with moral beliefs or argue about them. (This is not to say that non-cognitivism is a hopeless position: but this is the central challenge it has to meet.) The challenge to non-cognitivism is most explicitly developed in theories of ethics which use the idea of what John Rawls calls **reflective equilibrium**.

Central to this idea is the contrast between moral beliefs about particular situations and general moral principles. For example, you may have beliefs about which situations someone did the right thing in by not telling the whole truth to someone else (perhaps to spare that person pain, or even to save their life), and, contrasted with this, you have beliefs about when, in general, telling or withholding the truth is right. And these two kinds of beliefs may be hard to reconcile with one another. So we defend or criticize beliefs of each kind by comparison with the other, changing a general principle if it conflicts with many judgements about particular cases and changing a judgement about a particular case if it conflicts with general principles.

For example, if you believe the general principle that it is wrong ever to tell less than the whole truth, you may find that this principle conflicts with your reaction to a situation in which if information is not withheld from someone, they may become suicidally depressed. And enough conflicts like this may make you modify the general principle. In the same way, your judgement that, for example, some person is paid a fair wage may conflict with your general principle that people should be paid the same wage for the same work. And then you may change your judgement on the particular case. Eventually, Rawls hopes, by adjusting both judgements and principles, we will get a set of beliefs about justice (or other moral concepts) which is in harmony with itself. This is reflective equilibrium.

Rawls's idea of reflective equilibrium makes most sense in terms of a holist rather than a foundationalist picture of knowledge. For, according to this idea, a moral belief is justified when it fits well with the rest of our beliefs. It brings out, though, the basic fact that our beliefs usually do not fit well together, and that getting our beliefs into a coherent whole is nearly always a long struggle. There are many versions of the main idea, and related ideas are found in other modern ethical theories. (And also in modern versions of traditional theories such as Kantian ethics.)

One very basic fact about morality that Rawls's idea captures is that moral ideas are always open to debate. People argue about what to do in particular situations, and about what a good society would be like. These arguments go on, for generations, and change our moral beliefs. Among the strands in the pattern of moral debate is an important role for sceptical arguments. Mild moral scepticism suggests that many of our firm moral beliefs may be mistaken (perhaps there is nothing inherently wrong with telling lies). More fundamental moral scepticism suggests that the belief in morality itself may be an illusion (perhaps it is just out of sentimentality that we think there are constraints on how people can treat other people). The ultimate moral equilibrium would have answers to sceptical arguments as well as to differing moral views. We obviously are not there yet; the vital thing is that the argument goes on.

Cognitivism makes clear how much our use of our moral beliefs resembles our use of our beliefs about colour, humour, or for that matter the solar system. With regard to all these topics, we debate, produce evidence and arguments, make distinctions, and occasionally try a radical line to sweep away large chunks of belief. Seen in this way, morality and science look remarkably similar. Looking simply at the behaviour of people engaged in science and those engaged in moral debate, an observer might say: these both look like knowledge-gathering activities.

5. Knowing What you Know

Very few people can decide which philosophy of ethics they agree with. Most people have never even heard of any moral philosophy. So most people have no way of deciding what kinds of facts they are dealing with when they talk about right and wrong, good and bad, fair and unfair, decent and villainous. Indeed, when pushed even a little way with tricky philosopher-style questions about morality, most people run out of answers. They become inarticulate and bad-tempered. (You only have to push a little further on these topics to make philosophers inarticulate and bad-tempered.)

Does this mean that most people have no knowledge of right and wrong, only habitual opinions? Colour and humour again. Most people have never considered whether something's being red is a different kind of fact to its being square or weighing 35 grams. They have never compared weighing 35 grams to being red or to being hilarious. And if you sprang these comparisons on most people and asked their opinions, what they would say would be confused and uninformed. (The philosophers can do better?!) Does this mean that people do not know what colour socks they are wearing, or whether their parents' jokes are feeble? Of course not.

But what about witches? In a culture which believes in witches, people will confidently say that some people are witches and that others are not. They think they know these things. But they do not know, not only because there are no witches, but because the concept of a witch is confused and illusory. It describes fantasy rather than reality, and the evidence that these people cite for calling someone a witch points in fact just to their own self-fulfilling beliefs. If these people applied some philosophy and some science to their beliefs, they might find out just how hollow their supposed facts were. But might not our moral beliefs be like this?

There is a point here. The information available to most people is not enough to show that their moral beliefs are more like beliefs about colour than beliefs about witches. And while a bit of philosophy combined with a bit of science allows you to be better informed about such questions, the more you learn, the harder the issues seem. So perhaps no one has a completely trustworthy opinion here. If this is so, then no one knows whether we have moral knowledge. But this does not *show* that no one has moral knowledge. It is easy to get confused on this point. Knowing something and knowing that you know it are very different. You probably know the answers to all the questions in an average primary school arithmetic test. But you may lack confidence in your arithmetic skills, and so be uncertain whether you know the answers to any of them. In that case you know a lot more about basic arithmetic than you know you know. This is a common situation. And moral knowledge may be the same. Suppose that, in addition to the lack of confidence many people have in their knowledge of arithmetic, there were also sceptical philosophers who went around trying to persuade people that numbers may be mythical, or that when we calculate, we may really be guessing, and other philosophers with elaborate philosophies of mathematics, which most people cannot choose between. (Actually, both of these exist.) Then the situation would be like with our moral beliefs. We would know far more than we know we know.

This does not show that moral scepticism is false. (Nor does it refute emotivism and other non-cognitivist philosophies.) Instead, it suggests that we do not have to refute moral scepticism in order for some of our beliefs about right and wrong to be knowledge. It is enough that we can find evidence for them and defend them when challenged, and that this process links them with the facts, whatever they are, about which actions are right and wrong. If there are no such facts, then of course we cannot be linked with them; but if there are such facts, we can link with them whether or not we know that we do.

Similar issues arise with other kinds of belief. A sceptic about belief in the physical world may challenge you to show that you are not a brain in a vat of nutrient fluid being fed false information by a supercomputer (or some even harder-to-imagine source of consciousness being misled by some even more mysterious source of virtual reality). You may find that you cannot answer this scepticism. Does that mean that you do not know that you have existed more than a year, or that you have a nose and a mouth, or that you are on the planet Earth? One question here is whether the evidence you have that you are on the planet Earth can be good evidence if it cannot show that you are not a brain in a vat (where the vat is not on Earth). On many ways of understanding 'good evidence', this can be so. For if we reject foundationalism (see chapter 5, section 2), we can use evidence which is not itself completely certain. The evidence that you are on the planet Earth, although sufficient to make it reasonable to hold this belief, can itself be challenged – for example, by the possibility that you are a brain in a vat. (Bayesian approaches, discussed in chapter 9, give a similar diagnosis.) So you can have good evidence for a belief without having evidence that proves that your evidence can never mislead you. You can know without knowing that you know.

Reading Questions

1   Section 2 argues that since we can tell saxophones from flutes without being able to say how they differ, so might we be able to tell right from wrong. Which of the following is the important similarity here?
   (a) Some people cannot tell saxophones from flutes, just as some people cannot tell right from wrong.
   (b) You can sometimes know when something is of one kind rather than another, although you cannot put the difference into words.
   (c) Only expert musicians and psychologists know how flute-sounds and saxophone-sounds differ, just as only philosophers and wise people know how right is different from wrong.
2   Why can you know that someone is a liar even if the error theory of right and wrong is correct?
3   Why would someone with no sense of right and wrong not necessarily act in evil ways?
4   Specify more fully than the text does why knowing the colour of an object is in part knowing how other people will react to it.
5   How can people in the witch-punishing culture know that a particular woman is a witch when 'really' there are no witches?
6   Why does the fact that we can deny and argue about moral beliefs make a problem for emotivism (or other non-cognitivist theories)?
7   Which of the following is suggested in section 5?
   (a) We know which philosophy of morals is correct, but we do not know that we know it.
   (b) We know that we do not know which philosophy of morals is correct.

(c)   We know that many particular acts are right and many wrong, but do not know which are which.

(d)   We know of many particular actions that they are right and we know of many particular actions that they are wrong, but we do not know that we know these particular actions are right and wrong.

8   Why did the previous question say 'suggested' rather than 'asserted'?

Thinking Questions

9   Suppose you tell the liar that you have found him out and he replies: 'Sure, I'm a liar, but I don't want not to be.' He seems to know that he is a liar, but can this be moral knowledge for him?

10   Are there any properties that are not to some extent relative to the way humans apply them? Is there such a sharp contrast between 'green' and 'weighs 35 grams'?

11   Section 3 claimed that 'some people have definitely false beliefs about which jokes . . . are funny. So we do not simply make up the facts about humour.' How widespread could this be? For example, could a whole culture have a mistaken idea about what is funny?

12   Section 3 classifies 'witch' as less objective than 'funny', which was less objective than 'green'. Why should they be ranked in this order?

13   Suppose you think that what is right is what God commands. Could God have commanded differently? If he could have, would different acts have been right? If he could not have, is there some deeper source of morality than what God commands?

14   Is it true that if utilitarianism is right, then we can know what acts are right? Consider the fact that utilitarianism takes account of the effects of an act on all people during all future time.

15   Section 5 suggests that people with naive moral beliefs may be confused by exposure to moral sceptics and questioning philosophers. Perhaps this is like the situation studied in section 7 of chapter 6, where people do not have knowledge if there is confusing information that they could have encountered. If this is so, really naive people might have moral knowledge, but this would

be destroyed by the presence of philosophers, even if they are not exposed to their views. Could this be right?

Further Reading

There is no really simple introduction to these issues. J. L. Mackie, *Ethics: Inventing Right and Wrong* (Penguin, 1977), is a good place to start. The essays in Geoffrey Sayre-McCord (ed.), *Essays in Moral Realism* (Cornell University Press, 1988) introduce some new ideas. Recent work is described in Stephen Darwall, Allan Gibbard and Peter Railton, 'Towards *fin de siècle* ethics: some trends', *Philosophical Review*, 101 (1992), 115–90.

The source for reflective equilibrium is chapters 1, 2 and 3 of John Rawls, *A Theory of Justice* (Harvard University Press, 1971). Reflective equilibrium is related to ideas about knowledge in chapter 11 of Adam Morton, *Philosophy in Practice* (Blackwell, 1996), chapter 14 of which discusses issues about colour. The philosophy and psychology of colour are explored in great depth in C. L. Hardin, *Color for Philosophers* (Hackett, 1988). A deep reflection on the way in which intellectual reflection can erode moral certainty (see question 15) is found in Bernard Williams, *Ethics and the Limits of Philosophy* (Fontana, 1985), especially chapters 1, 2, 6, 9 and 10.

Selections from classic philosophical works relevant to this chapter can be found in John Cottingham, *Western Philosophy: An Anthology* (Blackwell, 1996). See part VII section 7, Henry Sidgwick, 'Utility and Common-sense Morality'; part VII section 8, Friedrich Nietzsche, 'Against Conventional Morality'; and part VII section 10, John Rawls, 'Rational Choice and Fairness'.

9 Bayesian and Naturalist Theories

1. Why Probability

Many questions in the theory of knowledge are questions about how strong our reasons for various beliefs are. Are our reasons for believing that other people are happy or sad as strong as our reasons for believing that the earth is round? Are our reasons for believing in science stronger or weaker than our reasons for believing in religion? Philosophers' answers to these questions give broad general pictures of what counts as a reason for a belief (empiricism, rationalism, foundationalism, holism). But they do not often supply the details which would allow one to decide how strongly particular reasons support a particular belief. How strong is the evidence for the theory of evolution? Is it stronger or weaker than the evidence that the earth is a sphere, or the evidence that influenza is caused by a virus?

Some brave philosophers have tried to describe the relation between beliefs and evidence with enough precision that strength of evidence can actually be measured. The obvious advantage of trying to do this is that it would help to give answers to questions about what we should believe. A less obvious, but important, advantage is that an epistemological theory that actually comes out and says which beliefs are more and which less justified is itself testable. If the theory says that beliefs which are clearly very uncertain are strongly supported, or if it says that there is only weak evidence for many beliefs which are intuitively very well supported, then we should consider the possibility that there is something wrong with the theory. So, by making precise versions of vague and general theories of knowledge, we can begin to get an idea of whether these theories could possibly be correct.

Rudolf Carnap (working on these issues between 1940 and 1960) was one of the first philosophers to see these points clearly. He wanted to construct definite rules which, given a belief and a statement of the evidence relevant to it, would determine how strongly the evidence supports the belief. In trying to do this, he came to some conclusions which have influenced all later attempts. One feature of Carnap's approach that has been retained by most later attempts to construct a precise epistemology is the centrality it assigns to probability.

This is a very plausible idea. There are good reasons why we might try to describe the strength of evidence for beliefs in terms of probability. In the next section some very basic probability theory is explained. For now, just consider the similarities between evaluating evidence and comparing chance events.

Assume that when there is evidence for two different beliefs we can compare their strength. We can say at least in a rough way which evidence supports which belief more strongly. Now suppose you have a bag with 50 green balls and 50 red balls in it. You reach inside and grab one at random, and before you can see it, you have to say what the probability is that it is a red one. You will say that the probability is 50 per cent, or 0.5. If instead there had been 10 green ball and 90 red ones, you would have said that the probability was 90 per cent, or 0.9. The important point is that probability can be taken as saying two things. On the one hand, as the probability of getting a red ball increases, so does the number of red balls you will on average get if you pick them at random over and over. (If the probability is 0.5, you will get a red one on average five times out of ten; if it is 0.9, you will get a red one on average nine times out of ten.) On the other hand, as the probability of getting a red ball increases, so does the strength of the confidence you should have that the next ball you will pick will be red. If your evidence about the proportion of red and green balls leads you to give a 0.5 probability to getting a red ball, then you should be less confident of getting one than if it gives a 0.9 probability. So probability can measure two things here: how often something will happen on average, and how strong the evidence for a belief is.

Probability is usually like this: the probability of an event can usually be taken as measuring the strength of evidence for a belief. Now remember our assumption that the strength of evidence for different beliefs can be compared. This means that if probabilities can measure the strength of evidence for beliefs about balls and bags, or roulette wheels, or tosses of coins, then they can measure the strength of evidence for anything. We can ask, for example, whether the evidence for the theory of evolution supports it more or less strongly than the evidence that a bag had 80 red balls and 20 green ones would support the belief that an arbitrarily chosen ball drawn from it would be red. So we can hope to measure strength of evidence in terms of probability.

Looking at strength of evidence in terms of probability brings a subtle shift of perspective. Familiar themes in the theory of knowledge begin to look rather different. In particular, issues about the role of background beliefs in reasoning become different and clearer. There are connections between this probability-based perspective on background belief and a different perspective, naturalism, which will be discussed in the final sections of the chapter.

Note: it is impossible to explain Bayesian epistemology without explaining some probability theory. For some readers this may be welcome. And this really is a very simple exposition. But if you want to avoid anything at all mathematical, you should read only sections 3, 5, 6 and 7.

2. A Guide through the Theory of Probability

Probability can measure both how likely it is that an event will occur and how strong the evidence is that a belief is true. These

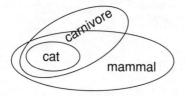

Figure 2. Venn diagram showing relations between three classes

are closely connected. Suppose that a belief concerns a possible event: for example, a coin's landing heads when tossed. If the event is very likely, then the facts that make it likely should be strong evidence for the belief. And if there is strong evidence for the belief, then someone who knows this evidence and knows no other relevant evidence should think that it is very likely that the event will occur. For example, if the coin has been tossed a hundred times and landed heads each time, then this is strong evidence that the coin is biased; so the probability that it will land heads the next time is very high, and the belief that it will land heads next time is strongly supported by the evidence of the previous tosses. So it is no accident that the likelihood of events and the strength of evidence for beliefs can both be measured by probability.

The basic fact about probability is that there is a limited amount of it: when one belief becomes more probable, then others become less probable. If you come to think it more likely that the coin is biased to heads, you should think it less likely that the coin will land tails next time. This can be visualized diagramatically with 'stretchy Venn diagrams'. The familiar Venn diagram represents the relations between properties, so that, for example, the relations between 'cat', 'carnivore' and 'mammal' can be represented as in figure 2.

When thinking about probability, it helps to use Venn diagrams where the areas represent not properties but propositions, possible beliefs or events. So, for example, we might make a diagram with the four propositions 'Heads next time', 'Tails next

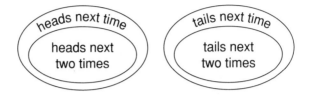

Figure 3. Relations between four chance propositions

time' 'Heads the next two times', and 'Tails the next two times'. We would then get figure 3. Think of the regions in this diagram as representing ways or scenarios in which the propositions could come to be true. You can see from thes diagram that there is no way in which the coin can land both heads and tails, and that all scenarios in which it lands heads (or tails) twice are also scenarios in which it lands heads (or tails) once.

Figure 3 does not yet have probability in it. To visualize probability, think of the sizes of the regions in figure 3 as representing probabilities: the larger a region is, the higher the probability of the proposition it represents. In some cases you can think of this as there being more ways in which the proposition can come to be true. This is illustrated in figure 4. As you can see, the probability that the coin comes down heads once (either on the first or the second toss) is the same as the probability that it comes down heads on the first and not the second toss plus the probability that it comes down heads on the second and not the first toss plus the probability that it comes down heads on both tosses. (Look at the diagram and see that the area must be the same.) This will always be true; that is, for any two propositions A and B, if we write 'Prob' for 'the probability that', we have:

$$\text{Prob (A or B)} = \text{Prob (A \& not B)} + \text{Prob (not A \& B)} + \text{Prob (A \& B)}.$$

Since there is a fixed area to the diagram, the total amount of probability is limited. To simplify things, it is standard to take the

heads, heads	tails, heads
heads, tails	tails, tails

Figure 4. The area enclosed by the heavy line corresponds to the probability that a coin will come down heads at least once. Given that the coin has landed heads once, (tails, tails) is ruled out, so the conditional probability of (heads, heads) is 1/3

total amount of probability as 1. So, since for any proposition A, any point in the diagram is either in the area associated with A or in the area associated with not A (since A is either true or false), another basic principle of probability is

Prob (A) + Prob (not A) = 1.

These two principles can be used as a basis for all of probability theory. If you understand them, you really can understand everything about probability. In fact, if you can think in terms of stretchy Venn diagrams, you can understand all of probability theory. But one more basic concept is also needed. For analysing the relation between a belief and the evidence for it, the most important notion used by probability theory is that of of **conditional probability**.

Conditional probability states how probable a proposition would be if some evidence were accepted. Suppose that you know how likely you think some propositions are, and then you discover that something you thought very unlikely is in fact true. You see a moose riding a motorcycle, or a coin landing heads twenty times in a row. One very simple way of adjusting your beliefs to the discovery goes as follows. Call the new discovery E (E for evidence). Step 1: give all propositions probabilities in accordance with how compatible they are with E, according to your previous probabilities. (This will mean giving probability 0 to all those beliefs which are now shown to be false: that is, to the denial of E and other propositions inconsistent with E.) Step 2: adjust the values so that E is the new standard of certainty, with probability 1, and all other propositions have probability in proportion to it.

This is called *conditionalization*. In terms of stretchy Venn diagrams, conditionalization is very simple. It means removing *not E* from the diagram and leaving everything else unchanged (step 1), except that the region that was previously just E now has to be considered the new diagram, with area 1 (step 2). So we wipe out part of the old diagram, the *not E* part, and stretch the rest so that it covers the whole area. (Consider, for example, how to get the conditional probability of a coin's landing heads twice in two throws, given that it has landed heads on the first throw. In figure 4, remove the area that corresponds to tails on the first throw, and notice that of the three remaining areas only one has two successive heads. So although if the coin is fair, the probability of two heads in a row is 1/4, given that it has landed heads the first time, the conditional probability that both tosses are heads is 1/3.)

The standard notation for the conditional probability of a proposition B given evidence E is 'Prob (B, E)'. (This says how much you should believe B given evidence E.) Prob (B, E) is obtained by considering just the probability of B & E (as in steps 1 and 2 above), and then adjusting the values so that the probability of E becomes 1 (step 3). This means taking the probability of B & E and dividing it by the probability of E. That is:

Prob (B, E) = Prob (B & E)/Prob (E).

This formula corresponds exactly to the stretchy Venn diagram description of conditionalization. The new probability of B (after discovering E) is the probability of what is left of the proposition P after removing the refuted proposition not E – that is, Prob (P & E) – which is then rescaled in accordance with its relative proportion among the non-refuted propositions: that is, divided by E. Part of the diagram is thrown away, and the rest is stretched to size. Suppose, for example, you see a coin land heads twenty times in a row – take this as E – and you had originally thought that the coin was fair – take this as B. Then your new probability for the belief that the coin is fair is the (old) probability for the proposition that it was fair and lands twenty times in a row divided by the old probability of the coin landing twenty times in a row. Unless the old probability for the coin's being fair is almost 1, the new probability, conditional on E, will be very small.

3. The Bayesian Picture of Evidence

An influential school of philosophers and statisticians believe that conditionalization, and other rules closely related to it, gives a model of how we ought to change our beliefs when we learn new evidence. These thinkers are called **Bayesian**. They use this label because their central idea about the force of evidence depends on a consequence of the definition of conditional probability first pointed out by Thomas Bayes in the eighteenth century. Bayes's theorem describes the probability of B given E in terms of the probability of E given B. More precisely,

Prob (B, E) = Prob (E, B) × Prob (B)/Prob (E).

This formula gives us a way of measuring how much support evidence gives a belief. It tells us to look first at how likely the evidence would be, given the belief. Then, the more likely the evidence would be if the belief were true, the more likely it is that the belief is true given that the evidence is true (with the ratio of Prob (B) / Prob (E) determining exactly how much). This is a simple and powerful idea, and it does capture many features of how we often understand the force of evidence. This can be made clear by describing three consequences of the theorem.

Less likely evidence gives stronger support. If a theory predicts that cats eat mice, then observing that cats eat mice does not give very strong evidence for the theory. On the other hand, if a theory predicts that stones subject to some novel influence will rise into the air, then observing that they do rise under those conditions gives strong evidence for the theory. If you think that a coin is fair, then you should not be very shaken in your belief by a series of eight heads and seven tails. But a series of fourteen heads and one tail should make you reconsider your belief. (Notice that as Prob (E) gets smaller in the formula, Prob (B, E) gets larger.)

Evidence supports beliefs that make it more probable. Suppose a geologist defends a theory which predicts an earthquake some-where on the Pacific coast of North America sometime in the next two years. Then if an earthquake occurs at a particular place and a particular time, the theory is somewhat supported. Suppose, on the other hand, that another geologist defends a theory which predicts an earthquake of force 5 on the Richter scale with its epicentre on the UCLA campus on 14 September (the anniversary of Carnap's death, incidentally) in the year 2,000. If this were to occur, it would be very strong evidence for the theory. Or consider the hypotheses that a coin is fair and that it is biased. Suppose that the coin is tossed and lands heads fourteen times and tails one time. This evidence is consistent with both hypotheses, but it has very low probability on the hypothesis that the coin is fair and much higher probability on the hypothesis that the coin is biased. So it gives much stronger evidence for the hypothesis that the coin is biased. (Notice that as Prob (E, B) gets larger, so does Prob (B, E).)

It takes very strong evidence to support beliefs with very low probability. Suppose that a bright light is seen moving at high speed through the night sky. Consider the reactions to this observation of two people. One of them thinks that it is possible that the earth is occasionally visited by alien spacecraft, and the other one thinks that this is very unlikely, almost impossible. For the first person the evidence will increase the probability of the alien visit hypothesis, while the second person will dismiss this possibility and provide other explanations for the evidence. Or consider two people, one of whom believes that a coin may be biased, estimating the probability of bias at around 1/2. The other completely rules out the probability that the coin is biased, estimating the probability of bias at around 0. They both observe a series of fourteen heads and one tail. For the first person this will move the probability that the coin is biased upwards, perhaps making it fairly high, while the second person will just point out that a fair coin can come down heads many times in a row, and leave the probability of bias near zero. (Note that if Prob (B) = 0, then Prob (B, E) = 0 for all E.)

These three consequences are relevant to issues about induction. In a way, they give answers to basic questions about the justification of inductive reasoning. To see this, consider more coin-tossing examples. You see a coin tossed five times, and each time it lands heads. You know nothing about the coin or where it came from. You are asked how likely you think it is that it will land heads the next time. The rule of simple induction, taken very simply and literally, says that since you have seen five instances of the coin landing heads and no instances of its landing tails, you should believe that it will always land heads. This seems a very rash conclusion. Of course, a less naive application of induction will remind you that you have often seen coins land heads for several times in a row and then land tails. Coins in general are usually fair, and when they are biased, it is as often to tails as to heads, so that, given a new coin, you should believe it as being as likely to land tails as heads. So you either treat this coin as a completely isolated case, in which case, if forced to decide, you say that the coin will come down heads, or you treat it as a coin among the zillions of coins in the world, in which case you say that heads and tails are equally likely. Both of these reactions seem wrong.

Contrast this with the Bayesian approach. Take it that the problem is that of determining what the bias of the coin is. Simplify the situation by supposing only three possibilities. Is it a fair coin, or a coin that always comes down heads (as naive induction might suggest), or a coin that always comes down tails? Call these three possibilities H-bias, Fair and T-bias. Suppose that before seeing the evidence you think that the coin is most likely fair, but it just might have one of the extreme biases. To be specific, suppose that your prior probability for Fair is 0.99, and for each of H-bias and T-bias it is 0.005. Then we can calculate the probability of each of them using Bayes's theorem. The probability of Fair, given the evidence, call it E, that it has landed heads five times in a row, is, according to Bayes's theorem, Prob (E, Fair) × Prob (Fair) / Prob (E). This is 0.861. Similarly, the probability of H-bias, given the evidence, is 0.139, and the probability of T-bias, given the evidence, is 0. So the hypothesis that the coin is fair remains the most likely one, but its probability has dropped considerably, and the probability that the coin has an extreme bias to heads is more than twenty times as likely as it was. The hypothesis that it has an extreme bias to tails has been refuted. In a more realistic case, with a large number of hypotheses covering many different degrees of bias, the result would be that a hypothesis of some smaller bias towards heads would have the greatest probability on the evidence.

(These figures are obtained as follows, if you really want to know. Prob (Fair) and Prob (E) are the probabilities *before* seeing the evidence, and Prob (E, Fair) is calculated in terms of them. Prob (E, Fair) is 1/32 = 0.0312. Prob (E, H-bias) is 1; Prob (E, T-bias) is 0; Prob (Fair) is 0.99; Prob (H-bias) = Prob (T-bias) = 0.005, as we assumed. And Prob (E) is the average of Prob (E, H-bias), Prob (E, Fair) and Prob (E, T-bias), where the average is weighted by the probability of each; that is, 0.005 × Prob (E, H-bias) + 0.99 × Prob (E, Fair); + 0.005 × Prob (E, T-bias) = 0.0359. So:

Prob (Fair, E) = Prob (E, Fair) × Prob (Fair) / Prob (E)
= 0.0312 × 0.99 / 0.0359 = 0.861.
Prob (H-bias, E) = Prob (E, H-bias) × Prob (H-bias) /
Prob (E) = 1 × 0.005 / 0.0359 = 0.139.
Prob (T-bias, E) = Prob (E, T-bias) × Prob (T-bias) / Prob (E)
= 0 × 0.005 / 0.0359 = 0.)

There are several striking contrasts between the Bayesian solution to the problem and the solution based on simple induction. The most important is that Bayesian thinking does not attempt to tackle the problem unless it first has some probabilities. Then it looks at the evidence and considers how the probabilities are changed by it. So you never reason from a completely blank mind; you start with some ideas and see how they are affected by what you discover. Another basic contrast is that the conclusions of Bayesian thinking do not tell you *what* you should believe. Instead, they tell you how you should spread your probabilities among the propositions you are considering, and therefore *how much* you should believe them. Both these contrasts are clear in the example above. We get no answers unless we assume some probabilities that the coin is biased, which we can then change when we see the evidence. And we do not in the end get told whether or not to believe that on the next toss the coin will land heads. Instead, we are told how the probability of its landing heads has changed.

So in a way Bayesianism gives a solution to the problem of induction, and in a way it does not. It solves the problem in that, given prior probabilities and evidence, it provides a clear and reasonable way to revise the probabilities in the face of the evidence. And in doing this it neither depends on any assumptions about the regularity of nature nor pretends that the world may not have sharp surprises in store for us. It does not solve the problem in so far as it assumes that we can start with prior probabilities; nor does it tell us where to get them from. (Some prior probabilities will be versions of assumptions about what kinds of patterns we can expect to find in the world: see section 4 of chapter 4.) And the conclusions it gives are not beliefs, but probabilities. It does not solve the problem as much as it transforms it. The question we must ask is whether the transformed, and solved, problem is a satisfactory substitute for the original.

4. Objections to Bayesianism

For all its advantages – its smooth scientific appearance and the clear thinking it brings – Bayesian epistemology has some problems. There is a lively debate in contemporary philosophy about whether the theory of knowledge can be shaped around conditional probability, and there are debates among Bayesian thinkers about the form their theory should take. Some of this discussion is very subtle and very technical. This section describes some very simple objections to the Bayesian point of view, and indicates how Bayesians might try to reply.

Beliefs cannot be measured in numbers. Often we do not know whether we are more sure of one belief than another. Can you say whether you are more confident that Washington is the capital of the United States than that dogs have legs? You know neither whether you are more confident of one than the other or whether they are both equally sure for you. Yet, if Bayesianism were right, you would have a probability for each of them which would be an exact number, so either one would be greater, or they would be the same.

This problem is particularly sharp when the beliefs are very uncertain. For according to Bayesianism evidence cannot support a proposition with probability zero. So if we think that there is any chance that there might be evidence for a proposition, however small, we should not give it a probability of zero. So consider the following propositions: the cube root of 1,728 is not 12; Nelson Mandela was not the first non-white president of South Africa; hydrogen is not a gas; brown is not a colour. Since there could conceivably be evidence for any of these, as any sceptical philosopher will tell you, you should hesitate before giving any of them probability zero. Instead you should give them very small probabilities, just marginally above zero. But can you really see such a fine structure in your beliefs, discriminating those a hair's breadth above probability zero from those which can safely be relegated to permanent disbelief? And among the almost-but-not-quite-zero propositions, can you really say which ones are more and which ones less certain?

Conditionalization gives the wrong answers. Consider the following example (adapted from Alvin Plantinga). Your probability for 'Maureen is tone-deaf' (M) is 0.3, and your probability for '90 per cent of people who go to heavy metal concerts are tone-deaf and Maureen goes to heavy metal concerts' (E) is also 0.3. But your probability for M & E, 'Maureen is tone-deaf and she goes to heavy metal concerts and 90 per cent of people who do that are tone-deaf', is only 0.001. Then, when we do the calculations, we find that Prob (M, E) is pretty low, lower than Prob (E). (In fact it is 0.0003.) So on Bayesian principles E is not evidence for M. But this seems wrong, since if you learn that Maureen goes to heavy metal concerts, and that 90 per cent of people who go to heavy metal concerts are tone-deaf, you should consider this to be evidence for the belief that Maureen is tone-deaf.

Bayesianism does not define the strength of evidence. The example above assumed that evidence supports a belief when the probability of the belief conditional on the evidence is higher than the probability of the belief on its own. But as the example suggests, this may not be the best way to understand evidence in terms of probability. And it does not fulfil one of the promises of Bayesianism, to give a measure of how much support a given piece of evidence, E, gives to a given proposition, P. Should this be measured simply by Prob (P, E), or by Prob (P, E) − Prob (E), or by Prob (P, E) / Prob (E)? (Some Bayesians choose to measure it by log (Prob (E, P) / Prob (E, not P))!) But until they decide among themselves, we cannot evaluate their theory. And the fact that all these thinkers cannot agree about the right measure might suggest that there is something fundamentally wrong here.

Bayesianism needs a fixed body of propositions. Much scientific progress occurs when someone finds a new concept. Space-time, genes, kinetic energy and even matter were concepts that had to be discovered. This process of concept creation continues, so we are always having to consider propositions that are completely novel to us. But we cannot have a prior probability for a novel proposition: when the proposition is first formulated and understood. So Bayesianism will have to say either that there can be no evidence for novel propositions or that their degree of support given any evidence is zero. Both are ridiculous responses, and prevent Bayesianism from connecting with the most interesting questions in epistemology and the philosophy of science, which arise when someone creates a completely new theory and we have to decide whether to believe it.

Bayesians have replies to all these objections. Very briefly, here are the outlines of what a Bayesian might say to each of the three points.

The objection that the sureness of our beliefs cannot be measured in numbers represents, according to Bayesians, a misunderstanding of their aims. They are not trying to describe how our minds actually work. In fact, when we consider what to believe, our minds are filled with illogicality and fuzziness. But we can keep before us an image of what a perfectly logical person would be like. Such a person would have definite numerical probabilities for all the propositions she considered, which she would change by conditionalization in the presence of new evidence. We finite and confused people can approach rationality even if we cannot achieve it, and we can see how near or far from rationality we are by comparing ourselves to this ideal.

The Bayesian answer to the objection that conditionalization gives the wrong answers is that it doesn't. Consider the example again. It assumes that the discovery that Maureen goes to heavy metal concerts and that 90 per cent of people who do this are tone-deaf is evidence that Maureen is tone-deaf. But suppose you believed that 99 per cent of all people are tone-deaf. Then the discovery that only 90 per cent of people who go to heavy metal concerts are tone-deaf would suggest that Maureen's going to such concerts is evidence that she is *not* tone-deaf.

The third objection was that Bayesians do not give us a single definition of how much a proposition is supported by evidence. A Bayesian would admit that this is right, and express the hope that Bayesian philosophers will reach more agreement on the matter soon. (In reaching agreement, they might discover that they did not all mean exactly the same thing by the support that evidence gives a proposition.) Then the Bayesian might go on to say that strength of evidence is in practical terms a side-issue. What we want to know is how much we should believe the propositions we are considering. And Bayesianism gives us a definite answer to this: we should believe a proposition in accordance with its probability, conditional on the available evidence.

The last and most serious objection concerned the difficulty of knowing what probabilities to give novel propositions. There are several Bayesian responses to this problem. One is to argue that we can rationally give a completely novel proposition any probability we like. Some probabilities may be more convenient or more normal, but if the proposition is really novel, then no probability is forbidden. Then we can consider evidence and use it, via Bayes's theorem, to change these probabilities. Given enough evidence, many differences in the probabilities that are first assigned will disappear, as the evidence forces them to a common value.

These replies raise important issues to which we will return: Issues about rationality, evidence and the nature of belief. They are issues that are hotly contested in contemporary epistemology.

It is more important to think through the tensions between the objections and the replies than to settle on a simple adjudication between them.

5. Background Beliefs

Bayesian epistemology can be understood so that it is not a rival to other accounts of how we should change our beliefs. Instead, it can be thought of as a way of making a model of belief and evidence in terms such that they can be easily understood and tested. (This is certainly not how all Bayesians understand their project. Many of them intend something much more threatening.) Bayesian ideas are easiest to apply when we are dealing with beliefs about tossed coins, dice, lotteries and other probabilistic processes. By making a link between the theory of probability and statistics that applies to these, and traditional issues in the theory of knowledge, Bayesianism can allow us to test our theories about belief and evidence on cases where there are definite numerical answers.

Seen in this way, Bayesian considerations support a mild holism with a very limited bias towards ignorance-avoidance rather than error-avoidance. (For both holism and ignorance versus error, see chapter 5, sections 1 and 2.) To see this, we can translate some Bayesian conclusions out of the language of probability into the language of *background beliefs*.

Background beliefs are beliefs which must be assumed in order for evidence for a proposition to have force as evidence. Suppose that we have a belief and some evidence. We might be considering whether some newly found evidence is evidence for or against the belief. Or we might be wondering whether some fact that we have known for a long time can provide a good reason for the belief. In either case, when we think about how the evidence might give a reason for holding the belief, we often find that it would give a reason for the belief only if we also assume some other belief.

For example, in the previous section we considered whether the proposition 'Maureen goes to heavy metal concerts and 90 per cent of people who go to heavy metal concerts are tone-deaf' is evidence for the proposition 'Maureen is tone-deaf'. The background belief then was: 'less than 90 per cent of the general population are tone-deaf'. If we deny this belief – for example, by supposing that 99 per cent of the general population are tone-deaf – then the evidence no longer supports the proposition. The belief that less than 90 per cent of the population are tone-deaf is a typical *background belief*. That is, it is a belief which affects the force which other beliefs have as evidence. Background beliefs are often, as in this case, beliefs which are considered to be obviously true. This makes it easier for them to function invisibly, since it will at first seem unnecessary to cite them among the reasons for holding a belief.

Three basic facts about background beliefs can be illustrated with Bayesian reasoning. First, the very existence of background beliefs. That is:

Background beliefs influence the force of evidence. You have a coin and you are considering the proposition that heads and tails are equally likely the next time it is tossed. Your evidence is the number of times the coin has landed heads in a series of preceding tosses. If you believe that the coin could not be biased – if you give it a probability of zero – then after seeing the coin land heads a hundred times in a row, you should still take heads and tails to be equally likely on the next toss. After all, a fair coin can come down heads a million times in a row; unlikely things happen. But if you give the proposition that the coin is biased a probability greater than zero, even only slightly greater than zero, then after a series of heads you will consider it more likely that the coin will land heads than tails the next time. So the probability of the coin's being biased functions as a background belief: it is essential for the evidence of a succession of heads to affect the probability you assign to heads and tails on the next toss.

Background beliefs are changed by evidence. Although background beliefs influence the way evidence supports or refutes other beliefs, they are themselves changed by evidence. As long as you think it is possible that the coin could be biased, by giving it a probability greater than zero, then as more and more heads appear, you will think it is more and more likely that it actually is biased, until eventually you think that it is more likely than not to be biased.

Some background beliefs make evidence powerless. If you think that the coin could not possibly be biased, then a hundred heads will not convince you. In fact, no number of heads will convince you. So the belief that the coin could not possibly be biased makes it impossible for this kind of evidence to change your beliefs about how likely another head is. But as long as you think there is even a very small possibility, enough evidence will eventually change your mind. So in a way it is better to leave open a very small possibility that the coin might be biased. If we can have beliefs about which of the things that we do not think true could be true, and which are more likely than others, then we have a better chance that, as more evidence comes in, it will direct our beliefs towards the truth.

These conclusions about background beliefs suggest a mild holism. Whether a person is justified in believing a particular proposition depends not just on the evidence that person might cite for the belief, but on a wide range of other beliefs, whose relevance the person may be completely ignorant of. This opens up an interesting function for the theory of knowledge: discovering these background beliefs and making it clear how our beliefs depend on many assumptions besides the ones we might suppose.

They also suggest a holism that is linked to mild ignorance-avoidance. The Bayesian-inspired attitude to background beliefs just sketched is based on the idea that the combined effect of evidence and background beliefs is to tell us not what propositions are certainly true, but how much confidence we should have in them. (And crucial in this is not the list of background beliefs that we think certainly true, but the exact degrees of confidence we have in different background beliefs.) This already shifts the emphasis away from error-avoidance, since it forces us to think in terms of less than perfect certainty. The shift becomes more definite when we consider that propositions with probability considerably less than 1 can still be used to guide actions – think of weather forecasts, or a doctor's guess of a patient's life expectancy – so that part of the aim in using evidence to revise our beliefs must be to get probabilities which can guide us in everyday practical life.

The most profound realization about background beliefs is that they can change in response to evidence. We need a rich background of beliefs in place before we can interpret evidence (see chapter 2, section 5), and before we can evaluate the support our evidence gives to propositions (see this section and the previous one). But this does not mean that we are stuck with the background beliefs we start with. They too change. So we can hope that we can use whatever background beliefs we have to find and evaluate evidence which will change all of our beliefs, leading to new interpretations of new evidence, so that false beliefs are, in the fullness of time, filtered out.

We may hope for this. But it is a hope, not a certainty. Some background beliefs, as we have seen, do not respond to evidence. (If you are absolutely certain a coin is fair, a run of a million heads will not change your mind.) In fact, it is a very hard problem to say which background beliefs will respond to evidence. In special cases we can prove, for example, that some assignments of probabilities will converge on the true values, given enough evidence; but the general situation is very hard to understand. This is another important task for epistemology: to find ways of describing those combinations of belief which will respond flexibly to evidence, and separate them from others whose unresponsiveness makes of them traps from which evidence cannot rescue us.

6. Rationality Naturalized

The last section suggested that we can rely on the evidence as it emerges to determine the shape of our beliefs. This attitude can have far-reaching consequences. Pushing it a little further, it suggests that the job of deciding what is to count as evidence and reasonable belief can also develop with our evolving system of belief as it grows and changes. We would then expect epistemology not to stand outside the rest of our beliefs judging whether they live up to its standards, but to be a set of beliefs like any others, changing as we make new discoveries. The natural fear about such a suggestion is that it would result in an epistemology that simply rubber-stamped our existing beliefs, judging them by no standard outside themselves. This fear is partly countered by the point about the changeability of background beliefs. The standards we apply to our beliefs can change, just as the rest of our beliefs do.

This is an intriguing – indeed, an exciting – suggestion. It is the suggestion that epistemology is part of natural science, the part that studies the information-gathering capacities of the human animal. It is thus a *naturalistic* suggestion, in that it takes human beings and their knowledge to be part of the natural world. But it is not obvious how to make it work. Since W. V. Quine made the first suggestion along these lines, there have been many attempts to push the idea further. The result has been a lot of interesting work; but the overall impact on the theory of knowledge is hard to assess. The greatest potential impact is on the way we think about rationality.

The theory of knowledge centres on ideas about rationality. For example, evidence supports a belief when a rational person who accepts the evidence would come nearer to holding the belief. (An irrational person might ignore the evidence, or take it as grounds for thinking that the belief was false.) And the theory of knowledge aims at discovering which of our beliefs we can hold rationally, and which we hold because of habit, prejudice or misunderstanding. But its attempts to give a clear picture of rational belief have not been very successful. We have a fairly clear understanding of logical reasoning, given by deductive logic. Though we do not know much about what happens in a human person's mind when conclusions are deduced from premises, we do have a definite idea of what the relation between premises and conclusion is when an argument is deductively valid. We know what standards we are applying. Inductive reasoning, on the other hand, is a much murkier business. We do not know how to describe the patterns of inductive reasoning that we find plausible, in a way that distinguishes them from the ones that seem ridiculous to us. (That is a conclusion of Goodman's problem, described in chapter 4, sections 3 and 4.) Most importantly, we do not have a clear statement of what we mean when we say that some inductive reasoning is good or valid, reasoning that a rational person ought to find persuasive. Should it be reasoning that will more often than not give a true conclusion? Or reasoning that will give a true conclusion in 99 per cent of similar cases? Or reasoning that most people with normal intelligence will find persuasive? All these answers have problems.

Other aspects of the theory of knowledge show the same tendency to leave rationality unexplained. Holist (or coherentist) theories do not say why it is rational to have coherent beliefs. (Are they more likely to be true? Are they easier to remember?) Empiricist and foundationalist theories do not give us clear reasons why it is rational to make perception the basic source of our beliefs. (At any rate, we do not have clear reasons when we no longer think that perceptual beliefs are never false or that people can know with certainty what is in their own minds.)

Naturalism can enter here. Instead of taking the concept of rationality for granted, we can try to approach it in terms of what we believe and can discover about human reasoning. We can see deductive reasoning, inductive reasoning, the search for coherence and the use of perception as some among the many ways in which people interact with their environment and arrive at beliefs about it. There are surely very many different belief-acquiring processes. For example, the ways in which people form opinions about one another's moods and characters on first meeting them are most likely not formed through step-by-step deduction but by some innate human social capacities.

When we focus on actual human information gathering, rather than on ideals of rationality, we are much less likely to think that many of our beliefs are the result of careful explicit reasoning which can be put into words and defended in the way that scientific theories or philosophical positions can be. At any rate, we want not to assume anything like this unless we can discover more about how human information gathering actually does work. Psychologists and philosophers are hard at work now, trying to put together a picture of psychological belief-acquisition processes, a picture that will link up with traditional philosophical questions about knowledge and rationality. There are two basic questions they face: What are the fundamental human capacities that are involved in belief acquisition, and what probability of producing true beliefs do they have under various conditions? And, given a particular belief, what processes (what applications of what capacities) can it result from, and what conditions are required for these processes to deliver true beliefs?

One example of this fits right into the themes of this chapter: our beliefs about probability. In everyday life people frequently have to think about how likely events are and how much they ought to believe that they might occur. So without studying probability theory, people have ways of thinking through problems that are really problems about probability. We can study these ways, and when we do, we find that they differ from 'correct' probability theory as described by philosophers and statisticians in several respects. Three of them are framing effects, base-rate fallacies, and persistent illusions.

Framing effects

Framing effects are found in situations like the following. A group of subjects is divided into two subgroups. Subgroup 1 is given question 1 below.

Question 1. Imagine that the country is preparing for the outbreak of an unusual disease, which is expected to kill 600 people. Two alternative programmes to combat the disease have been proposed. Assume that the exact scientific estimate of the consequences of the programmes is as follows:

If Programme A is adopted, 200 people will be saved.
If Programme B is adopted, there is a 1/3 probability that 600 people will be saved, and a 2/3 probability that no people will be saved.

Which of the two programmes would you favour?

At the same time subgroup 2 is given question 2 below.

Question 2. Imagine that the country is preparing for the outbreak of an unusual disease, which is expected to kill 600 people. Two alternative programmes to combat the disease have been proposed. Assume that the exact scientific estimate of the consequences of the programmes is as follows:

If programme C is adopted, 400 people will die.
If Programme D is adopted, there is a 1/3 probability that nobody will die, and 2/3 probability that 600 people will die.

Which of the two programmes would you favour?

The usual result is that most people in subgroup 1 prefer programme A, and most people in subgroup 2 prefer programme D. But programme A is the same as programme C, and programme B is the same as programme D. They are just described in different words, differing in whether they emphasize numbers dead or numbers saved. But most people prefer A when they read the first question and D when they read the second. Probability theory, by contrast, says that if you prefer A, you should prefer C, and if you prefer B, you should prefer D. This is called a framing effect, because it shows that when people think about probabilities, they are influenced not just by the simple probabilities, but also by the way the probabilities are framed by a story. Tell the story differently, and the same numbers produce the opposite reaction.

Base-rate fallacies

Base-rate fallacies are a way in which people often give too much weight to the evidence at hand rather than to their background beliefs. For example, consider your answer to the following question:

> George weighs 300 pounds and has very strong legs. He is either a sumo wrestler or a swimmer. Which is he more likely to be?

Your answer may be that George is a sumo wrestler. For he seems to fit that profile more than that of a swimmer. But this answer is wrong. There are more 300 pound swimmers with strong legs in the world than there are 300 pound sumo wrestlers with strong legs. That is because there are so few sumo wrestlers compared to swimmers, even though there is a much greater proportion of 300 pounders among them than there is among swimmers.

The mistake here may be a confusion of proportions with absolute numbers. Or it may be a more subtle confusion about conditional probabilities. Whatever it is, everyone is susceptible to it. It is in a way a framing effect, since it is sensitive to the way in which a problem is described. And it is in a way a *persistent illusion* – that is, a situation in which people can be relied up on to give what probability theory describes as the wrong answers.

Persistent illusions

Another class of such persistent illusions concerns risk. Given two situations, in one of which there is very little risk of a big loss and in the other of which there is a serious risk of a big loss counter-balanced with a corresponding possibility of a big gain, people will very often choose the 'no loss' option, even when the 'possible loss' option gives just the same average probability of loss or gain. (See question 19.) But the most striking case is the so-called *gambler's fallacy*. Suppose that you see a coin tossed ten times. It comes down heads every time. It is about to be tossed again. Which way do you expect it to come down? Inductive reasoning and probability theory suggest that you should either think that the coin is biased and so expect another heads, or put the run of heads down to chance and expect that heads and tails are equally likely. Yet some people will expect the coin to come down tails next time. They think: a run of eleven heads in a row is even more unlikely than a run of ten heads, so the coin will probably come down tails on the eleventh throw. But this is a mistake. (See question 13 below for more on why it is a mistake.) Reasoning like this, people sometimes shelter from thunderstorms under lightning-struck trees, thinking that lightning rarely strikes the same place twice. And in bombardments people sometimes sit in bomb craters, thinking that the probability of a bomb hitting the same place twice is very low.

The most remarkable feature of the gambler's fallacy is how universal it is. Psychological studies of probabilistic reasoning suggest that everyone, whatever their familiarity with probability theory, falls into the fallacy if it is sufficiently disguised. Most people fall for fairly simple versions, whereas professors of statistics fall for more subtle versions. It seems to result from some deep tendency in the way we process information about uncertain outcomes.

Framing effects, base-rate fallacies and persistent illusions all point to a single conclusion: that when people reason with probabilities – or about the kinds of questions concerning risk and uncertainty to which probability applies – they tend to do so in ways that diverge from probability theory as understood by philosophers and statisticians. It seems that thinking probabilistically is not something that we do naturally or accurately.

7. Bayesianism versus Naturalism

The Bayesian approach and the naturalistic approach have important similarities. Both emphasize the importance of background beliefs and the futility of trying to find evidence for our beliefs from a completely neutral standpoint. There are also important differences between them. The most basic concerns the concept of rationality.

For Bayesian epistemology it is rational for a person to believe a proposition to a given degree if that is the degree of belief (subjective probability) that results from conditionalizing on the evidence available to the person, starting with a set of prior probabilities that the person had before the evidence was available. It is the change of beliefs, rather than the degrees of belief at the beginning or end of the process, that is the focus of the theory; but it is definite in requiring that both the beginning and the end beliefs must fit probability theory, and that the end beliefs must be obtained from the beginning beliefs by conditionalization. In this way probability theory supplies the definition of rational belief that Bayesianism uses. And that definition is not negotiable; it is the most basic assumption of the theory.

Naturalism challenges this definition. It does so in both a broad and a narrow way. The broad way is by suggesting that instead of defining rationality by an unchangeable *apriori* definition, we should study the way human reasoning actually proceeds, to discover when it is more and when it is less reliable. The narrow way is by suggesting that reasoning about probability is not something that humans do very well. So the ideal of beliefs which model perfect probability and which change in accordance with conditional probability may not be a suitable one for human beings. It may not be an ideal which we are capable of following; it may not be an ideal which we ought even to try to follow, if we want to get true and usable beliefs.

Naturalism challenges standard ideas in epistemology in other ways too. One important dimension is the realization of the finiteness of human intelligence and memory. As psychologists study the ways in which we process, store and access information, it becomes clear that the ways of thinking that might be best for perfectly rational, intelligent beings are often not ways that human beings can handle. We are just too limited. So, for example, when we want to know what explanation of a phenomenon to accept, we cannot go through all the propositions we can conceive, comparing how well each one explains the phenomenon or how probable it is on the evidence. This would be too great a challenge for our powers of reasoning and memory. Instead, we have to consider the few possible explanations that our habits or our scientific traditions suggest are plausible. We can then carefully compare the advantages and disadvantages of each of these. Even that is often at the limit of our capacities.

Moreover, when we accept a new belief, we cannot check to see whether it is consistent with all the beliefs we already hold. A perfectly rational creature would do this before accepting a new belief, for otherwise, as beliefs accumulate, so may inconsistencies. But real human beings do not have the time, memory or reasoning power to do this. So we make only quick, superficial checks of this kind. Before accepting a new theory in geology, scientists do not check to see if there are un-obvious, complicated deductions showing that it contradicts theories in economics or medicine or history. They accept it if it seems consistent in the domains where trouble might be expected to arise, leaving it for future thinkers to iron out any surprising conflicts. As a result, inconsistencies are always being created in our beliefs. (A result of this is that there is always more work for philosophers.)

Another challenge derives from the inherently social dimension of human knowledge. Standard epistemology does discuss testimony, asking when it is reasonable for one person to believe what someone else says, and when this can give knowledge. But the emphasis is still on when an individual person knows a particular proposition. Social scientists, on the other hand, study the ways in which scientific traditions develop and interact, and the ways in which circles of co-operating and competing researchers find their way to new discoveries. Many of the relevant factors do not fit with the traditional image of rational individuals impartially considering what they should believe. For example, there is a division of labour between people who create theories and people who devise experiments to test them. Each of these tribes has knowledge and skills not shared by the other, and often the reasons for taking a theory or some evidence seriously lie more in the reputation of the scientist and the relation of one circle of researchers to another than in matters of intellectual content. It depends more on who knows who and who takes whose ideas seriously than on the objective force of evidence. Relating these factors to issues of justification, rationality and knowledge is not going to be easy.

Naturalism challenges epistemic ideals that do not take account of our actual capacities and limitations. It suggests that some of these ideals may be inappropriate for human beings to aspire to. These doubts are still only suggestive, though. We do not yet know enough to see how serious they are. More important is the very fact that doubts about the appropriate epistemic ideals can be based on facts about human information processing. Epistemology cannot stop with considering how the beliefs of perfectly intelligent creatures might develop. We also want to understand how real human beings, with human limitations and human resources, can succeed or fail in their search for usable true beliefs.

Reading Questions

1   Suppose you want to know whether you should believe the theory of evolution. How would it help to have a precise measure of the strength of the evidence for it?

2 Below are four assertions of probability. Describe each in terms of how often some kind of event happens, and also in terms of how strongly it would be reasonable to believe something? Are some easier to describe one way than the other?
   (a) The probability of rain is 0.8.
   (b) The probability of living to 80 at your age is 0.4.
   (c) The probability of this coin landing heads three times in a row is 1/8.
   (d) The probability that the terrorists will kill their hostages is 0.3.
3 Make diagrams like figures 3 and 4 for the propositions 'Speedy wins the race', 'Frontrunner wins the race', and 'Frontrunner drops dead'. Assume that it is very probable that Frontrunner will win the race and very very improbable that Frontrunner will drop dead. (Speedy and Frontrunner are race-horses, needless to say.)

   Find the areas of the diagrams corresponding to 'Speedy wins the race & Frontrunner drops dead' and 'Speedy wins the race & Frontrunner does not drop dead'. What area corresponds to 'Speedy wins the race & Frontrunner wins the race'?

   Find the areas of the diagram that represent the probability of Speedy wining the race conditional on Frontrunner dropping dead.
4 Suppose that the probability that Speedy will win the race and that Frontrunner will drop dead is 0.1, and the probability that Frontrunner will drop dead is 0.001, what is the probability that Speedy will win the race conditional on Frontrunner dropping dead?
5 Show how Bayes's theorem follows from the definition of conditional probability. (Hint: write out the definition of Prob (B, E) and the definition of Prob (E, B), getting the latter just by reversing the letters in the former. Then find a factor common to both of them so that you can solve an equation.)
6 How does the example about earthquake predictions fit the slogan 'Evidence supports beliefs that make it more probable'?
7 Consider the theory that everything in the world is affected by the actions of tiny invisible gremlins, whose actions are completely whimsical and unpredictable. Using the three statements in section 3, describe how strongly each of the following pieces of evidence supports the theory by comparison with the support they give to standard scientific theories.
   (a) A rocket which had been thoroughly checked before launch explodes shortly after blast-off.

(b) A person wins the lottery against 10 million to 1 odds.

(c) A teacher drops a heavy and a light ball before a class to demonstrate the laws of gravity. They pause in mid-air and hover for two seconds, then the light ball falls before the heavy one does.

8   Do the probability calculations in the example in section 3, assuming instead that Prob (Fair) = Prob (H-bias) = Prob (T-bias) = 1/3. Compare the conditional probabilities to those in the example. What conclusions are suggested?

9   The first objection to Bayesianism in section 4 mentions the denials of the beliefs that (a) Washington is the capital of the United States, (b) dogs have legs, (c) the cube root of 1,728 is 12, (d) Nelson Mandela was the first non-white president of South Africa, (e) hydrogen is a gas, (f) brown is a colour. All these are beliefs that you might want to give probability 1. If you had to rank them in order of certainty, what would the ranking be? Does this suggest that not all of them should have probability 1?

10   Make an exact calculation to back up the Bayesian reply to the example about Maureen and heavy metal concerts.

11   Use the calculations in the biased coin case of section 3 and question 8 to support the statements of section 5 that 'Background beliefs influence the force of evidence' and 'Background beliefs are changed by evidence'. Find some prior probabilities for this example that support the third slogan, 'Some background beliefs make evidence powerless'.

12   In the example illustrating framing effects, why will probability theory say that if you prefer A, you should prefer C, and if you prefer B, you should prefer D? (You do not need to appeal to anything deep about probability to answer this. Why, when you see questions 1 and 2 side by side, is it clear that these should be the preferences?)

13   You have a box with 90 coins in it. You know that 30 are fair coins, 30 strongly biased to heads, and 30 strongly biased to tails. You reach into the box and bring out a coin at random. You toss it, and it lands heads ten times in a row. Is the coin more likely to be a fair coin, biased to heads, or biased to tails? How is this relevant to the gambler's fallacy?

14   Why can geologists considering a new theory not check to see that it is consistent with all their other beliefs? Can they not go through

a limited number of other beliefs that are likely to be relevant, and quickly find any possible contradictions?

Thinking Questions

15 At the end of section 1 there is an argument as to why the strength of evidence can be measured with probability involving, on the one hand, hypotheses about random events and, on the other hand, scientific theories such as the theory of evolution. How is this argument affected if we deny that when some evidence supports one belief and other evidence supports another belief, the evidence for the one belief must always be either stronger, weaker or the same as the evidence for the other belief? Can we deny this and still say that some evidence is strong and some is weak?

16 Go back to the ravens paradox described in chapter 4, section 3. What might a Bayesian solution to the paradox look like?

17 In the biased coin example in section 3 the probability that the coin has an extreme bias to tails, conditional on the evidence, is 0. It would be zero if the evidence were only one toss in which the coin landed heads. If we now change our probabilities by conditionalization on the evidence, we will find that the probability of an extreme bias to tails remains 0 whatever the evidence. Is this an undesirable feature of the Bayesian approach?

18 The Bayesian response to the third argument against it was: 'We can rationally give a completely novel proposition any probability we like. Some probabilities may be more convenient or more normal, but if the proposition is really novel, then no probability is forbidden.' Suppose that a scientist comes up with a novel explanation of some phenomenon, and other scientists assign it a probability of zero, so that no evidence whatsoever will support it. Is this reasonable?

19 Suppose that you have to make both of the decisions below. Which choice would you make in each case?
    (i) Choose either (a) a sure gain of $60 or (b) a 80 per cent chance to gain $90.
    (ii) Choose either (c) a 25 per cent chance to win $60 or (d) a 20 per cent chance to win $90.

Many people will prefer (a) to (b) and (d) to (c). But if the average gain of (a) is greater than that of (b), then the average gain of (c) is greater than that of (d). (Average gain, or expected value, is the gain averaged over all possible situations weighted by how probable they are. Thus since (b) represents two situations one with probability 0.2 in which you gain nothing and one with probability 0.8 in which you gain $90, its average gain in money is $0.2 \times 0 + 0.8 \times 90 = \$72$. The gains do not have to be measured in money.) Some economists and psychologists use this as evidence that there is a persistent illusion in human decision making. Is this persuasive?

20   Issues of human finiteness and of the different roles that different people play in science link to the difference between rational and justified belief, discussed in chapter 1 (see questions 15 and 16 of chapter 1). Suppose that a geologist accepts a theory because there is a lot of geological evidence for it, no geological evidence against it, and she can see no reason in chemistry, physics or biology why it should not be true. However, it turns out that a basic law of physics combined with the new geological theory contradicts some well-known fact. (Perhaps it entails that the Sahara desert should have more rain than it does.) Showing this needs a lot of advanced mathematics which the geologist had no reason to consider relevant, and which had not been part of her training. Was she justified in believing the new theory (before learning about the problem)? What would Bayesianism say? What distinctions might a naturalist approach suggest?

21   Two naturalistic challenges to traditional epistemology, the challenge from human finiteness and the challenge from the social nature of knowledge, were described in section 7 as challenging much of epistemology. But they present particular problems for a Bayesian approach. Why?

Further Reading

Simple introductions to probability theory and the Bayesian approach to evidence are found in Brian Skyrms, *Choice and Chance* (Dickenson, 1966), and Richard Jeffrey, *The Logic of Decision* (2nd edn, Chicago, 1985). Good books giving Bayesian approaches to scientific method are Colin Howson and Peter Urbach, *Scientific Reasoning: The Bayesian Approach* (Open Court, 1989), and

Mark Kaplan, *Decision Theory as Philosophy* (Cambridge University Press, 1996). A classic source is Rudolf Carnap, *Logical Foundations of Probability* (University of Chicago Press, 1962).

A middle-level survey of issues about naturalism in epistemology is Philip Kitcher, 'The naturalist's return', *Philosophical Review*, 101 (1992), 53–114. Issues of human finiteness are discussed in Alvin Goldman, *Epistemology and Cognition* (Harvard University Press, 1986), and Edward Stein, *Without Good Reason* (Oxford University Press, 1996). Criticisms of the Bayesian approach are found in chapter 7 of Alvin Plantinga, *Warrant: The Current Debate* (Oxford University Press, 1993), and chapter 8 of his *Warrant and Proper Function* (Oxford University Press, 1993). The transmission of knowledge is discussed in Michael Welbourne, *The Transmission of Knowledge* (Aberdeen University Press, 1980). See also chapter 5 of W. V. Quine and Joseph Ullian, *The Web of Belief* (Random House, 1978).

10 Afterword: The Pursuit of Truth

1. The Inference to the Best Explanation

This is a guide through the theory of knowledge, not a comprehensive tour around it. Many topics have been left out, and many details left unexplored. One central topic that has been neglected is a kind of reasoning that is sometimes called ampliative reasoning, or abduction, or *the inference to the best explanation* – IBE for short. There have been a number of places in the past nine chapters where it would have been natural to introduce IBE. But I have refrained. One reason for refraining was that the separate issues may be seen more clearly if they are not brought under a single powerful idea with its associated problems. Another is that here, at the end of the book, is the place to look ahead to the large controversies that make the theory of knowledge still a live and central part of philosophy. IBE is at the heart of many of them.

Suppose that you come home expecting to find your friend there. She is not home, and you notice that her bicycle is gone. Moreover, you remember her saying that she was near to finishing a story that would have to be sent to a magazine in a hurry. So you suppose that she has gone to the post office on her bike. You set off in that direction to meet her.

The reasoning that leads to the belief that she has gone to the post office is an example of IBE. You begin with the facts that the bicycle is gone, that she was finishing the story, and that the story needed to be mailed to the magazine, and you see that they all fit together if you also suppose that the reason the bicycle is gone is that she took it to go to post her story. This belief explains these facts, and that is why you believe it. We reason like this all the time. The example is typical of IBE reasoning in several other regards too.

First, there could be other explanations. The bicycle could have been stolen, and she could have gone to report the theft to the police. She could have been abducted by terrorists who then disassembled the bicycle and hid the parts under the floor-boards. And so on. The conclusion that she took the bike to the post office is the *best* of the explanations available to you at the time, but that does not make it the only possible one.

Second, you do not have to believe it. You would be irrational to believe an inferior explanation, like the one about abduction by terrorists, given the facts. But you could refuse to venture any explanation at all. You could say: 'She's not here. There could be many reasons. I'll wait and see.' That would not be irrational. But it would leave you with no course of action if you wanted to see her as soon as possible.

Third, the reasoning can be rephrased in terms of probability. The various hypotheses about her whereabouts are not all equally likely, even before considering the evidence of the missing bi-cycle. So their conditional probabilities on the evidence could be considered, as described in chapter 9. It would turn out that the hypothesis that she had taken her bicycle and gone to the post office with it was the most probable one – the most probable among those that you had thought of and had the kind of attitude that could translate into a prior probability, that is.

Not all examples of IBE show all three of these features. The second feature might sometimes be missing. Some epistemologists argue that sometimes the best explanation is so obviously the best that it is irrational not to believe it. An example might be belief in the existence of a world of physical objects around us, inter-acting with each other and us via chains of cause and effect. We need to suppose this in order to make any sense of our experiences, and the option of refusing to accept any explanation and believing only in our experiences is not really open to us, since these beliefs would be too complex for us to handle. So, some argue, we have no alternative but to accept the existence of the physical world as the best (and only) explanation of our experience.

The third feature is (at any rate) not obviously present whenever the best explanation requires a new concept. Suppose we have an explanation in physics which refers to concepts, like curved four-dimensional space-time or subatomic particles that are both waves and particles, which are new in the theory. Then we have no degree of belief, no probability, for the explanation before it is invented. We have to assign it a probability, or at any rate decide how much we believe it, and the obvious way to do this is in terms of how well we think it explains the evidence. Something similar happens when new social attitudes bring with them new words to describe states of mind ('laid back', 'uptight', 'spaced-out' in the 1970s) to explain people's behaviour with. There is no previous set of beliefs in terms of which to judge how probable these explanations are; we just have to see how well they handle the data.

It is when explanations involve novel concepts that the inference to the best explanation becomes really interesting and controversial. Should we believe that the space around us really is part of a curved four-dimensional continuum, just because that is the only adequate explanation we can come up with for certain observations in physics and astronomy? Would it not be more reasonable to hedge our bets and accept the hypothesis temporarily as the best we can do, without putting too much faith in it?

2. Open Questions

Issues about the role of IBE connect with many of the open questions of the theory of knowledge. That is, in contemporary debates about the nature of knowledge and the choice of appropriate epistemic ideals, a recurrent theme is the status of IBE. It does not play a central role in all these debates, but it is always to be found somewhere among the cast. This section lists four large general issues that are currently very live and open in contemporary epistemology. One way to tie them together is to see how IBE crops up in connection with each of them.

What kinds of purposes are relevant?

The contrast between error and ignorance brings out the fact that truth is not the only feature we want our beliefs to have. We also want to be able to explain mysterious phenomena, predict scientific and everyday observations, control nature, cure diseases, create harmonious societies, live happy lives and so on. Is it rational to include all these aims in considering what to believe, and if so, how are they to be balanced against one another when they compete? Suppose, for example, that you are an unhappy person haunted by the cold and impersonal nature of the universe and by the difficulty of living with other people. Someone tries to sell you a set of beliefs centring around the worship of a guru. He persuades you that you can be happy if only you can make yourself believe that the guru has been sent from heaven to save humanity, give away all your possessions, believe all the very strange things the guru and her followers assert, and associate only with other devotees. You object that the benefits sound fine, but you can see no reason to believe that the things the guru says are true. 'Truth is only one good thing' says the missionary; 'you have to overcome your love of truth in order to achieve happiness.'

IBE is relevant here in two ways. First, we may wonder what is to count as the *best* explanation of the evidence. Is one explanation better than another when believing it will make you happier? Indeed, does an explanation explain better if it not only makes you see underlying causes of the phenomena, but also makes you feel that there is a satisfying human-oriented reason why they happened? (Suppose that all of a person's loved ones have died in apparently unrelated accidents. 'Why? Why?' To say that such things can happen by chance gives an explanation, but not a reason.)

IBE is also relevant in anther way. We might allow that scientific explanation justifies *accepting* a theory, while making your life feel good does not, while not allowing scientific explanation in itself to justify *belief*. Belief is only justified, we might say, when the evidence shows that it has to be true. Our need to have our curiosity about the world satisfied is not relevant. If this is so, then we are pushed back to error-avoidance, and IBE becomes a tool of superstition.

What is Rationality?

The whole enterprise of the theory of knowledge may be taken as an attempt to define rational belief, by working out what it would be reasonable to believe by discussing different classes of beliefs separately. But deep ambiguities in the concept of rational belief are now emerging. Might the ideal of rationality be one that we limited humans cannot achieve? The discussion of the Bayesian ideal in chapter 9 raised the possibility that probabilistic thinking may be the right way for perfect beings to operate, while being something that humans cannot do without making many mistakes. If this is so, how should people formulate less demanding ideals? How many concessions to their limited powers should they make? Can a precise, unambiguous ideal emerge from this retreat?

The relevance to IBE is that the more limited we see the human intellect by comparison with the complexity of the world, the less faith we can have that the best explanation – the best by *our* standards of the hypotheses that *we* are able to come up with – will have anything to do with the truth. Would an ant's best guess be worth much, or even a chimpanzee's? So why a human's?

How much can we choose what to believe?

Contrast two extreme pictures of rational belief. On the first picture there is in any situation a single set of beliefs which it would be rational to hold. It is irrational (in a sense which entails being wrong, foolish, undesirable) to believe anything that is not in that set. Such a view is often associated with a very definite sense of the power of evidence to give us rational beliefs. We can express it by saying that no one should ever believe anything without sufficient evidence. Call this the *compulsive* conception of reason. It contrasts with the *voluntarist* conception, according to which all that rationality determines is what it would be irrational to believe. In any situation, according to voluntarism, there are a few beliefs which it would be irrational not to believe; but most beliefs are such that we can accept or reject them as we choose, as long as we are careful to be consistent. (Bas van Fraassen, discussing these questions, cites US Supreme Court Justice Oliver Wendell Holmes who wrote that in Prussian law everything is forbidden except what is explicitly permitted while in English law everything is permitted except what is explicitly forbidden. Prussian law is compulsive, English law is voluntaristic.)

Again there is a link with IBE. A voluntarist is likely to be very doubtful that there is often a single best explanation of the data available to us. If the data are consistent, then we can explain them in many ways, and different people can choose to accept different explanations, or none at all. The link here is quite subtle, though. It is possible to believe in IBE, in the sense of thinking that when there is a single, clearly best explanation of the data, it is rational to believe it, while accepting that very often there is no best available explanation. Is this a voluntarist or a compulsive conception of reason? It is somewhere between the extremes, as a reasonable understanding of reason is likely to be.

Can we accept beliefs without thinking that they are true?

Suppose that someone accepts a hypothesis because it is the best of the available explanations of the data. But suppose also that this person doubts that any of the available explanations are true. The person may even doubt that any of the hypotheses that people will ever formulate on this topic are true. Can this person still go around asserting the hypothesis, teaching it to her students, acting as if it were true, and so on?

No, you might think. For to believe something is to think that it is true, and this person does not think that the hypothesis is true. But there is a reply to this. The person may say that she is not believing it. She is accepting it as the best explanation, and acting accordingly, but withholding judgement about its truth. Or, alternatively, she may say that believing something just is to act as if it were true, even though at a higher, more reflective level, we can doubt whether there are facts in the world that correspond to it. This is the attitude of many philosophers to advanced theories in physics, and of many people to moral and religious beliefs. It is perfectly reasonable, they say, to act as if they were true while being aware that the 'as if' is only that.

These are issues about *realism*. To take a realist attitude to a belief is to think that the world is literally as the belief describes it. The alternative is an anti-realist, or instrumentalist, attitude. The connection with IBE is clear. Beliefs gained by IBE give rise to the question. But there is another connection. IBE, combined with a mildly compulsive attitude to reason, is often used to suggest that we should take a realist attitude to our beliefs, particularly our scientific beliefs. Science gives us the best explanation of our experience; therefore we should believe it, therefore we should believe that it is true, therefore we should believe that the world is the way science says it is. Thus IBE can support realism. In fact, when people reason by IBE, they usually have already adopted a realist attitude to their beliefs. For, given some evidence, the number of hypotheses that could explain them is usually enormous. In order to discover the best explanation, we eliminate all those which we could not really think were descriptions of the real causes of the evidence. So realism and a faith in IBE usually go together.

3. Rules for the Direction of the Mind

These are the issues behind current debates in the theory of knowledge. They are very real and open questions, and it is not at all obvious what the answers to them are. Moreover, they clearly have implications well beyond epistemology. Well beyond philosophy, in fact. They are relevant to issues about religion, about the relation of science to common sense, about whether there is such a thing as scientific method, and ultimately to large imponderables about our place in the universe. They have one feature in common besides their connection with the inference to the best explanation. They all represent some kind of break with a core assumption of early thinkers in the theory of knowledge, from Bacon through Descartes to the British empiricists. All these thinkers assumed that there were easily grasped principles which, if we could follow them, would lead us to all the true beliefs we could have – 'Rules for the direction of the mind', as Descartes called them. The history of epistemology, and the history of knowledge itself, has shown that this assumption is at best ex-tremely dubious. When we realize this, we are led to ask the questions of the previous section. In this way epistemology is like our other beliefs: we begin with assumptions, use them to evalu-ate evidence and form new beliefs, and then eventually abandon the assumptions with which we began.

Thinking Questions

1   IBE was claimed in section 1 to be more controversial when the belief in question is a completely novel one. But is it so clear that there are any completely novel hypotheses? Theories about curved four-dimensional space-time use familiar concepts of space and time plus mathematics that, though advanced, is not new. Beliefs about subatomic particles just suppose that there are smaller things than what had previously been thought to be the smallest things. And there are definite limits to the concepts that human beings can

acquire. Perhaps the only concepts we can have are combinations of the innate concepts that are part of the human inheritance.

How plausible is this? If it were true, how would it affect the claims in section 1?

2   Describe connections between issues about the purposes that should be relevant to belief and issues about voluntarism (without mentioning IBE).

3   Describe connections between issues about the finiteness of human thinking powers and issues about voluntarism (without mentioning IBE).

4   In section 2 realism was said to follow from the combination of IBE with a mildly compulsive attitude to reason. Can IBE be combined with voluntarism?

5   Section 3 claimed that the issues of section 2 were relevant to questions about religious belief. What is the relevance?

Further Reading

Accessible treatments of issues about realism and the inference to the best explanation are found in chapter 1 of Paul Churchland, *Scientific Realism and the Plasticity of Mind* (Cambridge University Press, 1979); Ian Hacking, *Representing and Intervening* (Cambridge University Press, 1983); J. J. C. Smart, *Philosophy and Scientific Realism* (Routledge, 1963); and (of course) chapter 15 of Adam Morton, *Philosophy in Practice* (Blackwell, 1996).

A source of many ideas about IBE is Gilbert Harman, 'The inference to the best explanation', *Philosophical Review*, 74 (1965), 88–95. See also his *Change in View* (MIT Press, 1986). Some of the strongest criticism of IBE comes from Bas van Fraassen. See his *The Scientific Image* (Oxford University Press, 1980) and the much more difficult *Laws and Symmetry* (Oxford University Press, 1989), especially chapters 6 and 7. Alvin Plantinga's views on reasons for belief are explained and defended in *Warrant and Proper Function* (Oxford University Press, 1993). For the connections with issues about religious belief, begin with William James, 'The will to believe', in *Essays in Pragmatism* (Haffner, 1948), which is a reply to William Clifford, 'The ethics of belief', in his *Lectures and Essays*, vol. 2 (MacMillan, 1901).

Some of the sources of the ideas discussed in this chapter and in the works listed above can be found in John Cottingham, *Western Philosophy: An Anthology* (Blackwell, 1996). See part II section 6, George Berkeley, 'Nothing Outside the Mind'; part II section 7, David Hume, 'The Limits of Metaphysical Speculation'; part II section 8, Immanuel Kant, 'Metaphysics, Old and New'; and part II section 10, Rudolf Carnap, 'The Elimination of Metaphysics.'

Glossary

Below are definitions of some central terms used in this book. A definition is only the first step to understanding a word. A full understanding of a philosophical concept nearly always requires understanding the theories that use the concept; so after reading a definition, it is usually a good idea to use the index to find pages on which the word is used.

analytic   analytic sentences are sentences which are true because of the meaning of the words found in them. Analytic beliefs are true because of the concepts involved in them. Contrasted with **synthetic**. It is controversial whether there is a precise distinction between analytic and synthetic sentences or beliefs.

aposteriori   aposteriori beliefs are beliefs which cannot be known to be true or false without considering evidence from experience. Usually written 'a posteriori'. Contrasted with **apriori**.

apriori   apriori beliefs can be known to be true without considering evidence from experience. More often written 'a priori'.

argument from analogy   the argument that a person can know that other people have minds like her own by noticing relations between her own states of mind and her own behaviour, and then supposing that other people are in similar states of mind when they behave in similar ways.

ascent routine   the transformation of the answer to a question about the world into an answer to a question about a person's mind. For example, if you are asked, 'What do you think 33 + 777 is?', you give the answer to the question about your thoughts by finding the answer to the arithmetic problem.

basic beliefs   beliefs in terms of which other beliefs can be justified, but which cannot themselves be justified by any other beliefs.

Bayesian   the movement in statistics and philosophy which uses conditional probability to measure the strength of evidence.

cognitivist   theories which claim that some sentences do not express beliefs which can be true or false. See **emotivism**.

coherence   the relation between beliefs when they combine to make a unified and logically consistent system.

coherentism   the theory that it is reasonable to hold a belief when it increases the coherence of your beliefs. Same as **holism**.

conditional probability   the probability of a proposition given that another proposition has probability 1.

deductively valid argument   step-by-step reasoning from premisses to a conclusion, such that if the premisses are true, the conclusion must be true.

dispositional states of mind   states of mind which are defined in terms of their tendencies to cause behaviour, thought, or emotion. For example, an irritable mood is a disposition, because we understand it in terms of the typical behaviour and feelings of an irritable person.

eliminative materialism   the theory that everyday words to describe our minds, such as 'belief', 'desire' and 'memory' are so closely tied to false beliefs from **folk psychology** that they cannot be used to make any true assertions.

emotivism   the ethical theory that moral judgements are expressions of emotion rather than expressions of belief.

empiricism   the theory that a belief is reasonable if and only if it can be based on evidence obtained from perception.

epistemology   another name for the **theory of knowledge**.

error   false belief. Contrasted with **ignorance**.

error theory   a theory that explains why people hold some kind of beliefs in such a way as to suggest that these beliefs are false. Error theories of moral belief are common, but there can be other kinds. For example, eliminative materialism is an error theory of folk psychology.

evidence   reasons for holding a belief, usually derived from experience.

experiential concepts   concepts which can be learned by having particular experiences and seeing what they have in common.

externalism the theory that what makes a belief justified or qualify as knowledge depends on factors outside the person. (Beware: in other parts of philosophy 'externalism' and 'internalism' are used with similar, but different, meanings.)

fallibilism the theory that any belief could be false, however strong our evidence for it. Stronger or weaker fallibilisms take the possibility that beliefs we are confident of may turn out to be false more or less seriously.

folk psychology the beliefs, concepts and ways of thinking which we use in everyday life to understand ourselves and other people.

foundationalism the theory that a belief is justified only when it is based on a basic belief. See **basic belief** and **justified belief**.

Gettier examples examples which show that a belief can be true and justified but not qualify as knowledge.

holism the same as coherentism.

ignorance not having a belief you need. Contrasted with **error**.

induction (inductive reasoning) reasoning that begins with particular instances of a general pattern and concludes that the pattern applies to all instances.

inference to the best explanation (IBE) reasoning from the fact that a hypothesis is the best available explanation of some evidence or belief to the conclusion that the hypothesis is true.

internalism the theory that whether or not a person's belief is justified depends on factors within that person's mind. Contrasted with externalism. (See the warning under **externalism**.)

irrational belief A belief is irrational when it is rational to believe that it is false. See **rational belief**.

justified belief a belief which is supported by evidence, argument or other beliefs, so that an intelligent person who had made no mistakes in reasoning and, who had that evidence and those other beliefs would hold it. A justified belief is held for reasons which maximize the person's chances of having a large number of true beliefs.

knowledge belief which has the qualities we want beliefs to have. It is impossible to give an uncontroversial definition of knowledge, but any philosophical theory of it will try to explain it both in terms of the qualities which according to that theory beliefs should have and in terms of the situations in which people use the word 'know'.

Lehrer's principle the claim that for a belief to count as knowledge it must be true and based only on other true beliefs.

logical truth   a sentence or belief which is true because of the meaning of the logical words in it (such as 'and', 'not', 'all'). See **analytic**.

naturalistic epistemology   the claim that in order to understand when a belief is reasonable and when evidence supports a belief, we must understand the way that human beings process information from their environment. This position makes discoveries in psychology and biology relevant to the theory of knowledge.

necessity   the property a belief or sentence has when there is no possible circumstance in which it could be false.

occurrent states of mind   states of mind which are defined in terms of what happens in a person's mind at a particular moment. For example, when a person has a sensation, their experience begins and ends at a particular moment and is the same kind of experience whatever behaviour or thoughts it leads to.

other minds problem   the problem of showing how a person's beliefs that other people have minds similar to theirs can be justified.

perception, relational   the use of the senses to theirs a link between a person and a particular object which gives the person information about the object. For example, when a person smells a moose, the person is aware of changes in the moose's odour and proximity, even if they do not know that it is a moose that they are smelling. The person smells the moose, but they may not smell that there is a moose nearby.

perception, propositional   the use of the senses to gain information about objects in the environment. For example, when a person smells that there are moose nearby, the person learns that a belief about the presence of moose is true, but may not smell any particular moose.

perceptual appearance   the way the environment seems as a result of the use of the senses.

perceptual beliefs   beliefs obtained by use of the senses.

psychological beliefs   beliefs about thoughts, experiences, memories, emotions and other states of mind.

rational belief   a belief that a sensible and clear-thinking person would hold given the evidence available to them and their other beliefs. See **irrational belief**.

rationalism   the theory that many of our beliefs can be justified by the use of our power of thinking alone, without evidence from perception.

realism the theory that some beliefs are true or false of real things which are independent of our minds. For example, scientific realism holds that scientific theories describe objects, such as electrons and genes and gravitational fields, which would exist even if we did not have any theories about them.

reflective equilibrium a situation in which a person's intuitive beliefs about a class of particular situations are consistent with their theories and other general beliefs about those situations.

scepticism the theory that people have a lot less knowledge than they think they do.

sense–data information about what a person is perceiving which is so basic that the person has no alternative to believing it.

synthetic a synthetic belief or sentence is one whose truth or falsity depends on factors besides the meaning of the words or concepts. Contrasted with **analytic**.

theoretical concepts concepts which are used in a theory, and which are understood by learning the theory.

theory of knowledge the part of philosophy which discusses the desirable qualities of beliefs, such as **justification**, rationality (see **rationality**), and **coherence**, and the ways in which we can acquire beliefs with these qualities, such as by reasoning and by gathering **evidence**.

voluntarism the claim that different people with the same beliefs can respond to new evidence by changing their beliefs in different ways. (Warning: in other parts of philosophy 'voluntarism' is used with related, but different, meanings.)

Appendix for Teachers

This revised edition is very different from the first, though the difference may be disguised by the similar titles of many chapters. The book now covers more topics and describes a greater range of philosophical positions, and my own philosophical loyalties are less prominent and more clearly marked. The discussions of moral knowledge, Bayesianism and naturalistic epistemology are entirely new, but every chapter has been thoroughly rewritten.

My intention has been to provide an easily read book for a first course in the theory of knowledge that a teacher would not have to waste time quarrelling with. Students with a minimal background in philosophy, as in a one-semester introductory course, should be able to read chapters of the book on their own without much help or guidance. This should allow the teacher to concentrate on the exposition of classical texts or more difficult contemporary works. There should be no difficulty using this book in combination with either Descartes's *Meditations*, Hume's *Enquiry* or *Treatise*, Russell's *The Problems of Philosophy*, or other classics of the subject. In the further reading section of every chapter I have listed relevant selections from John Cottingham's *Western Philosophy: An Anthology* (Blackwell, 1996) which could be used to accompany the chapter. Equally, there should be no difficulty using it with contemporary standards such as Alvin Goldman, *Epistemology and Cognition* (Harvard University Press, 1986); Alvin Plantinga, *Warrant: The Current Debate* (Oxford University Press, 1993) or his *Warrant and Proper Function* (Oxford University Press, 1993); Laurence Bonjour, *The Structure of Empirical Knowledge* (Harvard University Press, 1985); or Bas van Fraassen, *The Scientific Image* (Oxford University Press, 1980). It would be impossible to use any of these books in an introductory course without also using something much easier to read, to give students something to hold on to.

A course also needs a core of books, usually held on reserve in the library, for students to use when writing essays or preparing for seminar presentations. The works by Descartes, Hume, Russell, Goldman, Plantinga, Bonjour and van Fraassen mentioned above could well have a place in such a reserve, as should Jonathan Dancy, *An Introduction to Contemporary Epistemology* (Blackwell, 1985); Plantinga, *Warrant and Proper Function* (Oxford University Press, 1993); Robert Schwartz, *Vision* (Blackwell, 1994); and Gilbert Harman, *Thought* (Princeton University Press, 1971), or *Change in View* (MIT Press, 1986); Peter Unger, *Ignorance: A Case for Scepticism* (Oxford University Press, 1975); Roger Woolhouse, *The Empiricists* (Oxford University Press, 1988); and John Cottingham, *Rationalism* (Oxford University Press, 1988). Of course the exact list will depend on the course you give.

In my experience, philosophy students like to appear to understand more than they do. So they semi-consciously fake it, learning sophisticated names and moves by rote, to disguise their bafflement. (I certainly did.) The expectation that intelligent students should be able to grapple with the most difficult issues and the most sophisticated writers at an early stage encourages this pretence, putting students in a situation where only years later can they admit how little they understood. I would like this book to encourage a style of teacher–student interaction where examples and counter-examples abound, where formulations are tested, and the aim is to understand rather than to impress. One device for encouraging this is the questions at the end of each chapter. As explained in the Foreword for Students, the reading questions test the students' comprehension of each chapter. They are suited for discussion groups accompanying lectures. Students who have done the reading should be capable of at least beginning to answer all of them. Some of them lead beyond bare comprehension and could be the basis for discussion. The thinking questions are more challenging. They could be used as essay topics, to provide more demanding material, and to raise doubts about whether the line in the main text tells the whole story.

In the chapter by chapter notes that follow, I list problems that may arise, teaching techniques that may apply, and sections of my *Philosophy in Practice* (Blackwell, 1996), that could be used or adapted to provide activities for teachers who prefer an activity- and dialogue-based style of teaching.

Chapter 1   One unstated aim of this chapter is to introduce the rather special senses of 'belief' and 'know' found in philosophy. These are best not approached very explicitly: that just causes confusion. Instead, if they are used in making other distinctions, they come to seem natural. The basic distinctions in section 3 are important; they are just the kinds of thing that students often seem to understand but do not. Sections 1.8, 1.10, 1.11, 2.1 and 3.2 of *Philosophy in Practice* contain activities that could be used with this chapter.

Chapter 2   Robert Schwartz's *Vision* contains additional material that fits well with this chapter. The mix of psychological and philosophical ideas about perception may well raise issues about naturalized epistemology that are not dealt with until chapter 9. Sections 1, 3, 4, 5, 7, 8 and 12 of chapter 9 of *Philosophy in Practice* contain activities that could be used with this chapter.

Chapter 3   The reading questions on this chapter seem harder than average, and students may need more patience with some of them. I have tried to present Quine's views so that they are consistent with his later writings, rather than sticking by the rather starker 'Two dogmas' formulations. I have listed a chapter of Quine and Ullian's *The Web of Belief* (Random House, 1978), under further reading: although this is an easy read, students may have to think to find the connections with the more traditional formulations in my chapter. The contrast between Quine's views and Kant's requires a sense of a quantifier alternation (as rehearsed in question 5 of this chapter) which some students have trouble grasping. The examples used to argue that not all apriori beliefs are necessary, in section 2, and the examples used to make it plausible that there could be synthetic apriori beliefs, in section 5, may be more controversial than the text suggests. You may want to expand on these topics. Question 11 covers Duhem's thesis, which you may want to mention. Questions 3 and 15 are in a way a pair, though 3 is rather hard for a reading question. Sections 2.8, 3.4, 9.8 and 9.10 of *Philosophy in Practice* contain activities that could be used with this chapter.

Chapter 4 This chapter presupposes a very basic understanding of deductive validity, such as would be given in the first three weeks of any logic course, or in sections 5.4–5.6 of *Philosophy in Practice*. The sections discussing probability do not presuppose any familiarity with probability theory. I switch from expressions like 'probability of 0.99' to '99 per cent chance' in a way that I think will be perfectly clear, but which just might produce some uncertainty. Some teachers will want to spend more time exploring possibilities of what Hume may actually have meant than I do. Question 10 should then be compulsory. The discussion of Goodman's problem tries to avoid the panic that it often induces in students by linking it to much more easily grasped examples than the notorious 'grue'. Grue is introduced in question 13, though. Sections 2, 11 and 12 of chapter 5 of *Philosophy in Practice* contain activities that could be used with this chapter.

Chapter 5 This is a shorter than average chapter, and serves to bring together themes from the preceding chapters while taking them to a higher level of abstraction. The ideas of holism and foundationalism, and the error/ignorance distinction, should be connected to the issues in the previous chapters. It is important to avoid identifying holism with ignorance-avoidance, or foundationalism with error-avoidance, even though there is a clear sympathy between each pair of views.

Chapter 6 Some of the material in this chapter is more difficult than average for the book. The most basic route through the chapter would be to read only the first four sections, de-emphasizing the conditional theory in section 4. The last section, 7, is also not difficult and could be included, but I should point out that it represents my views rather than current orthodoxy. (I don't want to give the impression that sections 5 and 6 are very difficult. They are not; but 1–4 are easier.) My version of the conditional definition of knowledge is worded to avoid Nozick's awkward use of a counterfactual with a true antecedent. One teaching technique to consider with the topic of this chapter is to present the students with thought-experiments in which they have to judge whether a person does or does not have knowledge. The examples in this chapter or similar ones would do. The point is that it is more enlightening for students to discover for themselves the remarkable similarity of our intuitions about knowledge and the difficulty of finding the pattern behind the intuitions.

Chapter 7   My characterizations of Cartesian (self-centred) and behaviourist positions are rather extreme. You may want to discuss how more moderate positions can be formulated. I have left conclusions about the force of eliminative behaviourism deliberately indefinite. Students tend to get enthusiastic for or against on this point, and it is as well to leave the initiative to them. My discussion of the arguments against folk psychology as a theory could naturally lead to a discussion of the Wittgensteinian attitude to mental language. Section 12.10 of *Philosophy in Practice* could be used as an activity for this chapter.

Chapter 8   The danger in discussing this topic is of getting bogged down in disputes about moral relativism or about the religious basis of ethics. The comparisons with humour, colour and witches are meant to prevent this. The idea of reflective equilibrium is used in this chapter to show how there can be a non-mysterious cognitivist theory of ethics. A number of other moral theories would have done as well. The point made in the very last section, that we may be able to say 'If there are facts of a certain kind, then we have moral knowledge' without being certain of the antecedent, and that this conditional can serve many of the functions that one would want an assurance of moral knowledge for, is fairly subtle. It does not matter if not all students get the point, as there is enough other material in the chapter for them to get their teeth into. Question 7 may help here, though. Question 5, 9 and 13 make links with internalism/externalism issues in meta-ethics, which are present throughout the chapter, but which I did not want to make explicit. Sections 11.4 and 11.5 of *Philosophy in Practice* could be used as activities for this chapter.

Chapter 9   This chapter combines a discussion of the Bayesian approach with an introduction to some ideas of naturalistic epistemology. The reason for combining them is that naturalism is just rhetorical without some psychological or biological facts to give it bite. This book is not the place to give an independent exposition of much psychology or biology, but facts about the psychology of probabilistic reasoning fit with the rest of the book very smoothly. So I use them and their obvious link with Bayesian issues as the springboard for naturalism.

Some students will find even the small amount of mathematics in the chapter off-putting. But others may find that philosophy is rehabilitated in their opinion by even this small quantitative element. To avoid the mathematics almost completely, you could stick to sections 1, 3, 5, 6 and 7. When teaching the material in section 6 on framing effects and similar phenomena, you may want to divide the class into groups and run the experiments on them, to make the issues vivid. Then they will see the results not as showing that people are stupid but as showing that they themselves tend to reason in ways that are hard to square with probability.

Chapter 10 The purpose of this chapter is to show how a number of areas of current debate in epistemology are related to each other, and how they arise out of the topics dealt with in the book. I have not included any reading questions, as the chapter, is so short. In writing this chapter, I found myself stimulated by chapters 6 and 7 of van Fraassen's *Laws and Symmetry*, though that book is much too confusing for all but the most bright and resolute undergraduates. One of the most profitable themes to pick up in discussion is the nature of explanation, and whether there is anything about a good explanation that gives us reason to believe in the existence of the entities it postulates. Another is voluntarism, and whether different people sharing most of their beliefs can with equal rationality react in opposite ways to the same evidence.

There are many courses with which this book could be used. Here are very bare outlines of four. I expect that no actual course will be identical to any one of them, but considering these may help you plan your own sequence of topics. For each one I give a sequence of topics linked to chapters of this book, and a list of other books that could be used as additional texts or for further reading. (a) is probably the easiest and (d) the hardest, in terms of demands on the students' sophistication. I should add that the simplest way to use this book in a course would simply be to read each chapter in order, centring the course on the book and choosing additional readings from Hume, Descartes and Russell, possibly augmented with Cottingham or Schwartz. I suspect this would work as well as any of the more complex plans below.

(a) *A guide through the theory of knowledge* The aim would be to understand why epistemology is central to philosophy and what the main ideas in it are. Topics: reasonable belief (chapter 1), sources of belief 1: perception (chapter 2), sources of belief 2: reason (chapter 3), problems about induction (chapter 4), escaping traditional constraints (chapter 5), what is knowledge? (chapter 6). And then two out of the following three: knowledge of minds (chapter 7), moral knowledge (chapter 8) and naturalism (chapter 9). Other books: those by Cottingham, Plantinga, Russell and Schwartz already mentioned.

(b) *Epistemology: a historical approach*   The emphasis here would be on the development of ideas about knowledge. Topics: the origins of epistemology (chapter 1), Cartesian ideas (chapter 3), empiricism (chapter 2), the Kantian revolution (chapters 3 and 5), beyond empiricism (chapters 3, 5 and 10). Other books: those by Cottingham, Schwartz, Tiles and Tiles (see chapter 1), Woolhouse, Descartes, Hume and Russell. This course could easily be given by reading chapters of this book and the relevant selections in Cottingham's *Western Philosophy*.

(c) *The variety of knowledge*   The aim would be to see the different problems of justification and analysis that arise with different kinds of belief. Topics: belief and justification (chapter 1), perception (chapter 2), mathematics and the apriori (chapter 3), induction (chapter 4), knowledge of minds (chapter 7), moral knowledge (chapter 8), knowledge via theory (chapters 5 and 10), knowledge in general (chapter 6). Other books: those by Dancy, Goldman, van Fraassen, Hume and Russell.

(d) *Current trends in epistemology*   The aim would be to get students to the point where they can appreciate current work in the subject. Topics: the tradition of epistemology (chapter 1), empiricism (chapter 2), breaking with empiricism (chapters 3 and 5), induction and the Bayesian approach (chapters 3 and 9), the definition of knowledge (chapter 6), naturalism (chapter 9), the inference to the best explanation (chapter 10). Other books: those by BonJour, Dancy, Goldman and Plantinga.

Index

A number in **bold** indicates that there is a definition or explanation of the word on that page.